What people are saying about ..
The AmerIcan Dream | HisStory In The Making

"There are storytellers and then there are those whose lives tell a story. 'The AmerIcan Dream' grabs you from the beginning and immediately transports you to a reality beyond your imagination. David Lee Windecher bravely narrates his life story with unparalleled honesty and unabashed emotion leaving the reader lamenting David's mistakes, grieving for his heartbreaks and rejoicing in his achievements. 'The AmerIcan Dream' is an awakening for us all."

Ozzie Areu, President, Tyler Perry Studios

"David Lee Windecher's rise from the gangs of Miami to the courtrooms of Atlanta provides a powerful argument for better rehabilitation efforts in our criminal justice system. As I read his memoir, I found myself cringing at times, tearing up at others, but always pulling for this underdog to make it. It's a timeless American story."

Jim Aucmutey, Atlanta Journal Constitution,
Author of 'The Class of 65'

"Inspired and chilling by turns. Windecher paints an unflinching portrait of what it's like to be poor, young and tempted by easy money."

Ana Veciana-Suarez, The Miami Herald

"It's a coming of age story about perseverance and survival in the face of abject adversity and poverty. It's a story of redemption and salvation. It's a story of hope."

Bonnie Berman, WLRN Miami, Florida

"'The AmerIcan Dream' is without question, a moving and profound read. One that should be read by every prison-reform advocate within the White House, United States Justice Department and Congress."

Kenneth Wooden, Author of 'Weeping in the Playtime
of Others – America's Incarcerated Children.

"David Lee Windecher is truly an inspiration to anyone facing serious life challenges. 'The AmerIcan Dream | HisStory In The Making' is a precious account of life on the streets and the frustrations facing today's impoverished youth. This book is a celebration of beating the odds and taking charge of one's destiny."

Sherry Boston, District Attorney, DeKalb County, Georgia

"This book is a must read for anyone. Windecher's memoir is not the typical story of someone succeeding and overcoming odds. This is a story of profound courage and belief in the values of change and education. Despite doubts, uncertainties and a societal attitude against him, despite all these walls, David perseveres. This is the story of a young man who should be dead or in custody, but instead journeys through the bottom rungs of society, drugs and gangs to become a licensed attorney helping others."

Alfonso Valdez, Director, Public Policy Laboratory, School of Social Science, University of California, Irvine.

"'The Amerlcan Dream' is a powerful testimonial of the emotional strength and guidance derived from one's faith in God. David recounts his life story with heartbreaking, yet encouraging honesty. Too many children are left to navigate the dangerous streets of America's impoverished neighborhoods. This book opens the window and allows every reader a peek into this dark world and likewise gives us a greater understanding of the challenges facing today's indigent youth. I believe in my heart it is the duty of every Christian to behold this knowledge and understand that there is hope for everyone. It is through galvanizing stories like David's we will come to understand this hope and begin to help bring the light of the Lord to those in need."

Michael Cox, Lead Pastor, Cornerstone Church, Anniston, Alabama

"David's book is now required reading for young offenders in my courtroom. I read David's coming of age book about how the development and realization of one's character and purpose superseded the instinctive desire to engage in criminal behavior for survival. At its core, this book will speak to everyone who wonders how a person might become involved in a life of crime and how with inner strength and a small community investment, redemption is possible."

Asha Jackson, Superior Court Judge DeKalb County, Georgia

THE
AMERICAN
DREAM

HISSTORY IN THE MAKING

DAVID LEE WINDECHER

TABLE OF CONTENTS

PART THREE

INTRODUCTION

"BE ASHAMED TO DIE
UNTIL YOU HAVE WON SOME VICTORY FOR HUMANITY."

HORACE MANN

What follows is the story of a gangster called Red. He is the son of Argentinean immigrants, the product of poverty and a broken penal system, and a child of the streets. He's the head of a drug ring and a convicted thief. Red witnessed his first murder in middle school. He dropped out of school on his sixteenth birthday, and was arrested thirteen times before his nineteenth. His knuckles are worn to nothing from years of gang banging and frequent visits to Florida's correctional facilities. For twenty years, he raged against the reality he was dealt, obeying the only rules that kept him alive: the code of the streets.

This is also the story of a man named David Lee Windecher.

A dual licensed attorney in Georgia and Florida, a God-fearing man, protective older brother of three, tutor to aspiring lawyers, and vocal advocate for impoverished youth. David is invigorated by his work, enjoys the company of dear friends, and loves his family more than life. Above all material things, he prizes character, discipline, and integrity. And he believes entirely in the power of young people to rise above their circumstances.

He believes it because he's done it.

Both of these stories are mine.

1

I grew up on the other side of white-picket-fence perfect. Raul Diaz Windecher and Laura Elena Montenegro Windecher, my parents, were Argentinean natives who immigrated to the United States in 1977. In 1978, I was born in East Los Angeles—the gang capital of America.

El Monte: home to Latin Kings, Bloods, Crips, Tres Puntos, and the Windechers. My parents tried to shield us—my brother, sisters, and me—from it, but there was no denying my home town was a scary place to grow up. Fewer than twenty-five miles Southwest of El Monte are the cities Compton and Watts, the African American equivalent of the Hispanic saturated East Los Angeles. The tracks, in this case, literally separated two worlds. On one side were Hispanic gangs; on the other were the African Americans. These two areas of Los Angeles County made up some of the most dangerous square mileage in the United States. The communities were filled with turmoil, violence, oppression, and an alarming lack of the necessary resources for communal progression. So when people say, "I grew up in the hood," I tend to laugh. Chances are they have no idea.

In America, my father always had blue collar jobs and blue collar hands to match. They were rough with the calluses he earned doing hard, honest work providing for his family. He was always about family.

In 1985, my father was painting industrial machinery as an independent contractor for a private company. For his six months of manual labor, my father received nothing. The company refused to pay him and, as the weeks passed, my parents' meager savings began to thin. With a wife and four children under the age of seven to care for, my father had no choice but to pursue legal action. He represented himself and sued the company for breach of contractual services in a bench trial—a trial heard by a judge, without a jury—and was awarded several thousands of dollars.

But my father never saw a penny.

The company employed a private attorney and appealed the judge's ruling. It took months to get back to court, and my father struggled in the interim to keep us above water. When the appeal was finally heard, my father lost. He couldn't afford to pay an attorney, and unlike in criminal cases, the court will not appoint public counsel in civil cases.

My father barely spoke English. He never stood a chance.

Justice was denied him, not because he was wrong, but because he was foreign and because he was poor. We were forced to leave California and move back to my parents' motherland of Argentina. My father's heart broke, and the first seeds of bitterness were planted in mine.

My first memory of the United States' legal system is of the day it told my father that opportunity was a luxury he couldn't afford. That was also the day I decided to grow up to fight that reality.

We lived in Argentina until I was ten years old. I learned to speak, read, and write fluently in Spanish. At that age, I had no idea what a tremendous impact living there would have on my life. Looking back, it's one of my most important experiences.

In the mid-80s, Argentina was a struggling Third World country. Believe it or not, living in El Monte, California was paradise compared to the dirt roads, lack of bare essentials, and extreme poverty that the Argentinean population endured. One full meal a day was often all there was. People slept on sidewalks and begged for food in the streets.

My father was fortunate to have access to gainful employment in Argentina, so for nearly five years, he was able to work and save money. Despite his setback in California, he wouldn't give up on America. In 1989, my parents decided to give the land of opportunity a second chance. This time, we went east to Miami, Florida.

Miami doesn't hold a candle to Los Angeles in terms of gang activity, but *Scarface* wasn't filmed there because Brian De Palma preferred the Southern palm trees and tropical climate. South Florida was, and remains, the hub of domestic and international drug transactions.

The on-screen depictions of gangsters and drug dealers you've watched from the comfort of your plush movie theater seats are inspired by the streets I grew up in. People are murdered daily as a result of gang affiliation and drug dealings, law enforcement officials are as crooked as the suspects they chase, and government plans to progress such areas are virtually nonexistent. I spent my formative years in the company of gangsters, drug dealers, users, and people that walked through life with a vengeful mentality born from cyclical, crushing poverty. And I was no different than the company I kept.

Except for the color of my hair and slight accent, you'd never suspect the connection between the volatile gangster and the reputable lawyer. Red is my past. The tattoos are usually tucked under dress shirts and slacks. My car of choice is no longer a low-rider Lincoln Town Car on fourteen-inch Dayton wire wheels. And when I'm in court these days, the trial isn't mine.

By all appearances, I am the embodiment of the American dream. I've achieved everything my father worked his whole life for me to have. I have risen above, reached higher ground, and become a success story.

But I can't stop there.

I didn't write this book to boast about my accomplishments or garner sympathy for my humble roots or even to rant about the unfairness of the hand I was dealt. I took responsibility for my destructive behavior a long time ago. Now I want to wake everyone else up to theirs.

I want to educate the middle and privileged classes so they might understand how difficult it is, as an impoverished minority, to obtain the American dream. I hope to remind the members of our legal system that their duty is not to only prosecute, but also, and more importantly, to rehabilitate our youth. Most of all, I want to show kids who are growing up in the grip of poverty, kids who have been beaten down by their circumstances, kids who think it's too late for them, that they too can overcome. Because if my time on this planet has taught me anything, it's that *no one* has more potential to rise than the person who starts from the very bottom.

PART ONE

"THINGS MAY COME TO THOSE WHO WAIT,
BUT ONLY THE THINGS LEFT BY THOSE WHO HUSTLE."

ABRAHAM LINCOLN

1

FIRST

JANUARY 16, 1990
PETIT THEFT[1]
ADJUDICATED GUILTY
SIX MONTHS COMMUNITY CONTROL

I was not raised wrong. I was raised in the wrong place. When people think of Miami they imagine the world's most beautiful beach resorts, multi-million dollar mansions on Star Island, towering skyscrapers overlooking Brickell, luxurious shopping experiences and upscale dining on South Beach, and some of the most popular nightclubs in America.

What you won't find in your Fodor's travel guide are the inner cities located west of the beaches and east of NW 57th Avenue. Starting just south of the Dolphin Expressway and ending as far north as County Line Road, Miami-Dade County's attractions include: Section 8 housing projects, frighteningly low employment rates, widespread criminal street gang activity, trap houses, and some of the most corrupt law enforcement agencies in the country.

This, as you might have guessed, is where my family relocated when we returned to the United States.

---

[1] See, Miami-Dade County State Attorney and Florida Department of Law Enforcement Case No. J90000572

Economically speaking, Miami wasn't any worse off than Argentina. The difference was that in Miami we knew we were poor. There were sixteen-year-olds cruising in Lamborghinis through South Beach, and less than ten miles away, my neighbors in the inner cities struggled to put food on the table. Being that close to such absurd wealth bred dreams of grandeur in our neighbors, dreams most could never manifest into reality. It stung. But the Windechers just felt fortunate to be back in America. In the midst of the squalor, my parents built a home.

The six of us—Dad, Mom, Christian, Giselle, Karina, and I—lived in a very small home in the city of North Miami Beach. In our neighborhood, all of the houses were small; there were no homes with a second floor, no pools, no yards to play in. Nearly all of the homes were shaped like a cube with a narrow driveway. Ours was no different.

Through our front door, was a living room that contained one couch and a little tube television. It was always hot in our house. There was a wall unit air conditioner in the living room that we never used because it rattled and didn't actually cool anything. The interior walls were covered with wallpaper and the floors with linoleum. At the end of the living room there was a hallway which led to two bedrooms, each about ten feet by ten feet.

My parents shared one of those bedrooms with my sister, Karina, who was only five years old, while I shared the other with my sister, Giselle, and my brother, Christian. We all shared one bathroom. Mornings in our house were mayhem. You could barely turn around in the kitchen, and fitting us all around the dining room table was comical. But that was home.

My father was proud. He left for work every day at 4:00 a.m., wearing the same clothes as the day before, to put food on the table. My mother was always there for us during the day. She cleaned our clothes, helped us get dressed, packed our lunches, and walked us to school every morning. I had no idea that wearing the same clothes two or three times a week was a sign of poverty until we moved back to the United States; in Argentina all students wore a uniform. I knew we did not have much, but I didn't feel different from other kids. Our parents made our home fun.

After school, my mom, who'd been a teacher in Argentina, helped us with our homework. When we finished, she sent us to go play outside until my dad returned home from work. We invented our own games because we did not have toys or video games. Giselle and Karina would pretend to serve meals with leaves, rocks, water, and whatever they could find outside. Christian and I would climb trees and pretend to fight villains and save the world like our favorite cartoon superheroes. Each night, my mom cooked a meal and we all ate dinner together. Our house may not have had much stuff in it, but it was full of laughter and conversation. We were grateful, and not having much money was okay. We had each other.

My brother, Christian Lee Windecher, or Keetee as my parents called him, and I were best friends growing up. I guess most kids are active, but Christian practically hummed with energy. He was more alive than anyone else I've ever met.

One night, back in Argentina, he saved a girl's life. We were out playing hide-and-seek and this girl fell into an open sewer hole. God knows how, but she managed to cling on to the edge, dangling over fifteen feet of darkness. My brother was the first to get to her. Another kid would have been too scared to act or would have left the rescue to a grown up, but not Christian. At the age of eight, he had the presence of mind to pull that little girl up onto the ground and out of danger. Christian was just like that.

He was only three years younger, and we did everything together. We climbed trees, played manhunt, started club houses, caught lizards and bugs; you name it. We were inseparable.

Playing outdoor sports was our favorite way to spend those humid Miami days, and our favorite sport was American football. We mostly played with the neighborhood kids at Greynolds Park on Miami Gardens Drive and West Dixie Highway. Unfortunately, Greynolds Park wasn't exactly just around the corner. It was actually a couple of miles from home, which made getting there a bit of a problem.

Christian and I shared one bicycle because my parents couldn't afford to buy one for each of us. Sharing wasn't just a matter of good manners in our house; it was an essential element of our family's survival. The trouble was that the bike Christian and I shared had a defective handlebar. The neck's grooves were stripped, so there was no way to completely tighten the device that fastened the handlebar to the bicycle's front wheel fork. The slightest push or pull of the handlebar would cause the entire device to fall forward or backwards. It was a precarious situation for a single rider, and it made Christian and me towing each other impossible. When we did hazard a try, the neck would give way and the person sitting on the handlebars spilled forward onto the asphalt. What we needed were bicycle pegs.

If we could just get our hands on a set of pegs, we could fasten them to the hub of the back tire, one of us could ride standing up on the pegs while holding on to the driver's shoulders, and we could both get to Greynolds Park at the same time without walking.

Pegs cost a measly twenty bucks. It was an easy, relatively inexpensive fix, but I knew my parents still couldn't afford it. I'd overheard more than one tense, hushed talk about money when my parents thought I was sleeping, and I understood what it meant when the refrigerator was empty by Thursday night. I knew that we needed money to eat and survive. And I knew that the pegs weren't important. But I wanted them.

It's a terrifying moment, realizing you're poor—especially for a kid. People say "money is power." I'm not sure about all that, but I know the opposite is true. No shackles are heavier than poverty's.

On January 16, 1990, Christian was in third grade, and I was a sixth grade student in my last year at Greynolds Park Elementary School. Despite the name, our school was pretty close to home and miles away from Greynolds Park. School had been buzzing all day about a huge football game that was going down that evening. This was the best time of the year for pick-up football games. It was playoff season in the National Football League, and the sport was all anyone could talk about. I wasn't going to miss this game.

When school let out at 3:30 p.m., Christian and I walked home together, and I made a decision.

It didn't seem like a big deal at the time, deciding to take what I believed I deserved, but that was the beginning for me. That was the day I started thinking like a hustler. The world wasn't fair by nature, but I could do something about that. I could stop waiting for the things I wanted to drop into my lap. I could stop going without. I could take what should be mine.

I picked up our BMX bicycle and told Christian to wait for me at home. I promised I'd be back in time to pick him up and that we'd arrive together when it was time to pick teams. I hopped on the bike and rode to Gary's Megacycle, the closest bicycle accessory and repair shop in North Miami Beach. It was located on the east side of 19th Avenue where it intersects with 182nd Street.

Inside, there were rows to my right and left of bicycles on display. In the middle of the store was one aisle with two sides, each facing one of the rows of bikes. The shelves were stocked with all sorts of bicycle accessories.

When I finally found the right section, I paused. There were too many options to choose from. I had no idea which type of peg would fit our BMX. I looked nervous, and I knew it. When I glanced up, the cashier was staring right at me.

"What are you looking for?" he asked.

He looked like he was about to come over to help. Or to bust me. My mind flipped through a million ways to answer, but before I could —

Bingo.

I snatched a bag of black pegs off of the shelves and locked eyes with him.

I froze for a moment. *What am I doing?*

But it was too late. Adrenaline was driving now.

I shoved the bag into my front pant pocket and bolted for the door. Through my heart pounding in my ears, I barely heard the cashier screaming, "Stop! You have to pay for that, you little thief!"

I made it outside, jumped on the BMX, and sped off toward home. I peddled like hell and didn't dare look back. For a moment, I thought I'd gotten away with it.

As luck would have it though, Gary—triathlete and owner of Gary's Megacycle—kept his bicycle handy and happened to be at work that day. Gary, it would seem, took the shoplifting of his merchandise rather personally, and he took it upon himself to chase me down and bring me to justice.

Even if I'd been able to outrun Gary, I'd forgotten one perilous detail.

When one is attempting to flee at any great speed on a bicycle, it is most efficient to stand up on the pedals. This will allow the rider to stroke the pedals at an optimal speed. Before attempting this, however, one better make damn certain that the handlebars are tightened so that they do not sway from the pressure applied by the force of one's body weight. As you might imagine, this tale is about to take a rather embarrassing and painful turn.

I focused on trying to pedal as quickly as possible, willing the BMX's handlebars to hold. But I failed. The handlebars pitched forward, I lost control and flipped over the front tire, hitting the ground shoulder first.

The next thing I knew, Gary the triathlete was picking me up off the ground like a wet towel. Out of pain and fear, I started to cry, choking out a refrain of "I am so sorry, sir," between sobs.

I begged Gary not to call my parents. I swore to Gary I would find a way to pay for the pegs if he gave me a chance. But Gary wasn't interested. Gary told me he was calling the North Miami Beach Police Department to have me arrested because I was a "little crook."

Sure enough, Officer Daniel Wilhite of the NMBPD showed up and read me my Miranda rights. Wilhite, a husky African American male, towered over me. He sported a flat top haircut with a pencil-thin mustache. He had beady eyes and the stare of a military sergeant. His cargo pants were tucked into shin-high boots with a flak jacket that read "NMBPD" across the back and "POLICE" across the front. He was an intimidating figure, but couldn't help thinking that his utility belt, packed with a gun, handcuffs, and a night stick, looked like he'd borrowed it from Batman.

To my great surprise, when he opened his mouth, his voice did not match his stature. Wilhite's high, whiny voice sounded like someone had clenched his ball sac with a tight rubber band. It was hard to take the large man's demeaning tone seriously when he couldn't keep his voice from cracking.

I hated him instantly.

When I got to the station, they charged me with Petit Theft and called my parents to inform them that I was under arrest. I remember sitting in a cell all by myself waiting for them to rescue me. It was cold. It was empty. I could hear the air conditioning humming through the vents.

Why had I done it? Why didn't we just walk? Why didn't I skip the football game? Why had it all been so important?

Officer Wilhite escorted my parents to the holding cell to see me.

The second my parents appeared on the opposite side of the grey bars, I burst into tears.

They were in shock. There was nothing I could have done to prepare my parents for that moment. I wasn't getting into trouble at school. I didn't have any behavior problems at home. My grades were always A's and B's. There were no signs for them to pick up on.

When the shock faded, my mother was distraught and my father was embarrassed. I will never forget the look on my mom's face. She did not deserve that pain. My father worked too hard to throw money away bailing me out of jail. He whipped my ass when we got home. And deservedly so. I knew better. I was raised better.

My brother and sisters should never have been exposed to things like jail and theft and arrests so young. Those concepts were abstract—the stuff of TV shows they weren't allowed to watch yet. Giselle and Karina were confused. I remember they both hugged me, vaguely worried looks on their faces. My parents grounded me for a long time. That first night of being grounded, I just sat on my bed and cried. Christian stayed with me. He always had my back. Even when I was wrong.

My case was referred to the Miami-Dade County State Attorney's office. After several hearings, a judge ordered me into the court's community control program where I was to perform fifty community service hours, write an apology letter to Gary, attend and complete theft-deterrent programs, pay court costs for such programs, and report to the judge every thirty days for six months. The community control program only made my parents' financial situation more difficult, and the burden of that guilt was too heavy for me to handle in a healthy, constructive way.

Placing an impoverished child into an expensive community control program is no way to teach him how to cope with poverty. I didn't steal because I enjoyed it or because I didn't grasp the moral issues at play. I stole because I was poor and I was helpless to change that. If ever there was an example of treating the symptoms and ignoring the disease, this was it.

That arrest and that court's ruling opened the door to the darkest eight years of my life. Overnight, I became a criminal. I was the child no parent wanted his or her children to be friends with. I was a petit thief. A little crook. I was the kid with a record, the kid placed on community control. I couldn't even play with the few friends who were allowed to talk to me because I had to spend my weekends performing community service hours.

I didn't learn how to accept my circumstances; I learned to resent them.

I seldom attended classes after elementary school. It wasn't that I didn't care about learning, but I had a reputation by middle school. I was a "bad kid." That's how kids deal with labels—they make them true. You tell a kid he's brilliant, and he'll prove you right. You tell a kid he's scum, and he'll act like it. It didn't help that I was being taught the exact same mathematics curriculum in ninth grade that I'd learned in my fifth grade year in Argentina. The teachers weren't engaging; the administrators were ignorant tyrants. It felt like they'd all given up, and I was bored.

Daniel Ortiz was the first gangster I befriended.

One day while we were standing next to each other in the John F. Kennedy Middle School cafeteria lunch line, I overheard him say that he'd forgotten his money and couldn't buy a cookie.

As Ortiz lifted the cookie off his lunch tray to hand it back to the cashier, I spoke up. "Here's a buck," I said, like it was no big deal.

Ortiz raised his eyebrows in surprise, and with a bit of suspicion, and asked me who I was. I told him.

"Naw homie you need you a nickname. Can't be walking around the hood looking that white and saying 'my name is David.' People gonna break that pretty-boy face." Ortiz looked me up and down. "From now on you go by Red."

Ortiz and I were friends from that moment on. He was a Latin King, and he always looked out for me because he knew I was Hispanic regardless of my white skin and red hair. Little by little, Ortiz introduced me to the majority of the Hispanic gang members living in the North Miami Beach area. Under his guidance, I learned that there were many paths to success and progression.

The older gangsters taught me that gang affiliation was a necessity because selling dope would inevitably make me enemies. And selling dope was what people in the hood did to make money. The Hispanic gangs had a strong presence throughout the Miami-Dade County area. Nobody crossed the Hispanics because an altercation with one member guaranteed violent retribution from the rest.

There were about seventy-five different gangs spread throughout the county, and every one of them was in some way connected to the South Florida dope industry.

The term "criminal street gang" refers to neighborhood groups who act collectively to achieve a common goal. Each criminal street gang has a two-fold objective. First, establish the gang's territory or "turf." Second, make money (primarily via drug trafficking). Each gangster plays a role. Those roles vary depending on the gangster's age, physical stature, and willingness to invoke violence to resolve disputes. The two principle factors in determining where a gangster stands in the gang hierarchy are his criminal history or arrest record and his ability to generate income for the gang. Most of the Miami-Dade County gangs operated informally with leadership given to those who had the balls to take control of their members.

The criminal street gangs born in the Miami-Dade County areas were made up of people with similar ethnic backgrounds and motivations. These individuals grew up together and bonded over similar needs. They formed groups with as few as five to twenty members and as many as several hundred members. The larger gangs broke up into neighborhood chapters to allow the gang to expand into various territories, generating more income.

Each chapter had a distinct gang language which consisted of verbal and visual ways to communicate. Verbal gang language included slurred speech or slang that could only be understood by gang members. Visual gang language included twisting fingers into hand signs, which is known as "throwing up" signs or "stacking." Stacking hands was the best way to communicate or claim one's gang and/or territory. A gangster could also claim his or her gang through other forms of visual gang language such as tattoos, specific colored clothing, or graffiti slogans displayed on public streets.

There were several ways to join a gang. The most common initiation for prospective members was to fight current gang members. This was known as getting "jumped-in." In Miami-Dade County, joining a gang was an expected and integrated part of growing up.

Once you became a gangster, the rules were simple: associate exclusively with other members, shift loyalty from family to gang, make money by participating in criminal activity, protect the gang turf and your fellow members, never snitch, never be the reason someone gets arrested, and never be the reason a fellow member dies.

I learned fast how crucial it was to never remain neutral when beef started. No matter the circumstances, the parties involved, or what was on the line, I always declared myself, without reservation, in favor of a side when a brawl was about to go down. Always. Whoever prevailed once the fight was over would not respect me if I wasn't willing to back them through it all. And whoever failed wouldn't back me the next time if I didn't come to their aid or get bloodied up alongside them.

The bottom line: a man takes a stand.

I started spending all my time with Ortiz and the Latin Kings, but one thing still stood between me and membership. If I wanted in for real, I would have to be "jumped-in."

To be jumped-in meant that I would have to fight five or more gang members for ten minutes straight and remain standing. That didn't mean I couldn't fall, it meant that for the entire ten minutes I had to keep getting up. Although it might be hard to imagine any good coming from willingly walking into a beating, good did come. Getting jumped-in taught me that it doesn't matter how hard I get hit or how many times I fall; what matters is willing myself to stand up again and again and, even when it hurts, again.

As scary as getting jumped-in to a gang might sound, it really wasn't too intimidating for me. By the summer of 1993, I'd grown accustomed to unfair fights. The African American Zoe Pound gangsters randomly jumped me on Cracker Day. At JFK, the student body ratio was 60% African American, 30% Hispanic, 5% Caucasian, and 5% various other races, such as Asian or Native American. I'd heard about Cracker Day while I was at Greynolds Park Elementary, but I thought it was a story that kids told to freak each other out. I soon learned it was as real as it was told.

On Cracker Day, when the final bell rang and students were sent home for the weekend, the African American Zoe Pound gangsters cornered the white kids and beat them into unconsciousness, just for kicks. Cracker Day was an opportunity for the African Americans to claim their turf. I learned to skip the last class period of the day on Fridays so that I could get an early jump on my walk home. But if there was a test, or I was all out of absences, I had no choice but to accept Cracker Day. No matter which route I took home, I was forced to walk through an African American area. If I took the main roads, they would walk with me until we reached a secluded area, and then jump me. Taking back streets home worked best.

The easy fix in the affluent home would be to arrange a pick-up service or a carpool with other kids. But in the hood, usually only one parent owned a vehicle and that parent was hard at work when school let out.

On the first Friday of middle school at JFK, I left walking toward home. Two African American kids, brothers named Pierre and Jean Pasquet, walked up to me and said, "Hey which way are you walking home? We will walk with you if you're going toward Greynolds Park."

My stupid innocent self thought they wanted to be friends. We made small talk while we walked. We exchanged names and talked about our favorite football teams. Then, when we reached a bridge that crossed us over the Snake Creek Canal, one of them threw a haymaker from behind and knocked me straight to the ground. I tried to get up but got kicked in the face just above my right eye. Blood came flowing out like a faucet.

I was scared for my life. I had no idea what was happening. So I balled up and took it. The next thing I remember was waking up on my stomach. My head was pounding. My book bag and its contents were gone. I was nearly naked. The brand new shirt, pants, and shoes my parents saved up for as a gift for my first day of middle school were taken.

The combination of terror and the concussion left me without my immediate memory. I got myself up and walked the rest of the way home in my boxers. When I got home, my mom called the police. They did nothing because I couldn't remember what happened. But as the weekend passed, I started to recall. Their faces and that experience were burnt into my mind for the rest of my life. I missed the entire next week of school because my face looked like ground beef.

I had been jumped at least twenty times before I even met Ortiz. As the beatings accumulated, I learned the less I fought back, the harder the whipping I would get.

So, I always fought back, but when I was outnumbered, there was very little I could do. It always started as a one-on-one, but a full-on jumping was inevitable. The instant I started to win a fight, two more would jump into the fray. There was no way I could win, but I always made it my goal to knock out at least one of the Zoe Pounders before I got concussed. Sometimes it wasn't so bad. A few times I didn't think I would survive.

My dad couldn't pick me up from school to prevent Cracker Day, so he taught me something that most affluent parents never have to teach their children: how to defend from and fight back against an aggressor.

My father did not teach me how to box so that I would become more violent. He taught me to fight because he wanted to make sure I made it home from school and could join our family for dinner every night. Most kids never have to face that type of reality. But that was my life starting at the age of thirteen.

It might sound sick, but I really started to enjoy fighting. I planned each move, gauging how much I could take before I got knocked out. Boxing became my hobby. My father taught me to keep my jaw locked to absorb hard punches. He taught me how to stand in defense and how to stand to attack. He instructed me to bait my aggressor, to allow them to hit me a couple of times so they would come in closer. As soon as they were within knockout striking range, I was to unload an uppercut to the chin or a haymaker to the temple. Most importantly, he taught me never to waste a single breath when I knew an altercation was inevitable. I took those lessons seriously. I never wanted to walk home in my boxers again.

But hand to hand fights weren't the only danger in the hood.

One weekend, Christian and I walked to the Skylake movie theater to see *Honey I Shrunk the Kids*. About halfway through the show, we heard an explosive argument out in the lobby. The voices got very loud and it sounded as if a fight broke out. Almost as if we'd rehearsed it, everyone cleared out of the movie theater in unison to see what was happening.

Christian and I jumped to our feet and followed. We pushed our way through the adults in the lobby until we made it to the front of the crowd. We watched, pressed against the tinted glass.

In plain daylight, right out in front of the theater, a gang fight had broken out. These kids were a lot older than us, probably in their late teens, and I could tell they were gangsters because of the tattoos and the clothes.

The fight was a four on one. Four African American gangsters pounding one Hispanic kid. As we arrived, one of the gangsters yanked the kid off the ground by his shirt and said something I couldn't hear. The kid spit in the gangster's face.

The gangster dropped him to the ground and pulled out a handgun.

It was like a vacuum had suddenly opened. All of the bystanders evaporated. But Christian and I didn't move. We stood transfixed as the gangster with the gun fired a deafening round into the kid's abdomen. We watched without moving as the gangsters fled. Our eyes grew wide as blood pooled around the still, still body.

It was just like a movie.

"Let's go home," I whispered.

Christian nodded, mutely.

I pulled open the door with a violently shaking hand, and caught a faint whiff of gunpowder and the sound of a muffled, anguished moan. I froze. The kid was still alive.

We stood there in the doorway, afraid to leave, afraid to go back inside.

That's something they don't show in movies. They make death seem quick. The soldiers get shot and then they're dead. The plane crashes and the passengers are dead.

But that's not how it goes in real life. Not always.

We probably stood there for five whole minutes, unable to look away, listening to the kid's moans grow softer and softer before he went silent.

I'd never seen anything dead before, but I knew when he was gone.

The sound of sirens echoed in the distance, and the spell was broken. I cried as we ran. That night I dreamt that I was the kid who got shot.

I knew, then, what I had to do.

The next Monday at school, I asked Ortiz to make it happen at 3:00 p.m. on Friday—the same day and hour that Cracker Day happened each week at JFK. I was ready to become a gangster.

2

SECOND

JANUARY 5, 1995
BATTERY; GRAND THEFT[2]
NOLLE PROSEQUI
FIFTEEN DAYS IN JUVENILE LOCK-UP

*S*tay calm and never stop breathing, David. Ball your fists with all your strength! Don't throw punches you can't land. Always keep one fist up guarding your face. Focus on the off buttons. Remember that the harder you try, the harder they will counter, and the more you will get hurt. Stay relaxed. But keep your jaw muscles tight. Breathe out when you punch and keep your eye on your target. Don't hold your breath and don't look at the ground. You have to learn to keep your eyes open.

The day of the jump-in came, and at 2:50 p.m. all I could hear was my dad's voice, patient but intense, coaching me through boxing technique on a loop.

By 3:00 p.m., when I pushed open the heavy doors to the parking lot, my mind was very, very quiet. Except for one thought.

Ten minutes. Get back up for ten minutes.

I stepped outside onto the blacktop and was instantly drenched in sweat. I blinked against the blinding Miami sun.

---

[2] See, Miami-Dade County State Attorney and Florida Department of Law Enforcement Case No. J95000367B

There they were—about fifteen of them—leaning up against cars, taking slow drags on blunts, and silently watching me approach.

As I got closer, Ortiz pushed off his car and walked to meet me. The broken pavement crunched loudly under our Reeboks.

He stopped about two feet away, looked over his shoulder at the waiting crowd, and turned back to me with a menacing grin. God help the gangster who crossed Ortiz. And suddenly, I knew: He was one of the five I'd have to fight.

My adrenaline spiked and ebbed.

Ortiz rotated his neck slowly from one side to the other. I felt a thick drop of sweat slide down my back.

"You ready, Red?"

Before I could answer, Ortiz's fist made sharp contact with my jaw. My fists sprang to life, all hesitation had evaporated. I did not utter a single word, but called up every lesson my dad had taught me. I focused on landing punches on Ortiz's off buttons: chin, nose, temples. One solid hit to any of those spots could put even the toughest man on his back.

Ortiz and I went at it for what felt like twelve rounds.

I felt my edge slipping. He was bigger, stronger, and had four gangsters waiting to jump in if I knocked him out.

Ten minutes.

Keep your jaw locked, David. Breathe through your nose.

Finally, I caught Ortiz with a haymaker to the chin, and he went down.

Even before he hit the pavement, another fist struck from the right. I felt the impact resonate through my fully compressed facial muscles. My training kept me conscious, but a clenched jaw can only do so much against five strong, amped up gangsters.

In an instant, I was on my back, the wind completely sucked from my lungs, blows landing from five sets of fists all at once.

Then they were kicking my legs and my back. I curled inward to protect my vital organs.

Ten minutes.

I had to get up. I could not go down like this.

I heaved with everything I had, but their weight was too much. I was trapped. I started swinging wildly, taking every shot I could, and one landed. Right on someone's nuts.

He yelled out in pain and keeled over, cupping his sac. The others jerked back, suddenly wary.

I picked my bruised body up off the ground, and struggled for a jagged breath.
Ten minutes.

I rushed at the group of gangsters, lunging at the closest one. I wrapped my arms around his back and flung him down to the ground. He fell on his face and I landed on top of his back. I started dropping haymaker after haymaker onto the side of his face.

After three or four heavy slugs, I was knocked harder than I had ever been hit before.

I dropped to the asphalt.

I fought for consciousness. My vision swam and my head was ringing, but I pushed myself up off the ground again.

I could barely stand. My knuckles were covered in slick, crimson blood, and I could taste it in my mouth. Was it even mine?

I raised my fists.

Ten minutes.

No one moved. I tried focusing on each of their faces, but darkness was creeping in from the corners.

I spit out a mouthful of blood.

"What the fuck y'all standing around for? Let's go!"

Ortiz stepped forward and I swung loosely at his head and missed. He was grinning again, but the menace was replaced with pride.

"You're in, Red," he said. "Welcome to the team, baby boy."

That night, I snuck into the house, moving as carefully as my stiff, aching carcass would allow. I grabbed washcloths from the closet, and slipped into the bathroom, locking the door behind me. I set the cloths on the side of the sink and leaned in to get a good look at the carnage.

I looked like I'd walked through a war zone. My shirt was torn and stained. My lip was split and caked with dried, blackened blood. My left eye was purple and swollen shut. My right eye wasn't far behind. There was gravel ground into my cheek, and I had a feeling that if I lifted my shirt, I'd see a nasty pool of internal bleeding spreading around my ribs.

This was the of face a gangster.

My seventh, eighth, and ninth grade years at JFK were an academic blur. I was never in school. I didn't need to read *Huckleberry Finn* and I didn't need to measure circles. What I needed was a way out of my family's poverty, and sitting in a classroom wasn't getting me there. Even if I did stick it out, what then? I couldn't get a job—no one would hire a kid with a Petit Theft conviction on his RAP sheet. And if someone did take a chance on me? I'd do what? Work some nine-to-five at minimum wage and fight through life, constantly sacrificing, constantly hungry, always wanting, barely getting by, and hoping for something better?

No way.

Doing things the "right" way was a dead end, and I was done wasting time. So I turned my focus to a more lucrative enterprise: the dope game.

In tenth grade, it was 1994—the year I turned sixteen—and it was decision time.

Ever since I was a kid, I dreamt that one day I'd become an attorney. It wasn't about attaining that cliché of occupational status. I wanted to be able to protect my family. I never again wanted to see a look on my dad's face like the day he lost everything back in California. I never wanted anyone to make my siblings feel small just because we were born into difficult circumstances. I knew that to fight the stigmas and the prejudice, I needed an education. I had to remain in school to become an attorney. I couldn't become a statistic of the hood.

But I was impatient. I felt stagnant and trapped at North Miami Beach High School, and I just knew there was more out there.

So one night, I'd had enough and I put an end to it. Christian, Giselle, and Karina were sound asleep, and my parents were talking in whispers in the kitchen. I tiptoed out and stood in the doorway, watching them for a few seconds. My mom was smirking as she packed our lunches; my dad was leaning up against the counter next to her, rubbing a knot out of his shoulder and trying to muffle a laugh at something she'd said.

They looked… happy, I guess. Like, even though Mom was wearing the same shirt she'd worn all week and Dad's knees were getting stiffer every day, they were doing okay in the ways that really counted.

I felt sick.

For a moment, I thought about crawling back into bed and sleeping one more night as the person my parents wanted me to be. But I've never been one to run from something difficult. And this conversation was difficult. More than I'd imagined.

My mom begged me to reconsider. My dad told me to give it more time. School could be interesting if I'd apply myself. I could get involved with clubs. I could test into honors classes. Anything. But just don't give up. Don't drop out. My dad reminded me of California, my mom reminded me of how hard they had worked, of how much they had gone through to give me the opportunity to succeed.

But my mind was made up.

I took my mom's hand and asked them both to trust me. I knew it didn't seem right on paper, I told them, but this was the right decision for me. Then I promised my parents and myself that this wasn't the end. I would get my General Education Diploma. I *would* go to college and then law school. I knew it in my bones that one day I would become an attorney. I had a vision. And I would find a way.

On October 16, 1994, when I was old enough to legally drop out of high school, I did. And I didn't look back.

I made a lot of promises that night—to my parents and myself. I knew there would be challenges, and I knew the climb would be long, but I also knew I had it in me to overcome.

From day one, the purpose of joining the gang was to make money.

I'd started hustling in the dope game long before I dropped out. As a fourteen-year-old jitterbug, an eighth grader at JFK, I sold weed for pocket cash. I did that for quite some time, making just enough money to eat and smoke for free. Almost every gangster I knew sold drugs to make money. The drug deals were mostly independent transactions; there was no real organization in place. It was a matter of eat what you kill.

I spent most of my time with older gangsters, especially Vernon Nickson. Nickson was my guide in the dope game. He told me to start by saving up just enough money—ninety bucks at the time—to purchase an ounce of marijuana. Once I had the capital for that first ounce, Nickson taught me how to break it down into smaller weighted portions and bag them in nickel or dime bags. Nickel bags, which held half grams, sold for five dollars. Dime bags, containing a full gram, went for ten dollars.

Based on this model, I could generate at least $280 from each ounce of marijuana and stood to earn a profit of about $180. That might seem like a decent payday, but the risk heavily outweighed the benefit. The margin was negligible given the amount of time and number of opportunities to get busted that went into moving fifty-six nickel bags or twenty-eight dime bags.

After I dropped out, I was ready to make serious money. Nickson always said that if I wanted to make "real money" I would need to work my way into moving quarter-pounds, half-pounds, or full pounds. I'd be able to purchase marijuana at a discounted rate, and I'd turn larger profits with less effort.

But enemies and danger are big money's ugly shadows. A gangster knows his number one, most basic need is to survive. Obviously, he has to make money to live, but if he gets greedy, if he lets the dead presidents call the shots, he creates a weakness in himself. And nobody knows how to exploit weakness like a rival gangster.

Before I could gain momentum in the dope game, I had to solidify my reputation as a formidable foe and valuable ally. With the right reputation, I could take more risks, and people base their first impression of a gangster on the people he keeps close. If those around me were known to be sharp and fearless, it would be assumed that I was of the same stock.

So I put a team together.

First, I wanted to recruit muscle. Joey Torres, Danny Martinez, and Edwin Echevarria were the obvious choices. They were some of the most intimidating Hispanic juveniles in the hood.

Joey Torres had three skills: fighting, cutting hair, and slanging dope. He was a stocky Puerto Rican who stood only five foot six, and he'd moved to Miami from the Bronx after getting expelled from three different New York schools for fighting. Joey was nicknamed Fade after the term for a one-on-one fight, and he was aptly named. Joey would fight anyone with the slightest provocation. A lingering eye was enough to set him on a war path. Beneath the anger, he was a person of strong character, but his father died when he was a kid and his mother worked as a K-Mart cashier to support their entire household. He didn't talk about it, but I knew it made him bitter. It also fueled the rage behind his hammer of a right hook. Joey was my best friend.

Danny Martinez was a straight up gangster of Colombian descent. He took everything, especially being a gangster, seriously. I don't think I saw him smile more than five times in all the years I knew him. The dude meant business. Maybe the scariest thing about him was his unpredictability. Like Torres, Martinez lived for fighting. I knew that first hand. We grew up on the same block, and we didn't always see eye to eye. Martinez and I fought each other on multiple occasions, but those fights bred mutual respect. I once saw Martinez get stabbed in the stomach with scissors during a fight. Before we rushed him to the hospital, he unleashed one of the worst ass-whippings I had ever seen on his assailant. I'd never seen someone gush blood like that. The stabbing sealed his reputation as one of the toughest gangsters in Miami-Dade County. Martinez was scared of nothing and no one, and I never met a single person who wasn't intimidated by him.

Echevarria was born in the Dominican Republic and raised in North Miami Beach. Echevarria was the poster child of a gangster. He sported an unruly beard with a mouth full of gold teeth and was built like a bodybuilder. He was jacked. All he ever did was work out. At the age of fifteen, he stood six feet tall and weighed 220 pounds. When Echevarria was not working out, he was out looking for fights. He was mostly known for starting full on brawls at nightclubs with bouncers, other gangsters, and cops. If Echevarria was around, you could count on fists getting thrown. It was all he talked about. He didn't pump iron for trophies; he did it for the power to knock people out faster. If Echevarria hit you with a clean punch, it was guaranteed that your body was hitting the floor. I lost count of the times I witnessed Echevarria knock someone out cold with just one hit. You could actually see fear in people's eyes when he walked into a room.

Second, I needed a man with connections who could acquire any type of drug we could possibly sell, and no one knew people like Nickson. Nickson was older than all of us. He was an African American who was down with all of the

Hispanics because he was a true businessman—an original gangster. Nickson was the first black person I believed I could trust. He didn't have time for nonsense or drama. He was all about making money. When I was first starting out, he was the one I purchased marijuana from. He was a mentor, and he had a ton of the right kind of connections. Most importantly, he was down with the notorious John Doe Dope Boys from Liberty City. The John Doe Dope Boys were the most renowned supply group for any illegal substance. They had the best supply and the best prices. No white boy could just knock on the door of the John Doe Dope Boys' trap house asking to get hooked up, but Nickson could.

Third, I needed someone who had an approachable personality and was well known throughout the hood in order to bring in new business. Dalwin Reyna was perfect for the job. Reyna was a pretty boy and very popular. He had this calm, easy way about him. He was of Dominican Republic descent and was one of the first people I met when I moved to Miami. We grew up riding bikes together. With his personality, Reyna could party with white kids, black kids, and everyone in between. He was also into the graffiti scene and made friends with various tagging crews. Reyna was a networking genius. He also happened to have an older sister named Adriana who was a magnet for attention. She was particularly attractive and was friends with everyone. Adriana introduced her little brother to all of her girlfriends, which, combined with his own friends, gave us plenty of relationships to capitalize on. Reyna was an important recruit because females loved him. Girls may be the single most powerful tool that can be exercised on a man: control the girl, and you control the man. If all the females Reyna knew would influence the other men in their lives to purchase drugs from us, we stood to make a lot of money. I knew Reyna would bridge the gap between supply and demand.

Fourth, I wanted Steve Toretto, a car man. I heard that chop shops in Miami paid good money for hot cars, and I wanted to find out. Toretto was Venezuelan. He was a mechanic practically from birth. He knew more about cars than anyone I'd ever met. Engines, transmissions, suspensions, brakes, tires, wiring harnesses, audio systems. Everything. When he was younger, Toretto a had purchased a car and taught himself all there was to know by taking it apart and putting it back together. He wanted to own a mechanic shop one day, but in the meantime, I put his skills to use teaching us how to unlock and start cars without keys. He could hotwire anything on four wheels, and he was a cool dude to smoke weed with.

Last, I wanted a capable grifter with a skill set that none of the other males had. I needed a female we could seamlessly work with on operations that required...a more delicate touch. For that purpose, I brought in Denise Aviles. Denise was one of the most attractive females in North Miami Beach. She was Puerto Rican and a straight hustler. She always had money on her mind. And she was willing to do whatever it took to get paid. We had that in common and became friends fast. This chick was a gangster at heart. Denise wanted to be down, and believe me, a trustworthy female is priceless.

In a matter of months, people started to recognize us. If anyone disrespected us in any way, we came after them. Our fights and retribution efforts were always carefully planned. We were never reckless, and everyone had a role to play. The combination of muscle, charisma, and an attractive gangster chica made our notoriety soar. The connections to purchase drugs in bulk and the skills to steal cars earned us income. The ability to network allowed us to expand quicker than most start-up businesses, and soon I was laying ground work for our own dope hole.

We were an eclectic group, but we all had one thing in common: poverty.

I had intense ideas on how to change that, and I jumped at chances others were not willing to consider. But I was not your average criminal. There were rules and protocols that any gangster on my team was going to follow. I wanted my people disciplined and mentally tough. I planned, analyzing each crime from every conceivable angle. There was no such thing as a small heist. If it could get us busted, it was scrutinized and blueprinted. We role-played each potential scenario. We studied our surroundings and brainstormed every possible setback. We outlined procedures to counter any surprise issues. We often planned for days, sometimes weeks, and even months if a payday was significant.

Hustling was a straight up job. From late in 1994 to the summer of 1997, we moved thousands of pounds of marijuana, stole hundreds of vehicles, and committed various forms of fraud.

On the day prior to my second arrest, I received a page from two kids from the Jewish upper-class neighborhood of Sunny Isles, asking for my help purchasing a quarter-pound of marijuana for a party. They were what we called "wannabes."

Even though they were brought up in well-off Jewish families, drove nice cars, and wore the latest fashions, these kids would parade around town with the wrong crowds, trying to act gangster. Frankly, it was pathetic.

But what did I care? They loved pot, and I knew they had plenty of money to spare because they'd become regular nickel and dime customers since I'd sold to them several months earlier at a party. This was my chance to sell my first quarter-pound of marijuana and make some real money.

My up-front cost would be $240 for all four ounces ($60 per ounce rather than $90 per ounce). At $500, I would make an immediate profit of $260 for a single transaction. *This* was the way to do it.

I quoted the wannabes $500, which they agreed to like it was nothing. We planned to meet in the parking lot at an apartment complex in Sunny Isles on 172nd Street and Collins Avenue. The transaction was to take place at 4:00 p.m.

At that point, I wasn't driving yet, so I called on one of my neighborhood friends, Josh Baron. Baron owned a beige four-door late-model Oldsmobile Cutlass Supreme with dark tinted windows. His nickname was Joker because, like Batman's arch nemesis, Baron had a sadistic sense of humor. He could transition from cool and collected to psychotic and dangerous in a split second. I offered to pay Baron to play chauffeur for the day's outing. When he picked me up from my parent's house, I handed Baron twenty-five dollars for his services, and we headed to the Star Creek Apartments to pick up Nickson.

Star Creek was my home away from home, as it was for many of the gangsters I associated with. The complex was located on NW 191st and NW 3rd Ave. The area was saturated with drug peddlers, drug addicts, and crooked cops. It was straight hood in Star Creek. Everyone that lived in that neighborhood was a gangster. Everyone was strapped. Everyone was a hustler.

Baron drove Nickson and me to the John Doe Boys' dope hole in Liberty City. When we rolled up, I handed Nickson the $265 that I'd saved selling nickel and dime bags to purchase a quarter-pound of marijuana and to cover his connection fee. Nickson walked into the dilapidated apartment complex while Baron and I waited in the car.

Unless the John Doe Boys knew you personally, it was out of the question to come near their doorstep. Baron and I kept a low profile until Nickson returned. Once he had, and the quarter-pound was safely in my hand, we delivered Nickson back to Star Creek, and I paged the wannabes to describe Baron's car and instruct them to bring a bookbag to conceal their purchase. I was about to make some real money. If all went as planned, I would walk away with $210 from a transaction that took less than a few hours to complete.

Baron and I arrived about an hour early to stake the complex out. Baron backed his Cutlass into a parking spot near the end of a narrow lot. I moved into the back behind the front passenger seat. Our plan was to have one of the wannabes sit in the back seat with me to conduct our business while the other wannabe sat in the front passenger seat next to Baron. I was worried that cops may get suspicious since we didn't exactly fit the profile of the average citizen in Sunny Isles. As it turned out, the cops weren't the only ones we should have been worried about.

Baron and I sat in the Cutlass with the windows up, scanning each car that pulled into and out of the complex. I swiped a layer of sweat off my forehead and rubbed my dripping hand on my damp shirt, only to have a giant droplet sting my eye. The hour crawled, and I was getting restless.

Suddenly, the doors of a black four door, new-model Nissan Maxima that parked about twenty-five yards ahead of us popped open.

I elbowed Baron and nodded toward the car and its two occupants.

These guys looked like they belonged here about as much as we did.

In fact, they looked like Hispanic gangsters. The driver had tattoos on his right forearm, and both of them sported the familiar baggy shorts, short sleeved Nautica button-ups, and Reebok Classics with matching leather hats. A few years younger, and they could have been us.

"I don't know these fools. You?" Baron whispered.

I shook my head once.

We watched as the two gangsters had a brief conversation in the parking lot near their car. After a few minutes, the passenger headed into a building inside the complex, and the driver got back into the Maxima.

About fifteen minutes later, a grey four door, new-model Oldsmobile 88 Royale pulled in. I strained to see through the tinted glass. It was one of the wannabes.

This didn't feel right. I'd been selling to the wannabes for months, and not once had I seen either of them driving an 88.

The wannabe backed the 88 into a parking spot—right next to the Maxima. With the driver's sides aligned.

"Red?" Baron muttered, "You seeing this shit?"

I didn't reply.

The wannabe sat in the 88 for about a minute before stepping out.

With each second that passed, I felt my body winding up, the way I felt right before a fight. When the wannabe finally got out, I saw his lips barely move as he passed the driver of the Maxima. I looked him up and down. No bookbag. And no sidekick.

I reached into my own bookbag and pulled out a Smith & Wesson 25 millimeter handgun. I placed it in my lap in clear view. As he approached, I lowered the rear right window just enough to be seen and heard.

"Back seat," I told him. "Driver's side."

The wannabe opened the door and froze, one foot in, one foot on the ground, eyes fixed on my 25.

"Relax, dawg," I said. "I am a businessman, not a murderer."

As long as everything was in order, there was nothing to worry about. I'd always carried the gun, including each and every time he and I had transacted for a nickel or dime bag, but this time something was off, and I wanted him to see what he was up against.

He slid in and closed the door. Baron clicked the lock button and the wannabe flinched.

"Where's your shadow?" I asked.

"I don't know."

Wrong answer.

I leaned forward and looked the wannabe dead in the eye. "Don't tell me you stupid motherfuckers are dumb enough to try to set us up?"

The wannabe went white. "I swear it wasn't my idea. I swear. Please don't shoot me. I'm sorry!"

My heart dropped. We were probably seconds away from being robbed. I grabbed my gun and shoved it into the right side of the wannabe's stomach.

"What the fuck are you saying? Talk!"

"He's gonna page me—"

"Who?" I snarled. "Your shadow?"

"Yeah," he said. I dug the barrel of the 25 deeper into his gut. "Yes. As it goes off, he's gonna block you in, and they're going to rob you, but this wasn't my plan! I told him no. You believe me—"

I slammed his body against the car door. His head smacked against the window.

"Do they have guns?"

"No! No guns." His face was twisted up in pain, and his eyes were glazing. "Please don't shoot us."

I tightened my grip on his shoulder.

"What are they armed with? Knives? Bats? What!"

He nodded quickly. "Bats. Please—" His voice cracked. "Please don't shoot us."

His pager sounded.

Tears puddled in his eyes and he started sniveling like a little bitch.

"I'm sorry. *Please*. I'm so sorry. Just—"

I struck him with the handle of the 25 in a close-fisted backhand to the jaw and he slumped forward. No more crying. In the same instant, Baron cranked up the Cutlass, but before he could throw it into drive, the other wannabe flew into the complex, blocking our exit.

I locked eyes with the passenger—it was the same Hispanic passenger from the Maxima. He must have met up with the other wannabe on the front side of the complex. He jumped out, but I saw it coming. Before he could take a single step toward Baron's Cutlass, I was out of the car, aiming at the other wannabe behind the wheel.

"Move that piece a shit or I am going to blow you and yo bitch ass homeboy away!"

Tires were squealing before the Hispanic could react. The other wannabe fled. He floored it all the way out of the lot, leaving the Maxima's passenger and his unconscious friend behind.

I turned the 25 on the passenger who was standing there like his mom just caught him masturbating.

"I don't know what the fuck you thought was gonna happen here, but it aint going down like that," I said.

He looked around wildly for a way out.

"Now," I went on, "take those chains off yo neck, whatever you got in yo pockets, put it on the ground, and get the fuck up outta here!"

The passenger threw his gold chains, beeper, and cash on the ground and ran toward the Maxima.

Only when their taillights were completely out of view did I lower my 25. I could suddenly feel my heart slamming against my rib cage. I took a deep breath and blew it out my nose.

Baron climbed out, popped open the back door and dragged the unconscious wannabe onto the ground. I stuffed my 25 in my pants and gathered up all of the Hispanic's discarded belongings from the pavement. I'd been wrong. Save for their appearance, there was nothing gangster about the two unknowns in the Maxima.

As I turned back to the car, I saw Baron stomping on the wannabe.

"Dawg," I called.

He looked up at me, sweat dripping from his face, and I nodded. I couldn't blame him.

Baron drove south on Collins Avenue while I stuffed my 25, the chains, beeper, and the cash into my bookbag with the unsold quarter-pound.

"There," I pointed. "Pull off."

Baron drove around to the backside of a strip mall off Collins Avenue and parked beside a dumpster. I threw the bag in, and we drove west on 163rd Street toward Star Creek. We needed to hide out until it was safe to go back for it.

"That was crazy, man," Baron said, but he was laughing.

I rested my forehead on my fist. How had I not seen this coming? I ran through every step again. What had I missed?

Baron cursed under his breath.

I looked up. "What?"

He nodded to the rearview.

I looked in my side mirror just in time to see lights swirl on and hear a siren blip. I slammed my fist onto the dashboard.

Cops.

3

THIRD

JANUARY 23, 1995
CRIMINAL MISCHIEF; CONSPIRACY TO COMMIT A FELONY[3]
NOLLE PROSEQUI
ASS-WHIPPING AT THE HANDS OF THE NMBPD

Nearly five full years had elapsed since my first arrest, and I could hardly remember the little kid who ran from Gary's with the stolen bike pegs. Here I was, headed to a police station again, this time facing charges of Battery and Grand Theft.

Baron and I were taken to the Miami-Dade Police Department on Biscayne Blvd and NE 156th Street. We were immediately separated. Interrogation ensued, but it was brief. I was asked if I wanted to voluntarily give a statement; I declined and asked to speak with my parents. I was denied. Instead, I was fingerprinted and placed in a holding cell. I was transported to the Miami-Dade Juvenile Detention Center where I waited to see a judge.

At my first appearance, the state objected to my release pending trial. The presiding judge agreed with the state and denied my release due to what he called "the nature of the charges."

---

[3] See, Miami-Dade County State Attorney and Florida Department of Law Enforcement Case No. J95001002B

What Baron and I did was illegal, and there is no justifying our actions. But the foundation of our crime was very different from the wannabes'. I was only trying to sell to them so I could buy myself some new clothes—not for vanity's sake, but so I could finally retire the five hole-ridden boxer briefs that I had been wearing on rotation for the last two years—and so I could buy food to help alleviate some of that burden from my parents. My intentions were never to hurt anyone.

The wannabes, on the other hand, were pretending to be something they didn't need to be. They staged a robbery for something they could pay for, placed us directly in harm's way, and got another strike added to my record. Exactly which part of my life did they want? If those wannabes were forced to spend one day in my shoes, they would beg for home and their well-secured bright futures.

What really got me was the pattern of wealthy kids pretending to live the life of someone who survives by committing crimes. It didn't make sense. Why did they do it? Was it a game to them? Did their daddies work too much at their white collar jobs and not spoil them enough? Were they bored with their video games and sports camps and family cruises to the Bahamas?

Or did they want to fit in? Were they breaking the law to gain social acceptance with people like me? Did their soft reputations bother them? Was it actually possible that rich kids, raised in multi-story homes with new paint and plush carpet and shiny cars in the driveway and college funds and closets full of clothes, actually wanted the approval of hoodlums?

How could I blame the wannabes for trying to be something they weren't when we are mentally enlisted to believe this grass-is-greener-at-the-top-of-the-hill garbage? Were they at fault in doing what they did? Sure enough. We are all responsible for the decisions that we make. The better question is, weren't they just getting in line, following the very clear cut path that our current idea of the American dream is leading us to? We're taught to admire self-destructive athletes with drug addictions and rappers who constantly prattle about gold chains with Jesus pieces and cars with shinny rims. America: the land of the dissatisfied and the home of the opportunists.

After they'd pulled us over, the officers had asked us to sit on the trunk of Baron's Cutlass as an unmarked police vehicle crawled into the Texaco station.

It was a detective driving, and in the front passenger seat sat the wannabe who'd tried to set us up. He was staring at his knees. I'd watched the detective's lips move as he lifted a finger and pointed right at us. The wannabe's eyes flicked up, met mine, and he quickly nodded before returning his stare to his knees.

My cheek was smashed against the trunk of the Cutlass and cuffs were slapped onto my wrists before the detective's car was out of the lot.

Baron and I never told the full truth. Not to the police, not to any detective, prosecutor, or even the judge. The wannabes walked after trying to rob us during what should have been a simple business deal, and we took the rap for it. But there were rules, and "never snitch" was one that, if broken, could have an irreversible effect on my reputation.

It wasn't like we had a choice, anyway. Who would believe us over "those poor innocent kids"? And, far more importantly, the true story would put a 25 in my possession, which could have upgraded the charges to Attempted Murder, Robbery, Possession of a Firearm, and Aggravated Battery. Without the gun and the rest of my bookbag's contents, the only evidence the state could turn against Baron and me was an out-of-court identification from the wannabe I'd knocked unconscious on the date of the incident.

As it turned out, there were no other witnesses who came forward. Whether someone saw something and didn't want to get involved, or somehow we'd actually avoided being seen, it was impossible to say. Either way, it meant that in order for the state to establish our guilt beyond a reasonable doubt, they needed in-court testimony from at least one of the wannabes to identify us as the perpetrators.

That would never happen.

Prior to trial, Torres, Martinez and Echevarria visited the wannabes and helped them to understand the consequences of testifying. My friends were very persuasive. When the wannabes suddenly stopped cooperating with the prosecutor, the state had no choice but to drop the charges. But I wasn't waiting for this decision at home. I spent the fifteen days it took the state to dismiss the charges in the Miami-Dade Juvenile Detention Center.

On March 18, 1963, the Supreme Court of the United States made history with their ruling in the landmark case of *Gideon v. Wainright*[4]; ironically a case that started in Florida and made its way up to our Supreme Court. Clarence Gideon requested and was denied counsel when he was charged with breaking an

---

[4] See, United States Supreme Court Case No. 372 U.S. 335 (1963)

entry with the intent to commit larceny. Much like my father back in California, Gideon could not afford representation and as a result was forced to act as his own trial counsel. A jury found Gideon guilty and the judge sentenced him to five years in a Florida state prison. Gideon appealed. The Supreme Court reversed the conviction ruling that every American accused of a crime is entitled to an attorney because to have a fair trial and equal justice there must be equal representation. Gideon's case was retried in Florida with the assistance of a court-appointed public defender. The jury acquitted Gideon of all charges but not until after he already spent over five months sitting in jail. Justice, right?

That was the beginning of public defenders.

I was appointed one such public defender to represent me during the criminal proceedings. With all due respect to public defenders, these court-appointed attorneys cannot hope to provide adequate representation because they are subjected to working in some of the most challenging conditions imaginable. They're drowning in an unreasonable number of cases, and they simply don't have the time or resources for exhaustive research and trial prep. They're known as "bleed 'em and plead 'em" attorneys because, in an effort to decrease their caseloads, they will counsel clients to enter guilty pleas without thoroughly examining the merits of the state's case or properly explaining the consequences of entering a plea to the client. Since the Supreme Court's ruling in Gideon, America has come to accept embarrassing low standards of representation for indigent people.

Since the state was clearly going to have difficulty meeting the burden of proof, any half-witted private defense attorney would have argued for my release to my parents so I could await trial without being thrown in a cell. There was no direct evidence; no gun; no money; no drugs. All the state had was testimonial evidence from the wannabes who I knew would never take the stand.

At my first appearance, my court appointed public defender had no clue what the case was about. I doubt he even read the file prior to the hearing. The judge hammered us, so I sat in jail awaiting trial. After my first appearance, the public defender visited me in jail only to attempt to persuade me to accept a plea offer of guilty to Battery that included sixty days to serve at the Miami-Dade Juvenile Detention Center.

"Fuck that," I told him. "Aint no way I'm doing sixty days for this. Take it to trial."

"They have eyewitnesses," he said. "If we go to trial and lose you could get a lot more than sixty days. The judge already denied your release. What do you think the judge will do if he hears that someone witnessed you do it?"

"Trust me," I laughed, "those two little punks will not show up for trial."

"Have it your way. It's your life. I'll see you in a few days."

That was the last time I spoke with the public defender until the day of the trial. Not one more visit. Not a single effort to follow-up with me. Nothing.

Early on the morning of the trial, I was transferred to the Miami-Dade Juvenile Court's holding cell and waited for what felt like an eternity. When I first arrived, the public defender sat with me for a few minutes and asked me if I was sure that I did not want to accept the plea offer. I declined and asked if the two witnesses had arrived. He said they hadn't, but that the judge saved trials for the end of the day so they had plenty of time to show up before our case was called.

I remained in that cold, smelly holding cell until late in the afternoon. There was no clock. I did not know what time it was. And even though it was freezing, I was sweating. I replayed the incident over and over again in my head.

Then all of a sudden I heard my name called by the corrections officers, "Windecher!"

I stood up as I heard the unlocking sound of the steel doors to my holding cell. The public defender walked in.

"You were right. Their witnesses never showed. The judge had the state call them and they didn't get an answer. So, the state agreed to a dismissal and the judge signed the order. They're going to transfer you back and release you to your parents."

I smirked. Had I listened to the public defender's advice, I would have spent sixty days behind bars. But just like Gideon, I had to sit in lock-up for fifteen days before my case was dismissed. Justice.

Nothing good comes from placing a kid in juvenile lock-up. There are really only two possible outcomes. Either the juvenile will decide that lock-up isn't as bad as it seems and cease to consider serving time a deterrent from further committing criminal offenses, or he'll learn how to commit more crimes by associating with advanced and hardened juveniles.

The Miami-Dade Juvenile Detention Center consists of two long corridors filled with holding cells connected at the end by a hallway. On one side, the hallway connects the two corridors, and on the other side grants access to the courthouse. The holding cells did not have bars. They were small rooms with a toilet, a sink, two beds, and a large metal door with a small glass window. It was always freezing inside the cells.

Each morning at 6:00 a.m., all of the inmates were awakened so the corrections staff could perform a head count. Then we were shipped off to the cafeteria for breakfast, handcuffed to our cellmate. My cellmate was a sixteen-year-old Hispanic nicknamed "Pucho." Pucho and I had a lot in common. He was impoverished, lived in the same neighborhood, and was a member of a local criminal street gang known as the Wylos. Pucho was an aspiring tattoo artist. He had more tattoos on his body than anyone I had ever seen. Pucho offered to tattoo me for free. I had no idea how such a thing could happen given we were sitting in juvenile lock-up, but I agreed.

That night, when the corridor lights were dimmed and we were supposed to be asleep, Pucho revealed a box that was taped to the bottom of his bed. The box contained a small bottle of India ink, a pack of sewing needles, and a roll of white thread. I had no idea how that box got in there, but I was all in. I asked Pucho to tattoo "Red" on my right ankle.

Pucho wrapped several layers of the white thread around the tip of the sewing needle. When he was finished, the needle tip was barely exposed under the white thread. It looked like a miniature Q-tip with a pointed end. He submerged the tip into the bottle of India ink to soak the thread. Then Pucho wiped the threaded end to remove the excess ink dripping from the tip. Pucho pricked at my ankle repeatedly until my gangster nickname appeared permanently on my skin. Pucho had a steady hand. The tattoo came out perfect.

During the fifteen days I spent incarcerated, Pucho and I became close. We rivaled with African American gang members day-in-day-out. We ate together every day. We talked about being poor and talked about what we wanted to do when we were released. Pucho was passionate about tattooing. He wanted to own a tattoo shop one day but that reality was starting to seem impossible. Pucho had been charged with Armed Robbery just a couple of days after I entered the

Miami-Dade Juvenile Justice Center. A few days later, his case would be bound over to the Miami-Dade County Circuit Criminal Court because the State Attorney's Office was planning to charge him as an adult. But before Pucho was transferred to the county jail, he taught me one more thing: how to execute a crime he called Presto.

Presto is a handy little trick if you're hungry and short on cash. Since I was always both, I jumped at learning it. Basically, it's the forced withdrawal of items and/or cash from a vending machine. It's remarkably simple, really, but more sophisticated than tilting the machine or busting the glass case. You attach a five dollar bill to an eight foot strip of clear adhesive tape to trigger the mechanical gears and sprockets inside of a vending machine to spin counter clockwise. The counter clockwise motion allows you to retrieve the bill and five dollars' worth of products without ever truly paying for the goods. Alternatively, you could retrieve the bill, products, and change for five dollars after the cost of the dispensed product.

According to Pucho, all I needed was the newest five dollar bill I could find, sixteen feet of clear Scotch tape, and his instructions:

Step One: Cover one long edge of the face side of a five dollar bill with tape, and loop the tape in half so both adhesive sides are facing each other. Then stick the tape along the same edge on the side of the bill without Abe's face and carefully stick the tape to itself. The adhesive-on-adhesive creates an eight foot strip with the bill laminated at the end.

Step Two: Run a plastic card downward and outward over the bill and across the strip of tape as many times as necessary to remove any air bubbles. The bill has to be as crisp as possible so the optical lens inside the vending machine will have no issue reading the currency through the tape. All of the bubbles have to be smoothed so the tape won't tear while traveling through the labyrinth of gears and sprockets inside the vending machine.

Step Three: Insert the bill into any vending machine as if making a regular purchase. The bill will travel nearly six feet through the vending machine and land inside the cash deposit box, leaving about two feet of clear tape sticking out from the payment slot.

Step Four: Make five dollars' worth of selections, or select the lowest priced product and request change.

Step Five: Once the products, or the product and change are in your possession, wrap your hand around the exposed strip of tape and slowly pull. Abe will travel back out of the deposit box, through those six feet of mechanisms, and into your hand.

Presto.

I was released from the Miami-Dade Juvenile Detention Center on January 20, 1995. I was arrested again three days later.

My third arrest was a prime example of "wrong place, wrong time." The wrong place was the Miami-Dade Juvenile Detention Center. The wrong time was at an impressionable age. Growing up in the hood there is *always* a wrong place and wrong time, and I'd been in plenty of trouble as a direct result from running the streets. But not this time. It was no experience from the hood that led to my third arrest. It was what I learned while incarcerated—while I was supposed to be being rehabilitated—that earned me strike three.

As soon as I was released, I walked to go see Torres who lived at the Star Creek apartment complex. I was itching to see if Presto actually worked, so I explained the operation to Torres.

I know it seems like a lot of work and unnecessary risk for free pretzels and some change, but when you're broke every dollar counts. I lost everything I'd saved on the drug-transaction-gone-wrong just a few weeks earlier, and my parents were worse off than ever. I was desperate, so Presto seemed like the next best thing to make money.

Torres was skeptical, but he had a five dollar bill and Scotch tape, and there was no way he'd turn down a good scheme. All we needed was a location to test it.

Torres suggested we visit The Woods. The Woods was an apartment complex on 24th Avenue and NE 173rd Street. It had two vending machines next to the pool area bathrooms, and though neither Torres nor I knew an actual resident at the Woods, we did know it was an easy place to sneak into. We'd made a habit of smoking blunts there at night. It was such a frequent routine that the thought of being charged with trespassing never crossed our minds.

That night, Torres and I took a bookbag each to The Woods. There was no one at the pool when we arrived. We staked it out for a few minutes anyway, checking inside the bathrooms, walking the perimeter, and looking for anyone out on their balconies. The place was deserted.

I pulled the Presto strip out from my bookbag.

Torres eyed it.

"You sure this gonna work?" he asked.

"Pucho swore by it."

"You talking about the same dude facing twenty years for Armed Robbery…" Torres muttered.

"Hey genius, if you have any better ideas I'm all ears."

Torres turned his attention to scanning the windows of the apartments overlooking the pool.

I kissed the bill and slipped it into the payment slot.

"Come on, motherfucker," I whispered.

The bill fed into the machine, and I watched as the strip followed it inside. It stopped abruptly with about two feet of tape dangling out of the slot like a clear tongue, just like Pucho said. The display flashed: $5.00. *It worked*. I punched Torres in the back.

"It worked."

Torres' eyes were gleaming. If we could streamline this, Presto could be big for us.

I selected a Coca-Cola and requested change. The vending machine dispensed the Coca-Cola and spit out $4.25 in change. *Now for the delicate part*. I wrapped my hand around the strip of tape and slowly pulled backwards. Within just a few seconds, the tip of the tape with the laminated bill was back in my hand.

"Thank you, Pucho," I said.

I just got myself a Coke and $4.25 for free. Well, save for the illegality behind the process. I was stoked.

"Alright," Torres said, grabbing the Presto strip out of my hand, "My turn."

Torres and I ran Presto almost twenty times before a tenant who probably heard the vending machine dispense one too many times called my old pals at the North Miami Beach Police Department.

In the hood, there is a general rule that, when doing something illegal, if you hear, "STOP!" "FREEZE!" "HEY!" or anything of the sort, you hightail it as far and as quickly as humanly possible. So when we heard a man yelling at us from outside the fence, Torres and I booked it out of there.

"Split up!" I yelled, flinging my now heavy bag over my shoulder.

"Let's meet back at the Creek!" Torres shouted before sprinting through the back of the complex into Greynolds Park.

I ran the opposite way through the front of the complex, out to 173rd street. The backpack, pounding against my spine, was slowing me down. Plus, it would be impossible to explain its contents if I got caught.

I couldn't believe this was happening again.

I detoured to 173rd Street and 21st Avenue—my friend Michael Klaiss' house. I stashed the bookbag under Mikey's 1976 Chevy Monte Carlo and kept running.

I needed to get off the main roads. Any police vehicle reporting to The Woods would pass me on its way in. I cut into an alleyway.

Bad idea.

I hadn't made it more than twenty feet before I was blinded by the headlights of a North Miami Beach police vehicle.

I pivoted without braking. My body's center of gravity nearly forced me to the ground, but somehow I kept my feet under me. I hurdled back in the direction of The Woods. I could feel the adrenaline slamming through my muscles, forcing my legs to pump and my feet to fly. The car was on my tail.

My mind sped through possibilities as I neared the mouth of the ally. If I could get to the main street, I had options. The car revved behind me, and I could feel the heat of the lights and engine on my back.

The front bumper was inches from my calves, and I was already gasping for air. If I stopped too quickly, it would barrel me over.

There was no out running the cop car.

Here we go again.

I threw my hands in the air and slowed to a jog. The car stopped behind me and I heard the doors pop open and shut.

"Police! Put your hands on your head. Turn around. Drop down to your knees."

I did as I was told.

The police officer approached with a saunter that made me want to drop a haymaker on his chin. This guy was a cocky piece of scum, but as I wasn't in a position to dole out insults or violence, I kept my comments to myself and hands on my head.

"What did I do wrong, officer?" I asked.

He didn't respond. Instead he walked behind me, placed his foot on my back, and kicked me down onto the asphalt. He handcuffed me from behind with my face down on the road and his knee digging into my back.

I figured I was going back to jail.

I figured wrong.

I blinked.

It was dark.

Where am I?

I turned my neck, and gasped as a spike of pain shot from my head to the base of my neck. I tried to take a deep breath, but could only manage to fill my lungs with a shallow breath under my aching ribs.

I lay there for a minute, fighting off the panic and the waves of nausea. I tried to figure out what had happened, but there was nothing. It was like waking up from a forgotten nightmare—all the fear was there, but none of the memory.

I started to take stock of my injuries, slowly moving each part of my body, noting searing pain and inflamed stiffness. No outer extremity seemed broken, though. I tried to lift my right arm, but my shoulder would not let me. I picked up my left. It seemed okay. I prodded my ribs and went into a profanity filled rant. They hurt like hell, but nothing was out of place.

I dropped my hand and was surprised to feel grass. Had I tripped? Did I fall and hit my head? I took a quick breath and forced myself up into a sitting position.

I sat for a moment, looking around. I was in a field. I knew this field.

It was Victory Park.

I fought back the bile rising in my throat. Victory Park was Zoe Pound turf. I was in the wrong place. Though I still couldn't remember, I assumed I was probably jumped by Zoe Pounders and left unconscious.

I quickly got to my feet and I started walking toward my parents' house because I did not want to get caught alone in Victory Park.

As I walked, taking in slow, painful breaths, I started to remember. It was all blurry, nothing concrete. I felt weird. Confused. Scenes from jail were mixing with images of a kid lying dead outside a movie theater.

I paused. I was lost. My head was throbbing. I could only open one eye.

I've had my hide thoroughly beaten on Cracker Day. I survived being jumped-into a gang. But whoever did this to me took it to a whole new level.

I took a moment to get my bearings.

I continued to walk toward my parent's house. There were other images now. Christian was sitting on his bed, silent. I was fighting Ortiz. Then I was fighting Pucho. I lifted my hand to my throbbing head. That didn't make sense. I'd never fought Pucho. Pucho was my friend. He'd taught me —

I stopped. *Presto. He'd taught me Presto. Torres. We'd gotten caught—the cops. The cops!*

It was all back.

Where was my wallet?

I patted my pockets and saw something yellow sticking out of one. I tugged the paper loose and stepped into the light of a street lamp.

I doubled over and vomited. When I was empty, I dry heaved, wishing I had more to push out, tears involuntarily springing to my eyes. My throat stung and my head pounded.

It was a carbon copy of an arrest citation issued by the North Miami Beach Police Department.

Signed by Officer Wilhite.

I felt trapped, like all the oxygen was suddenly stale, like metal rods pierced my feet and anchored me to the concrete. In jail, on the streets, it didn't make one bit of a difference. Government authorities could do whatever they pleased with me. Standing there under that streetlight on that deserted stretch of road, looking through a bent chain-link fence at yellow lights filtering through dirty blinds in the windows of broken down homes with dilapidated cars in crumbling driveways, I had never felt so utterly without hope.

Without Torres, who was never caught, the state couldn't prove Conspiracy, and without the goods or a witness, they couldn't prove Criminal Mischief.

The case would ultimately be dismissed, but the dirty cops had already made sure I received punishment for the wrong I committed.

I looked back down at the signature line and crushed the citation into a ball. I let it drop out of my hand and onto the ground.

Wilhite.

4

FOURTH

APRIL 20, 1995
MISDEMEANOR POSSESSION OF MARIJUANA[5]
TWO DAYS IN JUVENILE LOCK-UP;
WITHHELD ADJUDICATION; PLACED ON COMMUNITY CONTROL;
200 COMMUNITY SERVICE HOURS; COMPLIANCE
WITH DRUG COURT PROGRAM

A pril 20th is what some call a counterculture holiday, but that label is a bit of a misnomer. It implies that the celebration is at odds with the social norm. April 20, or 420, honors the cannabis culture, which, if we're honest, isn't really at variance with the American lifestyle. Pot. Ganja. Weed. Reefer. Devil's Lettuce. No matter what you call it, the fact is that marijuana is as common as alcohol in the recreational pastimes of people from every class of our society.

Growing up where I did, dope was a part of daily life. Most of the kids in our neighborhood started smoking marijuana at an early age. It wasn't a matter of peer pressure; smoking was as natural to us as sneaking out or breaking curfew was for others.

---

[5] See, Miami-Dade County State Attorney and Florida Department of Law Enforcement Case No. J95005125

I couldn't afford to buy marijuana in middle school, and even if I could, the Zoe Pounders weren't about to sell me anything. But when I started spending time with Ortiz, that problem disappeared. By the end of seventh grade, my friends and I would smoke while we hung out almost every day, courtesy of the ninth grade Hispanic drug dealers.

Once I crossed over the curve from demander to supplier, I found one of my favorite perks of selling to be the extra inventory for personal use. But after everything with the wannabes went down, I decided to cut my career as a dealer short. I wanted to make money, sure, but I wanted the payday without the possibility of getting robbed or killed for it. This meant if I wanted to get high, I had to pay for it like every other teacher, cop, and doctor.

In 1995, the week leading up to 420 left North Miami Beach in an inventory dry spell. Everyone I knew had sold off their supply. This was a problem for me and my friends. The morning of the 20th, I paged Nickson to see if he could round something up from the John Doe dope hole, but when he failed to respond, my friends and I had to resort to other options if we wanted to properly celebrate 420.

One of the more popular local places to purchase marijuana was a dilapidated apartment complex behind a Burger King on 163rd Street and 19th Avenue. The spot was (cleverly) called the Burger King dope hole. The Burger King dope hole only sold nickel bags of marijuana packed inside small manila-colored envelopes stamped with the word "DOJA" in red.

A watch-out would sit in a plastic lawn chair right out front to put buyers on notice that the spot was open for business. In order to buy, customers could simply walk up and ask the watch-out for their drug of choice. He would direct the buyer to the appropriate door. Door number one for cocaine, door number two for crack, door number three for marijuana, and so on.

Amongst the Star Creek crew, we decided to put me in charge of picking up the marijuana since I lived closest to the Burger King dope hole. We only needed two nickel bags, but with the dry-spell, I wasn't confident that they would even have that much to sell me. I didn't own a car, so I walked to the spot, and was relieved when I saw the watch-out at his usual post. It looked like they'd somehow avoided the marijuana shortage. I glanced around, subtly checking for narcs or cops before crossing the parking lot.

The watch-out wore a blue pair of Cross-Colours shorts with a black t-shirt that read "F Da Police N.W.A. (Niggas With Attitude)" and a white leather hat.

He had a thin chinstrap beard and sported a Figaro gold necklace with some sort of gold medallion hanging from it. As I walked up, the watch-out pulled out a Newport menthol box, placed a cigarette in his mouth, struck a match, and lit it. He took a single puff before I approached him.

"You know where I can pick up DOJA two times?" I asked him.

He looked up and nodded with a loose half-grin as he blew smoke out of his mouth.

"Go ahead to door number three, homie," he said. "It's all good. We got that 420 fire for you today."

I narrowed my eyes at him. The friendly commentary didn't sit right. In my previous visits, the watch-out wasn't usually so chatty. He'd just tell me the door number and that'd be it. Then again, this was the first time I purchased marijuana here on 420; maybe the man was just feeling festive. Another customer was walking up, so I shrugged it off and headed for door number three.

I knocked on the door and received a gruff, but muffled, "Whatchuneed?" in reply.

"DOJA two times."

The door opened—just enough to exchange bills for envelopes. I couldn't see anything further than the rusty chain link lock.

"Let me see the money," the disembodied voice said.

I pushed two five-dollar bills through the sliver of open space. A second later, two mini manila envelopes appeared. I shoved the envelopes into my front right pocket.

"Aight," I said and walked away. On my way back to the street, I saw that the watch-out was no longer in the chair. Maybe they were shutting down for the day, but my gut told me something was wrong. I reached into my pocket and pulled out the envelopes. I flipped them in my hands a couple of times only to realize that they were not stamped "DOJA" on either side.

I swore under my breath, scanning the street for anything out of the ordinary.

I got about ten yards down the sidewalk before a police van abruptly pulled up alongside me. I didn't even have time to consider fleeing before a North Miami Beach police officer was in front of me, weapon drawn.

"Stop! You are under arrest for the purchase of marijuana from an undercover officer."

Happy 420 to me.

I sat handcuffed inside the van for hours surrounded by suckers just like me. This wasn't exactly the 420 festivities I'd had in mind. Once the van was full with would-be buyers, we were all transported to the North Miami Beach Police Department for processing.

Later that day, while I was nodding off in my holding cell, a high, grating voice woke me.

"It was only a matter of time, David."

It had been years since our last face-to-face meeting, but Wilhite still wore that flat top haircut and a tiny line of hairs above his upper lip. He was still terrifying... until he opened his mouth.

"Now I have the privilege of calling your mother and letting her know what a wonderful young man you're becoming. *Again.*"

I flinched in my heart, but didn't even blink on the outside. I stared at the wall, refusing to even look in his direction.

Wilhite continued, "I thought I'd come down to say hello to you, David, since we're such old friends. That was a tough break today, buying from an undercover cop. But buying weed on 420? Come on, Dave. How stupid can you be?" He had a good chuckle to himself. "I'm just glad I was there to see it."

Wilhite's big, sharp teeth glinted. "It was a pleasure doing business with you, Mr. Windecher."

I snapped my gaze back to the wall and tried to block out the whine of his voice.

"Anyway, I know a judge is going to let you out in a few days, but I've made a little 420 resolution that I wanted to share with you." He paused, waiting for a response.

When I didn't move, he took a step closer, his voice a scraping whisper.

"You're a worthless piece of shit, David. The world will be a better place with you behind bars, and, though you're probably going to walk on this bullshit charge, you're going to slip up again. You think you're some criminal mastermind? You're not, David. You're a weak, pathetic excuse for a crook. I'm going to be watching. And sooner or later, I will put you away for good."

A shiver rattled my body.

When my mom showed up, she was *pissed*. The look in her eyes was as serious as I had ever seen. She showed up alone because my dad was still at work when this all happened. Wilhite walked my mom to the front of my holding cell so that she could see me caged like a criminal.

"Why can't you stay out of trouble, David?" my mom asked fiercely.

Wilhite looked like his show poodle had just won first prize.

I stood up from the bench inside the holding cell, stared right at Wilhite and responded in Spanish, "Ma, I swear I didn't do anything wrong. I was not causing any trouble."

Wilhite and I continued to stare at each other as he said, "We are in America. Speak English."

I bit back my retort.

I looked at my mom and said in English, "I am sorry, but I didn't do anything wrong." Wilhite scoffed. "Buying marijuana from an undercover officer is against the laws of the State of Florida."

My eyes narrowed, I looked back toward Wilhite. "What about abusing your power? How about beating a kid up and leaving him for dead in a field? Is *that* legal, motherf—"

My mom snarled, "Show some respect!"

I apologized to my mom in Spanish, as I sat back down on the bench.

Wilhite, still grinning, explained to my mom that this was an arrest for which he could simply issue a notice to appear citation and release me to my parents.

"However," Wilhite said, looking right at me, "David needs to learn a lesson. So instead of releasing him, I've decided to personally deliver him to the Miami-Dade Juvenile Detention Center to spend a couple of days in lock-up."

The State later withheld adjudication because I qualified for community control. After six months of pissing in a cup, astronomical fines, and 200 hours of community service, the case was closed.

Wilhite's plan worked, though. I did learn a valuable lesson, but it was certainly not to quit smoking marijuana. That lesson was to never underestimate police officers again. He'd beaten me, left me for dead, and now he'd tricked me into buying drugs, tried to turn my mother against me, and made it personal.

This was a war. Me against the cops.

They'd made a fool out of me one too many times. It was time to take it up a notch.

During the forty-eight hours I spent in juvenile lockup before I was released, I made a decision. Clearly, the only thing I could trust was something I never took my eyes off of, something I built and filled with the people I knew best and trusted with my life.

I needed to build my own dope hole: a drive through 24/7 operation.

This was the perfect way to minimize the risk and increase the rewards. It's way harder to get burned when you control all the variables. And I knew the perfect place to start it.

The first night back from jail, I was sitting alone with my dad in the living room. It was silent for a long time. I could hear the faucet dripping from the kitchen, one of the beds creaking under a restless sleeper. Finally, my father sighed a deep, heavy, tired sigh.

"Why are you doing these things, David? You are destroying your life. Do you know what you're doing to your mother? She barely sleeps the nights you aren't home. She thinks you're going to end up dead."

"I never wanted things to be this way, Pa," I said quietly. "I started to sell drugs so that I could have money to eat and buy clothes, so you wouldn't have to worry about me. So that you did not have to work so hard."

"That is not your decision to make for me, David. You think that I would not work a thousand hours if it meant you'd go back to school? I want to see you do the things I could not do. Get an education. Become someone special. Someone important. Start a career and your own family far away from here."

He looked down at the bubbled linoleum.

When he looked up he had tears in his eyes. "That is why I get up at 3:00 a.m. to go to work, so you don't have to sell drugs. I want you to focus. You are intelligent. You have a chance. Don't destroy your life, David. Please. Your brother and sisters look up to you. What can I say to make you stop this?"

Tears dripped down my dad's face.

"Please, Pa, don't—" I said, fighting tears of my own.

My mom walked into the living room, "What's going on?"

My dad rubbed his eyes on his sleeve and said, "We are just talking."

"Why are you crying?"

He looked me right in the eyes and said, "Because I don't want him to die."

I reached for my dad's hand. "I'm so sorry, Pa. Please don't cry."

"Well, this is your fault," My mom said to my dad. "I told you. We never should have come back here. We should have stayed in Argentina. Ever since we came back it has been nothing but trouble. How many times has he come home beaten and bloodied?! He disappears for days. He has been arrested *four* times. Look at him. Our son is a *gangster*. And you brought us here. You did this to him. You did this to us."

My dad started to sob. The pain inside my heart grew.

"You're right! You are right about it all. And I am sorry." My dad got to his feet and tried to take my mom's hand. She snatched it away.

He was silent for a moment. "What if we move back to California? We can start new."

"Again!?" She shouted. "Do you remember what happened to us in California? I told you we never should have left Argentina."

And then my mom started to cry.

I got up, wrapped my arms around her and said, "Listen to me. I love you, Ma. I am sorry. Really. I don't want you guys to cry. I am sorry."

She pushed me away. "No. You don't mean it. And you are going to turn your brother and sisters into the same gangster you have become."

I took a step back, stung by her words.

I would have given life and limb to protect Christian, Giselle, and Karina. My life was the last thing I wanted for them. I wanted to protect them, and I believed that alleviating my dad's expenses was a way to do so.

I felt crippled by poverty. I was ashamed of it. And I was angry at the injustice. How was it fair that my dad worked thirteen-hour days and still barely made ends meet? Why, toward the end of the week, did my brother and sisters have to eat bread with sugar on it for dinner? How could bare essentials such as food and clothing become scarcities when other families had them in abundance? This wasn't what America was supposed to be like. We were supposed to be able to do anything, be anything. Work ethic and character were supposed to mean everything here. There wasn't supposed to be a caste system in America.

I went to sleep that night with a heavy heart.

When I woke up in the morning, I learned that my parents had decided to sell everything and move back to California. But I knew nothing would change. My parents believed that California would be a fresh start for me. It would separate me from the bad influences I had in my life. But what they could not—or would not—see was that I was in deep. The gang life mentality had completely taken over. California was not going to stop our poverty, and an end to the poverty was the only thing that could have broken me free.

But they wouldn't listen.

My dad picked up several odd jobs, sold everything in a matter of weeks, and purchased six flights to California.

The night before the flight, I ran away. There was no logic in moving to a place where we would be stuck in the same situation. While I was acquiring some money through criminal activity, at least I had income.

After a couple of days away, I returned to an empty house.

My family had moved to California without me.

After they left me, I became numb. I did not speak to my family for three months; the gang became my family. I started to lose a battle within myself. My bitterness toward poverty and my hatred for police officers caused me to begin to lose hope. I started to accept that it was only a matter of time before I was locked-up for good or wound up dead. I tried to hold on to my family but, after this arrest, the gang life completely took over. I believed it was the only thing that could help me make money and protect me from crooked cops.

I was going to get money any way I could and live the best possible life until it was over. Whether my demise would come at the hands of crooked cops, rival gang members, or due to prolonged incarceration, it was coming. And I almost welcomed it. The most dangerous person is the one with nothing to live for.

One day, while Torres and I sat in a Star Creek stairwell smoking a blunt, a taxi pulled up and my dad jumped out.

I sat up straight and threw down my blunt. I could not believe my eyes. It was the first time in months that I'd felt human.

"Pa!" I exclaimed. I ran up to him and we embraced each other with a strong hug. "Where is everybody else?" I asked.

"They are in California, David. Come back with me."

What could I do? I missed my family. They are the single most important part of my life, and being away from them was torture. So I agreed.

When I arrived in California I was relieved to see my family, but the relief was overcome by grief when I realized we were living in Chino. Chino was the same, maybe even worse, than Miami. Nothing had changed, except that I was vulnerable and out of the loop here. There were gangs everywhere, and I was the new kid with no protection, no friends again. I had no network, no way to make money. If I stayed, what would I accomplish? I would sink. I would disappear. Or I would get killed.

And worse, I missed gangbanging like an addict craves his fix.

My parents enrolled me into Chino High so that I could finish my education. But I would never make it back home after my first day of classes.

After school, instead of walking home, I walked to the nearest Grey Hound station. I purchased a one-way ticket to Hollywood, Florida. I didn't say good-bye to my parents. It hurt my heart to leave my family behind, but I was addicted. And my fix was in Miami.

Five days later, I arrived in Hollywood Florida where Torres picked me up at the Greyhound station. When we got back to Torres' house, the first thing I did was call my mom.

"Ma, I am sorry but I am not going to live in California," I said.

"Are you crazy? Where are you? Your dad has been looking for you everywhere!" she shouted.

"I am in Miami."

"What?!"

"Joey picked me up. I just got here. Listen, I am going to send you some money so that you guys can come back too," I explained.

"Where are you going to get the money from, David?"

"I don't know, Ma, but I will send it soon. I love you."

One month later I mailed my mom $3,000 in an envelope stuffed inside a teddy bear.

It is said, "The road to Hell is paved with good intentions."

It's interesting how true that saying can be even for a sixteen-year-old.

You start out with the idea of wanting to help your family. Then you get some money in your pockets, so you put some nice clothes on your back. Then you get some recognition for the manner in which you went about getting the money. Girls start wanting to get to know you from what they've heard about you and your street cred. Before you know it, it's no longer about your family but more so about the money and the cred on the streets. And that becomes an addiction in itself. Somewhere in between you completely lose yourself.

Or maybe you find a new, darker piece of yourself that you never imagined was inside. And you like it. You like it because the darker you has options. Red could make things happen that David only dreamed about. Red didn't have David's inhibitions. Red wasn't a slave to David's conscience. David followed the rules, Red was above the law. David was a victim; Red was the one holding the gun.

5

FIFTH, SIXTH

JANUARY 10, 1996; MARCH 12, 1996
PETIT THEFT[6]; PETIT THEFT[7]
NOLLE PROSEQUI; NOLLE PROSEQUI
SIX DAYS IN JUVENILE LOCK-UP

The pros of community control include skipping jail time. The cons include expensive weekly trips downtown to piss in a plastic cup. During the six months of the program I was participating in as a result of the possession charge, if I submitted a single positive drug screen, the judge could revoke my community control sentence and the state would prosecute me on the charges of my last arrest. Obviously, I had no choice but to quit smoking marijuana cold turkey, which also meant that I could not immediately begin operating the Star Creek drive thru dope hole. I just couldn't be around marijuana; I loved it so much that if I was, I knew I would relapse.

I suddenly found myself with a lot of time on my hands and very little cash.

It so happened that a former marijuana client of mine, Roberto Montero, had landed a part-time job at The Check-Cashing Store located on the southwest

---

[6] See, Miami-Dade County State Attorney and Florida Department of Law Enforcement Case No. (Unrecorded)
[7] See, Miami-Dade County State Attorney and Florida Department of Law Enforcement Case No. J96003100

corner of Hollywood Blvd and State Road 441. He'd been working there for several months when Torres and I happened to find a blank check in a parking lot. It was too perfect.

I waited in the car as Torres strolled into the check-cashing store on a Friday afternoon dressed in a blue nondescript Dickies work uniform—he could have been anything from a mechanic to a painter.

I was feeling anxious. This was the big leagues. All we needed was for one of Montero's bosses to drop in unexpectedly, and this whole thing would go straight to Hell. When we talked to him about the plan, Montero had promised this would be the easiest con in the world to pull off. But that didn't stop him from requiring a hefty $200 cut "for the risk he was taking."

I couldn't stop checking the time. How long did it take to cash a check?

I was starting to consider going in to investigate, when a shiny midnight blue Grand Marquise rolled into the parking lot. I slid an inch down in my seat and watched the guy climb out of his car. I breathed a sigh of relief. It was just a middle aged man in khakis and a t-shirt. He didn't look like a cop.

Just as he got to the door, it swung open and Torres stepped through. Torres nodded to the man and shot a smug grin at me.

"Berto was right. That was as easy as fuck," Torres said as we pulled out of the lot.

"So, you got the bread?"

"I need to invest in one of them fancy suits." Torres said. "This janitor thing is bullshit. With a suit we could get more dough."

I looked at Torres, impatient. "The bread, Joey. You get it?"

"Calm down, Red. You nagging me like a bitch. It's right here." He reached into his pocket and pulled out an envelope. "You should have seen it! Berto took the check and my license and was going back and forth, playing along, like he was making sure it was legit."

"And then he just handed you a stack? Just like that?"

"Just like that."

I looked out at the neighborhood flying by.

"We need more checks."

I knew we couldn't just lurk around parking lots, waiting for people to drop their checkbooks. We needed something more solid, something we could count on.

What better method than to go straight to the source?

Torres and I started staking out United States Postal Service delivery routes the next day. We followed them out of the Star Creek Apartments to see how far their route would take us. We monitored where the mailmen parked their trucks, how much of their route was on foot, and how long it took them to get back to their vehicles from the furthest point. Once we learned the routes well, we plotted how to remove the mail bins from inside the un-manned trucks and get them into Torres' car.

A few weeks later, we were ready.

Just like usual, we followed a mailman to his first stop and Torres parked about a half block away. Then we waited.

"That's it," Torres whispered. "That's as far as he's going to get."

"Alright. Give me the spark plug," I said.

In case you lack experience in auto parts and/or glass-breaking, you should know that there is a porcelain section on a spark plug that's ideal for busting windows. When porcelain makes contact with glass, the impact is nearly silent and forms a web of cracks all the way to the frame. A gentle push is enough to peel the entire window out.

I crept up to the mail truck, plug in hand.

I paused and glanced back at Torres, suddenly struck with how serious of a crime this was.

He threw a hand in the air, as if to say "What are you waiting for?"

I couldn't believe I was about to commit a federal offense in broad daylight.

In one swift move, I shattered the glass, pushed the window inward, and signaled Torres. He flew up the road and jumped out of the car with the engine still running. I threw open the mail truck door and started tossing bins to him. In less than a minute, all of the mail was stowed in the trunk of Torres' car and we'd turned the corner before the postman made it halfway back to his truck.

Back at Star Creek, we spread out across Torres' living room floor to sift through the mail bins. We'd intercepted several envelopes with big fat checkbooks waiting to be delivered to owners who would never receive them. By the time they realized their checkbooks were missing, it would be far too late.

A couple days later, it was my turn to dress up and run the scheme. I walked into the check-cashing store wearing a button up shirt, slacks, and eyeglasses. The store was empty. When I walked inside, I instantly felt a cold gust from the air conditioner. It gave me a chilling reminder of the inside of a jail cell. I shook it off and looked around.

There were three clerk windows at the end of a square shaped room. On the sidewalls were advertisements for calling cards and money advance offers. Montero was sitting in the middle window facing me. The window to his right was closed. In the window to his left sat an old Hispanic woman. I made eye contact with her and smiled. Then I walked right up to Montero's window.

"Afternoon, sir," Montero said, his tone was polite but his face said *you look like a total douche.*

I pushed my glasses up the bridge of my nose and handed Montero a check for $750 with my own Florida identification card. Once again, Montero played his part perfectly, acting as if my identification matched the name on the check, and counting out the bills.

"I appreciate it," I said with a nod.

"My pleasure, sir," he said with a grin.

Torres was waiting around the corner in his car.

"What happened?"

I pulled the bills from the envelope Montero had given me and fanned them in front of Torres' face. "We straight ballin, dawg!"

Torres let out a manic laugh. "This is huge, my nigga!"

We were definitely onto something, and I wanted to believe this was as simple and good as it seemed, but my gut was churning. This was an easy crime to commit, but it was easy to get caught too.

"You don't think it's too risky?" I asked.

Torres snorted and turned the key in the ignition. "Chill man. We ain't gonna run this forever. We'll just cash enough checks in the next month or so to live off of for a while."

I wanted to be all in, but I kept thinking about Wilhite's last words to me. Even though this wasn't his jurisdiction, getting caught with stolen checks was exactly the kind of thing that could get me put "away for good," or at least a very long time.

"It's only a matter of time till somebody catches on."

"Okay," Torres said. He pulled out onto the road. "So make one of them plans you always braggin' about."

My mind started to turn. We had a pile of checks to use, but the only person who would take them without a matching ID was Montero. And how many times could we run the scheme at The Check Cashing Store before getting caught?

I looked over at Torres. "We need Denise."

For what I had planned, we'd needed fake IDs made to match the names and addresses on the checkbooks; then we could buy anything from anyone. Well, anyone who didn't care enough to question it or couldn't realize what we were actually doing.

Nobody had a network like our grifter, Denise. Denise was a hustler in the realest sense of the word: she was a fast thinker; clean cut, attractive and well spoken. Due to her tremendous appeal she was down with everyone. Denise could often be found at high-end bars and lounges in the company of older men with impressive bank accounts. Denise told me she was friendly with a gangster named Pepe Gutierrez who was in the business of identity fraud. That is who she got her fake IDs from in order to enter of-age establishments. I contacted Denise and asked her to put me down with Gutierrez. Gutierrez was immediately interested in working with us because he realized we needed IDs on a steady basis. He charged me $150 to produce fake IDs made to match our checkbooks.

From August 1995 through March 1996, Torres and I heisted one USPS mail truck per month. We staked out trucks all over Miami-Dade County. As soon as we were comfortable with our knowledge of a route, we would strike. It became an easy routine. Each time we robbed a mail truck and collected new checkbooks, we would immediately contact Gutierrez and have matching fake IDs made. Then Torres and I went shopping.

We did the most damage at the mall on 163rd Street. We knew a lot of the people who worked in the shops, and we took full advantage. You name it. We hit it. Champs. Footlocker. Service Merchandise. Mervyn's. Burdines. Herman's. Spec's. The plan was almost too simple to fail. Go into a store, browse for a few minutes, pick up a few things, pay, get out.

To prevent getting caught, we concealed the fake IDs directly behind our real ones, and the stolen checks were always neatly folded deep in a sleeve inside our wallets. We kept a small amount of cash and random business cards too, so nothing would seem off if we were searched. To keep from immediately being profiled, we dressed preppy with button-up shirts tucked in, slacks, dress shoes, hair neatly combed, and eyeglasses. Most importantly, we never purchased too many items because we knew that would raise a flag.

In case it all went south, we planned to stage a Petit Theft. When people—specifically loss prevention officers—get suspicious, they want to be right, and they won't stop digging until their suspicions are validated. If we raised an LPO's suspicions, letting them bust us for a staged theft was infinitely preferable to letting them search our wallets. We were willing to sacrifice being charged with misdemeanor Petit Theft and spending a day or two in jail to prevent a felony Identity Fraud charge.

For months, Torres and I compiled an inordinate amount of clothes, shoes, and tons of other crap we didn't need, but were able to sell for cash. This was what living on the other side felt like. For a while it felt kind of fulfilling. Any status symbol I wanted, I could buy. The money was stacking up. I finally did not have to concern myself with how I would get my next meal. The manner in which I was acquiring the money did not sit well with me. I felt like a criminal. But any time that sentiment crept into my mind, I would shrug it off by telling myself that these were the cards I was dealt and I was just playing the game the best way I knew how.

On January 10, 1996, I walked into Spec's music prepared to purchase fifteen cassettes at $15 apiece and a Sony Walkman at $150. The key to avoiding suspicion is to believe entirely that you've done nothing wrong and then act like it. Dress the part. Keep your cool. Don't break a sweat. Be courteous to store staff. Ask questions about the product you intend to fraudulently purchase. Ask if they will accept returns if you do not like it. Ask about product insurance and physical damage protection plans. Ask the sales rep if they would buy it themselves. Develop rapport. Get them talking. Then take them to the cleaner's.

I'd been there for about five minutes flipping through cassettes when a six foot tall stocky white male, who looked like he could not grow facial hair but knew exactly where to place the anabolic human growth hormone needle, walked behind me, pausing a few feet away. This guy looked like he wanted to be a cop badly, but the steroids had gone to his brain and he couldn't pass the spelling exam required to become an NMBPD officer.

I picked up another tape and pretended to be engrossed in the track names. After a few seconds, I glanced up. He hadn't taken his eyes off me.

Suddenly a female sales rep with crusty spiked hair and a face that reminded me why Proactiv had become such a popular product appeared next to me.

"Can I help you with anything, sir?"

I set the tape down. The LPO was temporarily distracted by a group of giggling pre-teen girls.

"Actually, yes," I said. "I'm looking for Tupac's *Me Against the World*. Do you have it?"

The woman pointed to a section two rows over.

I followed her finger, all the while keeping the LPO in my peripherals. He disappeared into a tall aisle.

About a minute passed, and I'd made my choices. I was almost ready to check out, when suddenly, there he was again. When he wasn't circling me, he was staring at me. This guy was like a shark to blood.

I'd just picked up the Sony Walkman when another employee stepped up.

"Is there anything you need help finding?"

Either this was the most attentive store in Miami, or they were on to me. How I'd raised any flags, I didn't know. I was dressed like all of these other middle class shoppers with cash to burn, wasn't I?

What worried me most was that Torres and I had hit that Spec's location a couple of times several months back. Could they have caught onto the scheme?

If they didn't see me take something, they'd search me, and there was no way I'd be able to conceal my phony ID at that point. I had no choice but to go to plan B.

I had enough money in my wallet to purchase two cassettes, so I grabbed two, pretending to deliberate. Then, with as much nonchalance as I could muster, I pulled my pager out of my pocket, slipped the cassettes into my back pocket and acted like I was checking a message on my pager. It couldn't have been more than ten seconds before the LPO attacked, demanding to see what was in my pockets.

The stupid bastard was practically gloating.

I reached into my pocket and pulled the tapes out in surprise. "Oh, shit. This is a mistake. I'm still planning to buy those." I pulled my wallet out. "See? Here's the money."

He folded his arms over his chest and sneered. "Cut the act. If you were going to pay, why were they in your pocket?"

Nothing gets past you, huh?

I lifted the pager in my hand and tried my best to look sheepish.

"My pager went off. I must have put them in my pocket as I pulled it out to check who was beeping me. It was an honest mistake, sir..." I trailed off. He wasn't buying it. "Is it okay if I just pay for these and leave?"

The LPO scoffed and took me by the arm. "I don't think so. I'm going to call the police."

I put on a brilliant performance pretending to be scared and pleading with him to change his mind. He was beaming as he escorted me to the room where I waited to be arrested. It went better than I could have hoped. The idiot LPO was so proud of himself for catching me red handed, he didn't bother to search me further. The cop who answered the call was so annoyed to have his lunch break interrupted, that he barely looked at me before slapping the cuffs on.

The arresting officer transported me to my home away from home, the Miami-Dade Juvenile Detention Center, where I spent nearly three days before a judge released me. Everything went exactly how Torres and I planned. When my property was returned, the fake ID and stolen check were undisturbed, exactly where I'd hidden them. And so, I dodged a felonious bullet.

We should have quit after that, but it's hard to shut down an operation that well-oiled. We ran it smoothly for about two more months after I was caught, but on March 12, 1996, I was arrested again under almost identical circumstances. This one was a wakeup call.

I'd been poking around the men's department of Burdines for maybe ten minutes, and I'd already noticed more than one member of the loss prevention team circle.

I couldn't believe they were on to me already.

I hadn't even pulled anything from the racks. I was just browsing. About the third time an employee walked by me, I was officially nervous. It was time for the exit strategy. I grabbed a button up shirt like the one I was wearing, a pair of slacks, and a brown belt. I walked into the fitting room and tried on the outfit. I walked out and circled in front of the mirror, making a point of looking like I didn't care for the fit. Then I changed back into my clothes—with one exception. I purposely used the brown belt and left my own with the clothes in the dressing room. If they were actually suspicious, they'd bust me. If not, well, a belt for a belt.

As I walked toward the exit, the loss prevention team showed up right on cue.

"Did you pay for that?"

I stopped and looked at the woman who had spoken. "Me?"

She raised an eyebrow and pointed a stubby finger at my waist. "Did you pay for that belt?"

I opened my eyes wide, "Yeah. Of course. I got it a few days ago. Why would you ask me that?"

The woman took a few steps forward and lowered her voice as if she didn't want to make a scene, "We both know you didn't pay for that, kid."

I looked down at the belt and looked back up in shock. "Oh wow. You're right. That was a complete accident. I tried an outfit on but I accidently put on the wrong belt. I'm so sorry."

I immediately reached down and started unbuckling the stolen belt. She smacked my arm down and looked around the store, her cheeks getting red.

Then she narrowed her eyes, got close enough for me to feel her breath and said, "Do you think I am stupid?"

Why do they always ask that question?

I knew better than to verbalize a response, but my eyes must have answered for me.

Her nostrils flared as she reached for my elbow. "Let's go."

"Oh, come on," I said. "Really! It was an accident. I put on the wrong belt. Look, I left my brand new belt with you guys. I just bought it a few days ago. Why would I do that?"

"I have no idea, but I know a thief when I see one."

After the officer arrived and my rights were read, the cop removed all of my belongings from my pockets—including my wallet. I held my breath as he quickly thumbed through the cards and cash. All he had to do was stick his fingers inside the plastic ID sleeve, pull out my real driver's license, and the fake ID would be exposed. That discovery would prompt him to search the rest of my wallet, which would lead to the stolen check. I would have been finished.

But that didn't happen. He shut my wallet, and charged me with Petit Theft. I spent another three days locked up. When my property was returned, just like in the previous arrest, the fake ID and the stolen check were untouched.

For reasons I can explain with nothing but assumptions, the two charges pending against me for Petit Theft were dismissed. I figure that because both involved the theft of items not exceeding fifty dollars and each instance could have been an accident, the State Attorney's Office decided the fight wasn't worth it. Without being able to prove a person's specific intent to commit a theft, there will always be reasonable doubt.

After my sixth arrest, I decided to stop playing with the check fraud fire for three reasons:

First, this was the second time I had been arrested for Petit-Theft while attempting to transact a felony. The only reason I had not been brought up on felony charges was because of dumb luck. Had the arresting officers had any investigative skills, I would have gone away for much longer than six days.

Second, after months of robbing USPS mail trucks, the mailmen had stopped parking their trucks and walking their routes. Each USPS truck we staked out started to pull up directly in front of the house it had to deliver mail to. Then the postmen would either place mail inside the mailbox while sitting inside their trucks, or would walk up to each mailbox individually. The gig was definitely up.

And third, a couple of months prior to my sixth arrest, I had fully complied with the terms of the community control sentence I was given on my fourth arrest. I no longer had to submit clean drug screens, which meant I could once again smoke and, thereby, sell marijuana.

In the spring of 1996, Torres and I used the cash we stacked from our check fraud operation to open up the drive-thru marijuana dope hole we'd been talking about since my fourth arrest. Torres, Martinez, Reyna and Toretto were already living in the Star Creek apartments, so we set up shop there. After only a few weeks, the drive thru was booming with sales on nickel and dime bags. Nickel bags were filled with the same amount of marijuana as there is tobacco in one cigarette. Dimes bags had two cigarettes worth. We were balling. We had expenses, of course, but we were straight stacking cash.

The Star Creek apartments had two ingress and egress points. On 191st Street was the main entrance and exit. On NE 3rd Avenue was the back entrance and exit. We placed one gangster at each access point to act as a watch out. The actual dope hole was located closer to the back entrance of the apartment complex. We strategized it that way because Snake Creek Canal was adjacent to the back entrance of Star Creek. If anything ever required us to flee on a moment's notice, we could run and hide the dope in the field next to the canal. Any marijuana and weapons we had on us could be stashed away under large rocks in the field. Then we would run back inside Star Creek to hide in one of the apartments.

When a would-be customer entered one of the access points, the watch-out would signal the dope dealer on duty by making a "skeeeeuuoooooo" sound. The alert indicated that a buyer was driving in.

In the alternative, if a police vehicle drove in, the watch-out would signal the dope dealer on duty with a screeching whistle.

Once buyers drove into the complex, a second gangster approached and asked for the amount the customer wanted. The customers would respond, payment was collected, and they were informed to keep their vehicles running with the passenger window or door open. A third gangster, the on duty dope dealer, would walk up to the vehicle and drop the marijuana bags inside the window or open the door and drop the bags inside the vehicle. The buyers were then instructed to drive off as the dope dealer walked away. There was never any chatter or time to keep people around. We moved buyers in and out as quickly as possible to keep the flow of traffic at a minimum.

Little by little our entire crew moved into the Star Creek apartment complex. We rotated shifts, and I made sure someone from our crew was always on duty. We had a large group of gangsters working for us, but the core of the Star Creek crew always remained the same. We meant business. Word spread about our operation like it was mid-July and we were the only place in town with running water. People from all over knew about us. Within months, Star Creek was the preferred dope hole. We had weed all day, every day.

Cops never tried anything with us. In fact, some of the hypocritical pigs took a kickback to keep quiet. There was nothing more satisfying than paying those "law enforcement" scumbags in exchange for protection. We paid them well, too. Torres and I understood that contributing funds to what we called the 'Citizens Safety Project' was a necessary evil. As long as nothing crazy went down, we were in the clear. Torres and I ran Star Creek like a corporation; we paid everyone a decent salary and we incentivized customers with marijuana if they referred new business. We were running one of the most profitable drive-thru dope holes in Miami-Dade County.

Re-upping the supply was not a problem either. Nickson used his connection with Corey Smith of the John Doe Boyz to feed us all. This was the real key to our success. The John Doe Boyz ran the drug ports in Miami and were the best hook-up for cocaine and marijuana. It was a precarious relationship, though. They were powerful allies, but fierce enemies too. If you crossed them, not only would you not make money in the drug trade, but you were likely to find yourself bleeding out in an alley. It took a couple of months to build the relationship with the John Doe Boyz, but we hustled hard and it was well worth it.

By the summer of 1996, Torres and I were making thousands of dollars in profits per week. We never took the next step into selling cocaine, though. I knew that if we did, it would draw in an entirely different customer base, and I wasn't interested in putting everything we'd built in the hands of cokeheads. I saw the consequences of that when Nickson and I went to pick up our supply down in Liberty City. Let me tell you, we weren't anywhere near well-enough armed to handle the dope fiends who come crawling into those types of dope holes. Plus, the statutory minimum imprisonment sentence for cocaine possession, distribution or trafficking were much higher than for marijuana. We stuck with what we did best.

The marijuana trade became our bread and butter. We got addicted to the hustle.

Make no mistake: The hood *is* an addiction. An addiction that pulls as seductively and fiercely as the drugs hustled on its streets. And living in it is a daily exercise in survival.

Survival depends on reputation. The stronger your reputation, the better your chances of making it out alive. Every action, every failure to act, reflects on your credibility. And, believe me, someone is always watching.

A strong reputation is founded on respect: the respect of your friends and the respect of your enemies. There are two ways to earn it: through admiration or through fear. Once you choose, though, you can't look back.

I chose path number three. A combination of admiration and fear.

Love is a choice, in my experience. So earning admiration for my brains and skill was a fine method for family and friends, but nothing I did or said could make people love me if they'd made up their minds not to. Fear, on the other hand, was entirely within my control to inflict on someone else. Fear is a sentiment created with actions, and I always acted with my reputation in mind.

Sometimes that resulted in ugly deeds, but there were too many gangsters, dope dealers, graffiti crews, and crooked cops that—love me or fear me—needed to respect me. There was no such thing as emotional debt in the hood. Action was the only currency we had. Inaction earned you scorn and an orange jumpsuit.

If you were lucky.

6

SEVENTH, EIGHTH, NINTH

MARCH 14, 1996; APRIL 11, 1996; MAY 14, 1996
DRIVING WHILE LICENSE SUSPENDED OR REVOKED[8]
GUILTY ON EACH CHARGE
SIX TOTAL DAYS INCARCERATED

The marijuana drug trade generated consistent income for us, but there was nothing like selling stolen cars to make fast cash. During the carjacking span of our criminal racket, we successfully stole and resold, in whole or for parts, at least twenty-five high-end cars. None of us ever got caught stealing a car, and those were easily the most exhilarating heists we pulled.

There were three ways we stole cars: (1) my personal favorite: the old fashioned way, show up, slim-jim the door or spark plug the window, and crank up an empty ride right off the streets; (2) drive em' right out of the dealerships; and (3) Denise would persuade successful businessmen to leave bars with her in their cars.

---

[8] See, Miami-Dade County State Attorney and Florida Department of Law Enforcement Case No(s). 860320I, 175590O and Broward County State Attorney and Florida Department of Law Enforcement Case No. 451852P

From time to time, the local chop shops would make irresistible offers for brand new cars. These heists were the biggest paydays we could imagine: one-third of the car's price tag.

Star Creek was a short distance from US Route 441, which was basically a ten-mile stretch of new car dealerships. Torres and I thought long and hard about getting into this type of car theft. Each hit would require extensive planning and a team of at least five. We could never hit the same dealership twice. It was a huge risk, but we finally agreed that the ends justified the means.

Toretto, the gang's car man, had taught each of us how to quickly and effectively slim-jim a car. The first step, he explained, was to peel back the rubber seal of the driver's side window and slide the slim-jim down in between the window and rubber seal directly above the door handle. Second, slowly slide the slim-jim downward until it made contact with the door lock mechanism. Third, move the slim-jim in small circular motions until its arm hooked onto the internal lever which opens the door. Fourth, pull up slightly on the slim-jim to ensure that the arm is securely hooked onto the lever. Fifth, gently pull up on the slim-jim to operate the lever to unlock the door. Finally, pull the door handle open.

Once we'd all mastered that skill, we went to work.

Several dealerships on 441 had a long strip of wooded land on the backside, separating the dealership from a residential subdivision. In the middle of the night, the five of us—Torres, Toretto, Nickson, Martinez, and I—were dropped off inside the complex. We kept to the shadows, silently creeping through the palms and brush. We were dressed in black all terrain gear, our faces covered with ski masks, and our bags filled with the car thief's toolkit: slim-jims, screw drivers, rubber mallets, vice grip pliers, slide-hammers, burner phones and guns. We were not getting arrested. We were not getting locked-up. No matter what.

We made it to the wall at the backside of the dealership without incident, and scaled it one at a time, giving each person the chance to take cover and warn the rest if necessary.

Then we slim-jimmed each of the cars we wanted to steal and prepared them to drive off without actually cranking them on. We needed to keep noise down to a minimum until each car was ready to exit the dealership.

There were two ways we stole cars from dealerships. The method simply depended on the type of ignition device that was installed on the car we planned to steal. And no, neither option involved touching two peeled and exposed wires together. That was long outdated for the type of cars we were interested in.

Most American cars required that we use a rubber mallet to destroy the steering column's casing. Removing the casing made it easier to manipulate the ignition device. Once removed, we looked for two thin steel rods, one on top of the other, which connected to the ignition device. Using bolt cutters, we snipped the steel rods. Then we clamped vice-grip locking pliers onto one of the rods. A simple pull on the lower rod, or a push on the upper rod, would crank up the American car.

Most foreign cars, and some American cars, required that we use a slide-hammer to remove the key insert portion of the ignition device. The slide-hammer is a tool with a screw on one end, a handle on the other end, and a rod in between both ends that has a sliding weight used to exert force. We screwed the slide-hammer into the key insert portion of the ignition device, and when the screw was completely inside, we forcefully tugged on the sliding weight a couple of times until the ignition device ripped out. Once the ignition device was removed, all we had to do was insert a flat-head screwdriver into the hole, turn clockwise, and she'd spring to life.

One of the cars was always prepared as a sacrificial lamb, of sorts. The plan was to crash open the gated front entrance of the dealership with it like the lead car in a NASCAR race. I hated to ruin a perfectly good car that we could sell, but we needed to bust down the chained fence to get access to the main road as quickly as possible.

A few blocks away from the dealership—the opposite direction of the exit route—we had Echevarria waiting to create a diversion. This was back when burner phones were untraceable because cell site triangulation wasn't as common as it is today.

Once the cars were ready, I called Echevarria.

"We ready," I said.

A few seconds later, we heard the faint echoes of shots being fired into the ground.

I handed the phone off to Torres. He dialed 911.

"Hello?" he whispered into the phone, his voice frantic and quivering. "Please... Please send help," he winked at us. "There's been a robbery at the Citgo on Miami Gardens Drive off of 441...Yes. Yes, I'm fine but he had a gun and I think someone's been shot—"

He snapped the phone shut and everyone started laughing.

"Alright dumbass, I get it, you want to be an actor," I said. "Now ya'll stop fucking around and get ready to get this show on the road."

"Get to the whips," Torres said.

One person per vehicle, we waited for the sirens. As soon as they were close enough to muffle the sound of our exit, we fired up the cars and got into position. Torres was in the lead car, and I brought up the rear. He plowed right through the fence, pulled off onto the curb, and immediately jumped out. The next three flew past him. I swung out of the lot, slammed on the brakes beside the abandoned vehicle, and popped open the door for Torres.

We flew up the service road and another member of our crew driving a legit vehicle fell in behind and tailed us all the way out to the chop shop.

We made a killing off of the cars we stole from dealerships, and I won't deny it was an incomparable adrenaline rush to do it that way, but, it was far easier to catch the mouse with a mousetrap.

Denise stood about five foot five and weighed maybe 110 pounds. She had a beautiful face with piercing brown eyes, long brown hair, large breasts, olive skin, and curves to die for. She knew she was a dime, and she knew how to make anyone eat out of the palm of her hand. She didn't have the kind of insecurities that plague so many women these days. Men wanted her attention like nothing I'd ever seen before. The best part was that there were no boundaries to it. Businessmen. College students. Thugs. Foreigners. Even other females. They all fell for her.

I wasn't one to waste the talents of my crew, so after I saw Denise con a completely sober man into giving her his Rolex, I put her to work. Denise used her fake IDs to get into various upper echelon clubs to work her magic. The man was different every time, but the scenario always played out the same way.

Denise, dressed in something that clung to the curves of her breasts and hips, would take a seat at the bar and order a drink. In a matter of minutes, a guppy would bite her line. He would play it cool at first, just testing the waters, but in the end they were all infatuated. Her low voice would offer him a seat, and her vixen's eyes would promise so much more. When he asked to freshen up her drink, she'd order a twenty-dollar cocktail and watch his face for smug approval. She would touch his hand and look for Ivy League class rings. As she brushed his arm, she'd check the brand of his watch. She searched for designer insignias as she ran her fingers down the buttons on his shirt. Sometimes he made it too easy. He wanted to impress so badly, he would purposely place the keys to his car right in front of her on the bar.

Once Denise was certain she'd hooked a guppy with luxury wheels, she abandoned flirtation and went straight for seduction. She would put her hand on his knee and slide it slowly up his thigh as she leaned in to whisper in his ear. She'd tell him exactly what he wanted to hear. She'd make the guppy feel like he had the biggest dick on the planet.

And it never failed.

As Denise and the guppy left the club, three of us would be waiting inside our own car outside the club. We'd follow them out to the car, and if he was parked in an isolated lot, we would strike immediately. It usually wasn't that simple, so we often had to tail them to another destination.

That was usually a deserted public beach parking lot. Denise made sure of that. She'd ask the guppy to pick up a bottle of wine on the way and park on the beach because she couldn't wait to get undressed. Never did one resist, nor did they ever catch on to the fact that they were being followed. All they were thinking about was Denise. Once the guppy parked the car, he would uncork the wine, and the two would pass the bottle, fingers brushing against fingers. Denise would turn up the heat, knowing that the guppy would never have a chance to touch her.

One of us would stay in the getaway car parked within walking distance of the guppy's car, while I would walk up and knock on the driver side window. The guppies always jumped, then rolled down their windows and spat something rude and sarcastic.

"I am sorry to interrupt," I would say, "but I need you to get the fuck outta the car. I'm taking her."

If they weren't out within five seconds, I would pull my gun and ask again.

They never needed further persuading. These businessmen never met anyone that meant business quite like we did.

What happened next never ceased to amuse me. In every case, once the gun came out, the guppy was suddenly a valiant knight intent on saving his damsel in distress. They truly were all the same. In all the years, in all the dozens of times we ran this con, every guppy conceded whatever we asked for, "so long as we didn't hurt the girl."

Suckers.

As they stepped out of their cars they would adopt this shaky, artificially calm voice and instruct Denise to step out with them.

I would say, "Nah homeboy, yo bitch coming with us!"

Denise would scream, "No. No. Don't let them take me!" fling open her door and pretend to try to run for it.

Before she could escape, a third gangster would appear with a gun pointed right at her.

"Bitch, you ain't heard what he said! Yo ass coming with us. And if you scream, you both dead. Now jump in the back seat and shut the fuck up!"

Denise always threw desperate looks at the guppy, but the third gangster would shove her head down, push her into the back seat, and jump in behind her. Then I would dive into the driver's seat, start the car, and take off.

The look on the guppy's face was always hilarious, but never priceless—there was a very measurable stack of cash waiting for each of us at the end of those nights.

Perception is reality. At least that is what we tend to believe. Fancy cars are a status symbol for gangsters just as much as they are for lawyers. We tend to assume that he who drives the nicest car must be the most successful. No matter the socio-economic environment, perception is one screwed up thing in our society because the car you drive, the clothes you wear, the house you live in and the characters you associate with supposedly say something about the person. This skewed perspective predominates despite class, rich, poor or in between.

It drove me mad growing up poor as a kid having to watch my dad drive a raggedy-ass deteriorating bucket of rust that could barely travel the roads and looked like it belonged in a junkyard compactor. My dad's car said he was broke; that he was not worth much; and that his lifestyle was undesirable just like his car.

In the hood, the type of car you drove was important to your reputation because it said whether or not you were willing to do things others can't do or won't do. If you can come up from nothing and drive a nice car it put others on notice that you were balling. Even if you lived in dilapidated areas of Miami-Dade County, your reputation was enhanced if you drove a nice car with custom rims, tinted windows, a bumping system with bass, a candy paint job, loud exhaust pipes and or hydraulics. Nice cars also meant dime pieces. Nice cars allowed us to hook up with the often better looking but materialistic gangster chicks. Just like the lawyer, his BMW, and his trophy wife.

I decided that if I was forced to go travel through the valley of the shadow of death, then I was going to ride through it in nicer cars than any of the other gangsters. With the money we made, I purchased various vehicles and refurbished or customized them, modified the motors, equipped them with aftermarket rims and installed high-end sound systems. I owned an 81 Buick Regal, 81 Cadillac Deville, 83 Buick Regal, 84 Oldsmobile Cutlass Supreme, 84 Honda Accord, 86 Cadillac Seville, 90 Audi A4, 93 Mazda 626, 94 Ford Explorer, 94 Mazda Protégé, 94 Lincoln Town Car, 96 Mazda 626 and my favorite, a 1969 Chevy Impala. I kept the cars in Star Creek. Females could never figure out which car we'd roll up in. Haters wondered how we got our money. Rival gangsters understood that high-end artillery accompanied a high-end set of wheels.

We started living an extremely fast life. We had money. We had the cars to go along with the money. We had the females' attention. And we developed an infamous reputation as gangsters you did not want to cross. But while I was gaining street credibility, it was my soul that was being impacted. I felt as if I'd sold my soul for materialistic possessions. I was deep into the game. I had no fear. Only ambition. I was willing to do anything. Driving nice cars helped us enhance our reputation and in turn helped us generate more income. But driving nice cars also generated the wrong attention. Attention from the police.

On my seventeenth birthday, October 16, 1995, the Florida Department of Motor Vehicles issued me a driver license. By October 31, 1995 I received my first citation for having a tinted cover over my vehicle's license plate.[9] I went to court and reported to the judge that I'd removed the tinted cover, plead Nolo Contendere, paid the court costs, and the case was closed.

---

[9] See, Metro-Dade Police Department and Florida Department of Motor Vehicle Citation No. 861099I

On January 9, 1996, I received my second citation, this time for obstructing traffic.[10] I was in the middle of changing a flat tire on I-95 when a State Trooper pulled up. He said my car was too close to the highway where I'd parked in the emergency lane. There was nowhere else to pull off, other than in the grass, which would have made it impossible to change my tire. He issued a citation, but I never showed up to court because I didn't received the notice to appear. My license was suspended as a result.

Of course that didn't mean I stopped driving. I didn't exactly drive like a sweet old lady on her way to church, and I certainly didn't drive her car, so avoiding police attention was more than a little difficult.

On March 14, 1996, the same day I was released from the Miami-Dade County Juvenile Detention Center on my sixth arrest, I was pulled over by officer Mario Gutierrez and issued four citations, one being Driving While License Suspended or Revoked.[11] Officer Gutierrez placed me under arrest for the seventh time because a failure to appear warrant had been issued for my arrest after I failed to appear in court for the flat tire incident. So, the same day I was released from juvenile lock-up, I went right back in and spent two more days there.

On April 11, 1996, I was pulled over for speeding in Broward County. I was issued two citations and arrested for the eighth time because—as you may have guessed—my license was still suspended.[12] I spent two days incarcerated and was released from the Broward County jail on April 13.

On May 14, 1996, I was pulled over by officer Linda Ann Dohring and issued two more citations, one—again—being Driving While License Suspended or Revoked.[13] Officer Dohring placed me under arrest for the ninth time. I spent another two days incarcerated and was released on May 16.

For those of you keeping track, yes, I was arrested three times in three months for driving with a suspended Florida driver license. I plead guilty to each charge in July of 1996.

---

[10] See, Florida Highway Patrol and Florida Department of Motor Vehicle Citation No. 765934B

[11] See, Metro-Dade Police Department and Florida Department of Motor Vehicle Citation No(s). 860320I, 860321I, 860323I, and 860324I

[12] See, Broward County State Attorney and Florida Department of Law Enforcement Citation No(s). 451851P and 451852P.

[13] See, Metro-Dade Police Department and Florida Department of Motor Vehicle Citation No(s). 1755890 and 1755900.

Less than one year from receiving my driver license I began to serve a twelve-month suspension. I was not allowed to reinstate my driving privilege until July of 1997.

The philosopher Kierkegaard said, "Life can only be understood backwards but must be lived forward."

It was idiotic to not pay the fines. I know that now. In that moment, I completely lacked trust in law enforcement authorities and the American jurisprudence system as a whole. I'd started believing Wilhite's promise. I would go away for good one day, and there was nothing I could do to stop it.

All I could see in those crisp black police uniforms and silver shields was corruption. Judges, prosecutors, public defenders, probation officers and correctional officers were just the same. They were all dirty to me, and they were out for blood. I was running along a crumbling cliff-face, and they were below watching, hoping for my fall. It was inevitable. It was fact.

I couldn't stop the arrests because there was nothing I could do to prevent cops from profiling me as a criminal. I looked the part, I acted the part, but I didn't feel it. There were days when I looked around me in the middle of a drug deal, as if I'd just been jolted awake and had no idea how I'd gotten there. I'd always clung to the belief that I was smart enough to be and do anything I wanted. But day-by-day, I was losing that vision of my future. I felt trapped by the cards I was dealt. Poverty put me in this situation. Doing the things I was doing in the streets was the only way I saw myself escaping.

When I was very young, and we'd just moved to Miami, my dad drove us all to Vero Beach. It was for my mom's birthday, and that family trip to see the ocean was what she wanted as her gift. It was as beautiful as a postcard. I loved that America, the one I was promised. It was clean and the air was fresh and the people were happy. Christian spent the whole car ride reading his comic books, and Karina went on and on about her plans to dig in the sand like a paleontologist.

Giselle and I raced to the water the moment the car stopped. We heard Mom shout about staying close to shore, but forgot her warnings the moment our toes splashed into the surf. We dove in and swam out as far as we could. We flipped over onto our backs and just floated, staring up at the pale blue sky. I'd never felt so vast. I wasn't just one person, I was part of the Atlantic—an ocean that touched shores I may never see.

In the next moment, I was underwater, ripped from the surface. My lungs were filling with frigid, salty water, and my eyes and nose were burning. I couldn't breathe.

I fought to the surface, choking up water and screaming for my sister. But in an instant, I was under again. I had to find Giselle. I had to get to shore.

Again and again, I was pulled violently from the surface, swam as hard as I could, swallowed water and gasped for air, searched frantically for my sister, and was dragged under again. I was losing strength and every muscle in my body was cramping in on itself.

I was helpless.

The lifeguard who pulled me out told my mother that it wasn't getting pulled under that killed people. People drowned from exhaustion trying to escape the current. It's useless to try, he told her. The harder you try, the quicker you'll die. The rip will always win.

Trying was pointless then, and struggling against my fate was equally so now. So I did the same thing I'd done as a kid, half-drowned in the ocean: I quit fighting.

Today, I can't help but be afraid for a society that just accepts the idea that the fittest are the most prosperous—the let-them-fend-for-themselves mentality— while we sit back in our lofty towers and leave disadvantaged people to drown. That kind of uncompassionate thinking makes for a self-centered population, *especially* the portion of the population we abandon.

Why would a kid like me bother complying with a judge's order? Why would I apply someone else's moral codes to the manner and form in which I gather my personal assets, if it is the strong that will prevail? If I need break a few rules to get to the top of the ladder, who is society to judge and condemn my actions? If society doesn't care about me, then why should I care about society?

Don't tell a person to pull himself up by his bootstraps and then condemn him for following your instructions.

7

TENTH

JULY 15, 1996
BURGLARY OF AN UNOCCUPIED CONVEYANCE;
CRIMINAL MISCHIEF; GRAND THEFT; AGGRAVATED BATTERY[14]
NOLLE PROSEQUI
NINETY DAYS INCARCERATED

In our line of business, we sometimes made allies, but more often we made enemies. By the summer of 1996, Star Creek was known all over Miami-Dade County. We were the most reliable twenty-four-hour drive-through dope hole in the area, stories of our ballsy auto thefts were retold for months after they'd gone down, and we'd solidified our reputation as a force that was to be reckoned with—a reputation each of us vowed to preserve at any cost. It was that reputation that drew in regular customers with disposable incomes. We saw more money in a year than my parents made in ten. That kind of money is powerful, but it also bred envy. Being the area's most popular drug-dealers opened us up to robbery and gang wars.

We never knew when or how a hater would react to our success, but it was only a matter of time. When haters did strike retribution was an obligation. We

---

[14] See, Miami-Dade County State Attorney and Florida Department of Law Enforcement Case No. F96022280B

didn't seek out violence, but pacifism and peaceful resistance are not options for gangsters. Turning the other cheek didn't make us bigger men, it made us soft. And a soft gangster is a dead gangster.

Early one morning, I was driving my 94 Lincoln Town Car and stopped to fuel up on my way to Star Creek. The Lincoln was in immaculate condition. It was pearl white with a snowy leather interior and pitch-dark window tints. I dressed up all of my vehicles with after-market rims, wheels, and sound systems. For the Lincoln, I'd purchased a set of fourteen inch Dayton wire wheels with low profile whitewall tires. I had the car lowered to just a few inches from the ground so that the wheels hugged the fender's lip. The Alpine system I had installed was state-of-the-art and featured the best JL Audio subwoofers, highs, and tweeters money could buy. The Lincoln had bass so powerful it made buildings shake.

I pulled into an Amoco gas station on Miami Gardens Drive and NE 19th Avenue. I had the windows down with the sound system turned up as high as possible, the beats vibrating through my chest.

The station was very busy. I circled the entire station waiting for a pump to become available. The Amoco had a central hub for the cashier with eight gas stations on each side of the hub, and all of them were full. My music was making car windows throb and people were staring—some frightened, some annoyed. I couldn't help smirking. Finally I spotted an open pump. I left the windows down with the music blaring, and walked toward the cashier to pay.

As I stood in line, I watched the station's windows wobble like they were made of Jell-O. I reached the cashier just as the song ended. I handed him a few bills, waiting for the next track to start. It didn't. I glanced back at the Lincoln, worried I'd blown one of my amps.

Sitting in the passenger seat of the Lincoln, staring right at me, was Jesse Perez.

Perez was affiliated with a rival gang known as the 15th Ave. Boys. Perez was a Hispanic about my age, stood close to five foot four and was kind of a thin guy, and had a massive chip on his shoulder stemming from the worst case of Napoleon complex I've ever seen. We'd crossed paths on numerous occasions, and he had earned his place on my list. This was the last straw.

I ran out of the cashier hub, eyes locked on Perez. The instant I hit the blacktop, Perez jumped out of the Lincoln and dove into the driver's seat of a car parked a few feet from mine. As he squealed out of the Amoco, literally burning rubber, I spotted at least one other member of the 15th Ave. Boys in the front passenger seat. I made it to my car just as the getaway car sped into the flow of traffic. I knew that car. It, like the Lincoln, was designed to garner attention, and I'd seen Perez's beige two-door 1983 Oldsmobile Cutlass Supreme more often than I'd like.

I circled the Lincoln once, looking for damage. The tires weren't slit and he hadn't keyed it. I slid inside the open passenger door and started checking for my valuables.

My Motorola StarTAC phone was gone. It wasn't just that the phone was pricey, but it was inside a leather case that had five $100 bills hidden inside. I sat back and brought my fist to my forehead and shut my eyes. Freaking Perez. I was really going to have to teach him a lesson this time.

I flicked open my eyelids.

My sound system. He stole the detachable face from the Alpine sound system. Without the face, the whole thing was useless. This wasn't just a theft. This was an insult. I got out of the car and slammed the door.

I yanked the pump out of my car and snapped the cap back into place. I could feel angry heat creeping up my neck and my fists were involuntarily clenched. My mind was consumed with thoughts of retaliation. I couldn't give chase then because I was alone and unarmed. But I knew exactly how to find Perez.

When I arrived at Star Creek, Nickson and Torres were hanging out with a good friend of ours, Mikey Klaiss. It so happened that Klaiss' sister, Shannon, was acquainted with Perez's sister, Jenny, so we called her up to get their address. Shannon told us that Perez lived in a yellow house with a water fountain on the north side of NE 181st Street off of West Dixie Highway. It appeared Perez lived adjacent to Greynolds Park, which was ideal. We knew the area well and decided to canvass before making our move.

Nickson, Klaiss, Torres, and I took the Lincoln to check things out. There was only one yellow home with a water fountain on NE 181st Street, so we figured it had to be Perez's even though his Cutlass wasn't in the driveway.

Later that afternoon, Torres and I went back to Perez's house in the Lincoln. Klaiss and Nickson followed in Klaiss' pick-up truck. Perez's Cutlass was still not in the driveway. However, I did notice a blue and white Suzuki GSXR motorcycle parked under the front porch. I pulled into the driveway, got out, and walked toward the front door where I got a good look at the GSXR up close.

"Not bad," I said to Torres.

He nodded, "So let's ransom it."

I banged hard on the door. "Let's see if anyone's home first."

We waited about thirty seconds before an adult woman of Hispanic decent cracked the door.

"Who are you?" Her voice was a harsh whisper and there was a thick triangle-shaped crease between her eyebrows.

"I'm here to see Jesse Perez," I replied with an easy smile. "Does he live here?"

The triangle between her eyes relaxed, and she opened the door wider. "You are friends of Jesse's?"

"We sure as hell ain't friends. He robbed me today, and I want my stuff back."

I went on to detail the encounter for the woman, and with each word, her shoulders sagged a little deeper.

"Jesse is my son. He's a good boy," she said with a heavy, raw sigh. "He has been very troubled with gangs and drugs lately. His father—"

"That's really none of my business, ma'am. I don't need an explanation. All I want is what rightfully belongs to me."

She nodded. "Let me beep him."

After about ten minutes, Perez had yet to respond.

"He will make this right," she promised. "I know he will. He is a good boy."

Torres and I exchanged a look. "Yea, I'm sure he ain't a crook," I said. "But I'll be taking his bike as collateral, just to make sure."

She squared her shoulders and looked at me with the ferocity that only a mother protecting her child can summon. "If you touch that bike, I'll call the police."

I laughed. "Go'head. Call. I'll probably get my stuff faster that way."

She tightened her lips and squinted at me.

"When Red gets his stuff back, we bring the bike back," Torres called. "For now, it's our insurance policy."

She closed her eyes for a moment, and I knew she'd resigned herself to the situation. She flicked her hand at the bike. We later found out that an arrest would have been Perez's second probation violation, which meant he would likely serve the balance of his probation behind bars.

I waved to Klaiss and he backed his truck into Perez's driveway. Nickson, Klaiss, Torres and I lifted the GSXR into the bed of Klaiss' truck, Mrs. Perez watched us from the porch with her lips pursed and arms folded. Once the GSXR was secured, I gave her my pager number and told her to contact me when Perez returned. On the way to Star Creek we picked up a few beers and blunts. We unloaded the bike and then drank and smoked and waited.

Around eight o'clock, I received a page with the code 911 from a local number. Back in the pager days, 911 codes didn't always mean emergencies, but they always meant the situation was urgent. I used Nickson's StarTAC to call the number back.

Perez answered after one ring. "Red you bitch ass mother—"

"I'm on my way to yo house right now. You betta have my shit." I immediately hung up and looked around at the other three.

"We best not take the Lincoln," Torres said to me.

I nodded, "Or Mikey's truck."

Nickson spun his keys and grinned. "Let's go watch Red bust this motherfucker up."

Nickson's 1990 black four-door Chevy Caprice Classic was the signature gangster mobile. It was black-on-black with jet black tints and no hubcaps or white walls on the tires. The Caprice looked every bit like a drive-by vehicle.

As the four of us rode over to the Perez home, Klaiss suggested that violence be a last resort since the North Miami Beach Police Department was only a few blocks down the road.

"Fuck that," Torres said. "I say we just drop 'em. Fool disrespected you, Red, and we ain't letting that shit get out."

He had a point. When others heard about the 15th Ave. Boys' gas station robbery, that story had to be followed with one about Star Creek's violent counter. Our reputation depended on it.

"First order of business is to get my shit back," I said. "Then I take care of Perez."

Nickson circled the block a couple of times to ensure we weren't walking into a trap. The first time we cruised past Perez's block I could see his car parked directly in front of the porch on the driveway. It was the only one there.

"Park on the corner," I said. "Let's watch it for a minute."

After a span of no activity, we decided it was time to approach. As soon as we stepped into the front yard, Perez materialized on the porch with a gun in his right hand.

"Put it down, Jessie," I said. "We ain't armed."

"Y'all motherfuckers coming out here to my mama's house? I oughta bust one in you. Where the fuck my bike at, nigga? Gimme my shit back or I'm gonna blow you away!"

My eyes were trained to Perez's gun hand, "Whatcha gonna do? Shoot me right here with all these people watching so you can go straight to Dade County? Put that down and give me a fade, 'cause we all know you ain't gonna shoot nobody."

Perez paced back and forth a few times, staring at me with murder in his eyes. Finally he stopped. "Jenny! Get out here."

Perez handed her the gun and told her to hide it inside. Jenny paused and gave me a look that was part pleading and part anger—the same look her mother had given me—before she disappeared into their little yellow house.

Perez must have thought I was soft because he stepped off the porch with his guard down, spitting insults. I almost laughed.

Since the gun was gone, I knew my risk of death was too. Perez was angry which would make him powerful, but it also made him wild. I had training and control on my side. I ripped my Polo shirt off and threw up my set. As soon as Perez was within reach, I threw two quick rabbit punches that landed right at his chin and knocked him straight to the ground.

I towered over him. He was still conscious, so I waited for him to get up. My father taught me never to hit a man while he was down. There was a glazed stare in Perez's eyes, which any trained fighter knows means his opponent is a few hits away from taking a long nap. Perez rushed at me with jerky, lurching steps. I stepped out of the way and Perez stumbled back onto the ground.

I leaned over him. "Where's my shit? This can end right now."

Perez struggled to his feet, looked at me, and uttered, "Fuck you! I aint got it no mo'."

He lunged at me again, and I met his advance with an uppercut that caught Perez directly under the chin. He arched backwards landing awkwardly on his back with his legs twisted. I moved toward Perez to finish it.

Suddenly hands were on my back, pulling me. I immediately thrust my elbow back with force.

I heard a girly scream of pain and my heart dropped. I flung around to see Jenny in a heap on the ground, clutching her chin.

This was getting out of hand. "Stay out of this! Get back in the house—"

I took a punch to the left side of the face, mid-sentence.

I spun to meet Perez, completely focused. I was done wasting time. I threw punch after punch after punch until I backed Perez up against his Cutlass parked on the driveway. He started to crumble. I heard Jenny screaming at me to stop. I pulled Perez upright by his shirt so I could hit him as many times as possible without him falling back onto the ground. Finally, his body slumped. I let him fall onto his car and slide onto the driveway.

I ran a fist over my chin, wiping away blood. I looked up at Nickson and the others. We had to make an example of him.

"Get me a bat."

Nickson grabbed one from the trunk of his car and handed it to me. Jenny started screaming and crying hysterically, and trying to lunge at me, but Torres and Klaiss held on to her.

I balanced the bat in my hand for a moment. It had to be done.

I swung the bat down with all the force I could muster and shattered the windshield of Perez' Cutlass. I butchered that car until every window, headlight, and taillight was decimated.

I lost track of everything but the rage I felt, the absolute fury at his disrespect. I hated him. I hated myself for hating him.

I didn't stop until I heard, "Freeze! Hands in the air! Hands! Now!"

I didn't freeze.

The rage fueled my feet, and I bolted for Greynolds Park. If I could make it inside, it would be nearly impossible for the cops to find me in the dark. I saw the six foot gate ahead, but I didn't slow. Anger and adrenaline gave me wings. I cleared the fence like an Olympian. Once inside, I sprinted for the most heavily wooded area. After years of playing there, I knew those park trails like I'd blazed them myself. The largest oak tree in the center of the most wooded area was my destination. I used to climb it every day as a kid. I knew from experience that it was the perfect hiding place. If I could make it there, I could wait the cops out until it was safe to escape from the park.

At the highest fork in the tree, I crouched and waited. I took long, even breaths through my nose, and took a full ten seconds to push them out through my mouth. I could feel my pulse throbbing in my neck, and willed my heart to slow. After some time, when my mind was quiet again, I listened to the sounds of the woods.

In the distance, I heard a rhythmic hum. As I listened, it got heavier—like a washing machine that had gotten off balance. The winds started shaking trees, and the chop of the blades grew deafening.

They'd sent a chopper.

A huge flash of light illuminated the open meadow not twenty feet from where I hid. I had to get out. Moments after the flash, I began to hear the faint sound of dogs barking.

I was trapped.

There was no question; the dogs would definitely sniff me out, and I'd have no choice but to surrender. I had to run for it.

The quickest way out of Greynolds Park was by accessing NE 174th Street. To get there, I would have to run across a wide-open golf course and risk being seen from the air. It was a long sprint from the center of the wooded area, but I had no options and my time was limited, so I went for it.

At the far edge of the golf course, I could see the fence that separated the inside of the park from the adjacent residential neighborhood. If I got out of the park without becoming dog food, and if I could make it to Klaiss' house without running into the cops who were undoubtedly surrounding the area, I could hide in Klaiss' backyard until the coast was clear. I raced through the course, leaping over sand traps and dodging flags, careful to keep to any shadows I could.

Finally I reached the fence, planning to clear it in the same manner I'd entered. I placed my foot on the fence, pushed upward, planted both hands on the horizontal pole, and flung my body over the fence. But, in my haste, I failed to observe the spike protruding above the pole.

As I thrust my body over the fence, my right hand did not follow.

The force of my jump yanked my body and slammed me back against the outside of the fence, and I hung from my right arm like a puppet.

That was pain like I'd never felt.

Blood was running down my arm. I needed a hospital. I could still see the police helicopter hovering over the park, searching methodically. My adrenaline and strength were fading, and I heard the dog barks getting closer and closer.

I suddenly had flashbacks to the shadowy night in the field the last time I'd run from cops. Warm blood was still sliding down my arm and onto my chest. It was time to make a decision.

I climbed up a few inches and tried to push my hand upward. I had to stifle a cry of agony. Any slow movement felt as like someone was shoving a knife into my hand and twisting it. I looked closely and realized the piercing was not between the fingers. It was only on the outside of my palm on the outer part of my right pinky finger. I didn't recall much from anatomy class, but I was pretty sure there wasn't anything vital in there.

I firmly placed both feet inside the gaps in the chain-link fence and used my left hand to grab the top of the horizontal pole. I took a deep breath and pulled down as hard and as fast as I could, throwing all of my weight onto my right hand, ripping it free. I fell to the ground, the breath nearly knocked from my chest. There was no time to recoup. I looked at my hand and choked back bile. I yanked my undershirt off and wrapped my hand as I ran the last leg of my journey to Klaiss' house.

It was close to midnight when I arrived, but with the way I was bleeding, there was no way I could just lay low. I knocked on Shannon's window. A few seconds later, she appeared outside.

She took one look at me and rushed to take my hands.

"Oh my God, David!" She said. "You're covered in blood. What happened—?"

"No time! You hear the ghetto bird in the sky? That's for me. You gotta help me hide."

She nodded and hurried me inside. We tiptoed into the bathroom, locking the door behind. I sat on the toilet and she perched on the edge of the tub. She poured peroxide on my hand and I swallowed the scream that threatened to escape.

"Sorry," she said. "I know it burns."

I just nodded and watched as the tiny bubbles rose out of the crater in my palm.

"You have to tell me what happened. Is this about Jesse? Is this why you called me?"

As Shannon poured another cap full of peroxide, I began to narrate the events that put me on her doorstep. She spread a thin layer of Neosporin on both sides and wrapped my hand with a gentleness and sureness that made me think she'd done her fair share of dressing wounds. She held my hand softly as I spoke, and I was suddenly very sorry to have given her another burden.

When I finished my story she looked me in the eye. "You're all so fucking stupid. And you don't know where Mikey is?"

I shook my head. "You know how it is, Shannon. Cops show and it's every man for himself."

"So fucking stupid," she said. She tossed the first aid kit into her purse. "Let's go find my brother."

On the way back to the scene, we passed Nickson's Caprice, still in the same spot where we parked. Halfway down the street, we saw two cop cars with their lights pointing at the Perez's yard. Nickson, Klaiss, and Torres were all sitting, handcuffed on the ground. We drove on.

Early the following morning, almost exactly twenty-four hours after Perez had started this whole thing, I turned myself in. My hand needed serious medical attention, and after Perez, Jenny, and their mom provided an accurate description of me, a warrant was issued for my arrest. I was going to pay for this one, that was clear, but I wasn't going to let the cops beat me to a pulp first.

When I walked into the North Miami Beach police station, I barely spoke.

I offered no excuses and no emotion. They could never understand. *They couldn't bear to understand why I did what I did*—to comprehend would shatter their perfectly constructed illusions of what life was. They had the luxury of living by the laws of civilized people in a black and white, right and wrong world. In my reality, good and bad were relative, and at the end of the day neither mattered.

Good was alive and bad was dead. The hundreds of individual decisions we made between sleeps were all immaterial grays in the war to survive the hood.

8

NINETY DAYS

The maximum statutory sentence for the crimes I was charged with carried fifteen years behind bars; the mandatory minimum was two. Though the case was ultimately dismissed, I still served ninety days in the Miami-Dade County Pretrial Detention Center.

Three months incarcerated is an eternity when you're seventeen. I saw and heard things worse than anything I'd experienced in the streets and I spent my days in the company of some of Miami's most reprehensible criminals. But more terrible than any act I witnessed or any of the lowlifes I encountered, was the slow realization that I was becoming one of them.

I did a lot of thinking while I was locked up. That might be the most excruciating part about jail—the relentless time alone in your own head. Silence is like this magnetic cavern that draws out every memory and regret and thought we try to keep tucked away in the deepest folds of our minds. Regret is the real prison.

Again and again I saw the childhood vision I'd had of my life, that plan to use the law to protect good people like my father, that dream of giving my brother and sisters a future. Those had been my reasons for living once, hadn't they?

It all seemed so distant now. Had I really once believed that someday I could wear a suit and live in some ritzy house and drive a car I hadn't bought with dirty money? Had I honestly believed that someday I'd marry a kind, honest girl and raise our innocent kids in some deed-restricted suburb?

David had been such an idealistic fool.

But he was gone. Life had devoured that smart kid with dreams bigger than his circumstances, and all he'd left me with were the shadowy remnants of his hopes.

I was Red, and I was destined to live on the wrong side of justice.

After I turned myself in, I was transported to the Miami-Dade Juvenile Justice Center and immediately scheduled for a detention hearing. At a detention hearing, the circuit court judge exercising jurisdiction over the case determines whether to grant a conditional release or temporary custody to my parents during the pendency of the court's adjudication of the case.

The Public Defender assigned to represent me at the detention hearing argued, "Your Honor, we ask that Mr. Windecher be released to his parents pending adjudication of the case because this was a matter of self-defense. In addition, Mr. Windecher does not have a single delinquent adjudication on his criminal history."

The judge looked over at the State Attorney's table. "What is the State's position?"

The prosecutor stood up, cleared his throat and answered, "Judge, the State vehemently objects to this defendant being released back into the community. We have reason to believe this matter was gang related and not an issue of self-defense."

The prosecutor continued, "In addition, I want the court to understand that this defendant is an evasive flight risk. He caused the North Miami Beach Police Department to employ the assistance of a police aviation unit before his twenty-four-hour manhunt concluded. Further, Your Honor, there is a significant possibility that he will cause serious injury to others. That is evident by the violent and destructive behavior that led to these charges. We believe he will attempt to seriously injure the victim in this matter, Mr. Jessie Perez. Finally, Judge, this defendant has been on a warpath for *eighteen* consecutive months. I was appalled when I reviewed his criminal history. While he does not have any delinquent adjudications, the defendant has amassed *nine* arrests over the previous eighteen months. That is one arrest every two months, Judge. It is only a matter of time before an innocent person's blood is on his hands."

"Objection, Your Honor!" boomed the Public Defender, getting to his feet. "This is unnecessary characterization and badgering. This is a detention hearing, not a disposition."

"Sustained," the judge said. He shot a warning glance at the prosecutor. "Stay within the scope, counselor."

"Your Honor, the State will prepare an information and direct file this defendant so that he may be charged as an adult. In the interim, we ask that he be transported from the Miami Dade Juvenile Detention Center to the Miami-Dade County Pretrial Detention Center."

"Understood," said the judge.

The judge turned to the Public Defender and stated, "As it is within the discretion of the State Attorney's Office to decide whether or not any juvenile under eighteen years of age may be charged as an adult, I grant the states motion to bind the matter over and, order that Mr. Windecher be transported to the Miami-Dade County Pretrial Detention where he will await his day in court, that is, unless he is granted bail by a judge with jurisdiction over this matter. This court no longer has jurisdiction over Mr. Windecher's case."

I was immediately transported from the Miami-Dade Juvenile Detention Center, where all of the inmates were adolescents facing charges with maximum sentences of five years, to the Miami-Dade County Pretrial Detention Center where everyone was an adult and the majority facing serious charges with lengthy sentences.

At the bond hearing, I was denied bail due to the nature of the charges and forced to sit in jail until the date of my trial. And just like that, I was facing fifteen years in prison.

This tenth arrest proved to be my most challenging obstacle later in life because it impugned my character, nearly preventing my matriculating into law school, sitting for the Georgia and Florida bar examinations, and being sworn-in to practice law as a licensed attorney. Even though I was not convicted, I would never have been able to overcome the crippling effect these charges could have had on my life had it not been for a few breaks that fell my way. All too often these types of charges cause American youth to never reach their life or career potentials due to the limitations such a criminal record will impose.

In due course, the State decided to drop the charges against Nickson, Klaiss, and Torres. The State offered each of them a dismissal in exchange for incriminating testimony against me. None of them accepted the offer. The State eventually dismissed their charges because it did not have any other choice. Their charges were dismissed for the same exact reason mine were.

My case was ultimately dismissed because the State's material witnesses refused to take the stand against me. Prior to trial, a few of the other Star Creek gangsters dropped by the Perez home to explain that testifying was not in their best interests. They reminded them that it was Perez who created the entire issue, and explained that if they were to continue in their efforts to make me pay for his stupidity, the result would be far, far more painful than the beating I'd served Perez. My boys left no doubt about what they were prepared to do if any of them took the stand and testified for the State. In late September of 1996, the Perez family informed the Miami-Dade State Attorney's Office that they no longer wished to prosecute or cooperate. The Perez family intimated to the State that if they were subpoenaed they would simply not show for court, despite any legal consequences.

Right before the trial, the State requested a status conference with the judge to inform the court that it feared its material witnesses would not show for trial due to the fear of retribution on my behalf.

"Judge," the prosecutor opened, "we fear that if we set this case for trial, our material witnesses, Mr. Jessie Perez and his family, will not appear before the court because their lives have been threatened by the defendant's gang."

"Your Honor, this is absurd," responded the Public Defender. "Mr. Windecher is not a gangster. The State's case is tentative at best because we have a colorable self-defense argument, and now that the truth is coming out their witnesses no longer want to cooperate. So they pull this stunt hoping you impose some sort of witness tampering sanction. They should have left this case where it belonged: in juvenile court."

"Counselor, what evidence do you have that Mr. Windecher, or someone he is associated with, has tampered with the witnesses?" asked the judge.

"Judge, we do not have any direct evidence—"

"Have you informed your witnesses about the consequences of disregarding a court ordered subpoena?"

"Yes, judge, but—"

"But what, counselor?" demanded the judge. "If you do not have any evidence of witness tampering and you properly subpoenaed the witnesses, then there is nothing further to address."

Before the judge concluded the status conference, the Public Defender requested, "that the State be placed on terms if it intends to announce ready for trial at tomorrow's calendar call because there are no reasons to further continue this matter beyond this term's trial calendar."

"We will see about that tomorrow, counselor."

At the calendar call, the State had no choice but to announce ready for trial if it intended to pursue the charges against me. The Public Defender requested that the State be placed on terms. The judge granted the motion. The case was set for trial on October 15, 1996. All the State could do was hope that one of its material witnesses would show.

None did.

Without their material witnesses, the State was unable to prove its case against me beyond a reasonable doubt. So the State had no choice but to dismiss the charges. I was released from the Miami-Dade County Pretrial Detention Center a few hours shy of my eighteenth birthday.

The ninety days I served while awaiting trial were desperately dark, but they were nothing compared to what could have been. Had I been convicted and served the full fifteen years, there's no telling what kind of man I'd be today, or if I'd even be alive. While I'm grateful my time wasn't longer, it was long enough to eliminate any doubt about the effects of incarceration on adolescents. Any adolescent who spends a significant amount of time incarcerated with adults is guaranteed to be released a hardened criminal.

Only the strong survive in jail, and I don't mean just physically. You wake up each morning in a small concrete cell with a person you don't know anything about. You cannot get up and walk out because you are barricaded in with steel bars. When the cell gate does open, it gives way to a jungle filled with dangerous and unpredictable animals. If you've never been incarcerated, it might be impossible for you to understand.

Can you imagine standing in the lunch line waiting for your food when suddenly the person ten feet in front of you gets stabbed in the neck with a shank and all you can do is watch the blood spew out like a water fountain? Or how about playing a game of cards when three inmates appear out of nowhere and stab your opponent more than twenty times until he collapses? How much sleep would you get laying in your bed at night and listening to the muffled cries of a grown man being raped? And how would you respond to corrections officers screaming at you, their faces inches from yours, while they rip up your family photos?

There are no comforts in jail. You wear an orange jumpsuit that, no matter how many times it's washed, will always smell like sweat and cause every inch of your body to itch. Every morning you're jolted awake by deafening alarm buzzers for the 4:00 a.m. head count. On your way to count, you get screamed at repeatedly while being pushed around by autocratic corrections officers. If you even consider reacting, you will spend a good portion of the foreseeable future in solitary confinement, known on the inside as "the box."

After the head count, you have thirty minutes for breakfast where you're served some sort of barely edible substance that vaguely resembles food. Then it's back to your cell. You sit in the cell until rec time. You have one hour of recreation each day. This is the most dangerous hour to survive. Anything can happen. Riots. Gang wars. Murder. Anything.

After rec hour, you're sent back to the cafeteria for lunch. The cafeteria is safer than the rec yard because it's a smaller area with much more security, but again, anything can happen.

When you're done eating, it's back to the general population quarters where you remain until lockdown. Each day at 7:00 p.m. you are locked in your cell to await the next day when it all starts again. This is the time you spend alone with your cellmate. I did not make friends with mine until the day I returned to my cell after serving a week in the box for fighting during rec hour.

"Ain't no man can keep his wits in the box," my cellmate said.

We hadn't spoken much before, and I hadn't spoken much at all in the last week. I looked at him for a moment before responding. "Trapped in a box inside of a bigger box. When I get out this bitch, I ain't never coming back."

"The penitentiary ain't for me neither, homie. I'm an artist, not a criminal. I'm gonna get out of this shit hole too." He paused for a moment, sizing me up. "My name is Ernesto Flores. My boys call me E."

Flores was facing a life sentence due to Criminal Mischief, Robbery and Weapons charges, but he was incarcerated because he got caught doing what he loved: graffiti.

He was Puerto Rican and moved to Miami from Los Angeles when he was very young. He was a gang member, but was also a highly skilled and notorious graffiti artist in the Miami-Dade County area. Flores was several years older than me and had been gangbanging for nearly a decade.

Flores had been bombing, or spray painting, a blank advertisement billboard in the middle of the night when an off duty police officer happened to drive by in an unmarked vehicle. Flores took notice of the vehicle as it slowed down, but did not flee because the unmarked vehicle drove off. Plus he was almost finished with the artwork.

But the off duty officer called his buddies who swarmed Flores and apprehended him. When he was placed into custody, the police officers searched his book bag and discovered an unregistered nine millimeter handgun. Later when the State Attorney's office investigated the weapon, it was determined the firearm was used in a robbery several months back.

Flores and I became close friends while we waited for our days in court. If I had commissary funds, I would buy him something good to eat, and vice versa. If either one of us received a book from our families to read, we would take turns reading chapters and discussing them. We talked about our families. We talked about our dreams. We talked about our girlfriends. We talked about gang life. We talked and talked and talked. We looked out for each other, too. We were not just cellmates; we were the only persons we could each trust inside of that jungle.

Everyone has a reason for coming into our lives. After a few weeks of knowing each other, Flores told me a story that rewrote my history.

We were lying in our bunks one night after lockdown. The days with serious bloodshed made Flores contemplative.

"Yo Red, you ever think about quittin' this shit?" Flores asked.

I stayed quiet. I'd learned that he didn't really expect me to answer. He just needed to talk.

He continued, "I mean. What we doin' this shit for anyways? Look where we at!"

I still said nothing.

"Look man, I'm just saying, what's the fucking point anyways? You're the first person I been real with in a long time. I haven't thought of any outsider as one of my boys since I got jumped-in. It took you and me getting thrown in the county before we could get down. Why it gotta be like that out there?"

I turned over on my side. "Whatchu saying, E?"

He was quiet for a long minute. Finally he responded, "A few years ago, I thought about getting out. Me and my homie talked about it. We was roll dawgs. We came up together. We got jumped-in on the same day. He was like a brother to me. We done did a lot of dirt over the years. When we caught beef, he had my back and I had his. One day he told me he wanted out because of a female he fell in love with." Flores laughed. "He wanted a family. He tried to convince me to get out too. I told him I couldn't. I told him I loved it too much."

"We all love it. That's who we are," I said.

"I lost touch with him," Flores went on. "I never talked to him after that day. Everyone said he turned his back on us for some hoe. Everyone said he was a mark-ass-bitch. But he wasn't; he always had my back."

It was a moment before he spoke again, and when he did I could hear the poorly masked emotion in his voice.

"One day I was at 163rd Street Mall and I seen his mom so I walked over to say 'what's up.' She said 'Ernie, I haven't seen you in so long, I can't believe you didn't come.' She told me he was killed, Red. He was with his girl at Skylake. Tony was just buying popcorn when four niggas he used to have beef with started to fight with him. He tried to fight back but they shot 'em."

I felt my blood turn to ice. I could still smell the faint scent of gunpowder, still see the pool of blood around the kid at the theater and Christian's ashen face and unblinking eyes.

"Ain't nobody had his back anymore. Zoe Pounders caught word and they acted. I shoulda been there with em. You know what I'm saying? They wouldn't have tried anything if there was two of us. He was alone——" Flores' voice broke. "He died and I never had a chance to tell him that I wanted to be like him. That I wished I could have the balls to get out too. I never talked to him again after that day he said he was going to quit. I turned my back on em. And for what?

For money? He was my only real friend. Ain't no one come to visit me in this bitch, you know what I'm saying? Only my O' G."

I was having trouble forcing shallow breaths into my lungs.

After a long pause, Flores continued, "The night I got caught was Tony's birthday. I was tagging the billboard with a mural in his memory. He's dead and I might die in here. I shoulda gotten out before it was too late."

I lay awake all night, haunted. When I closed my eyes, the thick smell of butter and salt filled my nose just as it had that day. I saw it all. The lines at the bathroom. Laughing with Christian in the empty movie theater while we waited for the future release trailers to start. The old lady in front of me with big, puffy white hair who smelled like baby powder. The sudden shouts from the lobby. The crowd running. The single shot.

That night, for the first time in a long while, I dreamt that I was lying in a pool of my own blood. Ortiz was there, standing over me. I reached out my hand to him, slick with blood.

Ortiz leaned down and whispered in my ear, "For life, Red."

I never told Flores about the kid I watched die at the Skylake Movie Theater. I had no idea if he was Tony, but I thought about it constantly. There wasn't much else to do besides think between breakfast and dinner, other than bobbing and weaving interactions with other inmates that were more trouble than they're worth. So I thought and thought some more. I counted down the days, hours and minutes, waiting for my day in court to finally arrive. The uncertainty was enough to drive a person mad. Was this my new life? Or would I be released into the world and sent back to my old life?

If they did let me out, could I go back to the way things were? My two possible futures played out again and again. If I stayed in the gang, I would end up incarcerated for life and die in prison. If I got out of the gang, I would be at the mercy of my enemies, constantly looking over my shoulder.

I was at an impasse.

Sure, I was starting to have some cash flow and I'd built a strong reputation on the streets for Star Creek's and my exploits. I was no longer shackled to the chains of poverty. But what had I really accomplished? Hadn't I really just traded one prison for another? Would I go on like this until I made the ultimate exchange for a wooden box and six feet of earth?

It all came down to two basic questions: How could I help my family locked away? And what benefit was it to me if I ended up with a lengthy prison sentence?

The answers to those questions planted the seed that helped me grow into the man I am today. However, to act on those thoughts and begin to change into that person took time and three additional arrests.

As soon as I was released from the Miami-Dade County Pretrial Detention Center, my aspirations of living a righteous life became a distant memory. Gang life reality waited for me on the outside. High-minded thoughts were all well and good, but you had to be alive to live right.

9

ELEVENTH

FEBRUARY 22, 1997
DRIVING WHILE INTOXICATED; DRIVING
WHILE DRIVER LICENSE SUSPENDED[15]
GUILTY
TWO DAYS INCARCERATED; SIX MONTHS
DRIVER LICENSE SUSPENSION

After I served my ninety days, I swore I was not going to drive until I was allowed to reinstate my driver's license. I knew I needed to start getting things right. But knowing isn't always enough. Knowing alcohol is bad for your liver does not mean you're going to forego indulging in a social drink. Knowing that smoking is a leading cause of lung cancer does not mean you're going to skip puffing a celebratory cigar with a friend. Knowing your driver's license has been suspended does not mean you're going to give up getting behind the wheel if your girlfriend needs you.

Back in the early summer of 1996, before the Perez incident, I started dating a girl named Jennifer Anton who went by the nickname Lil Jen. Lil Jen was a petite Italian at five foot four and only 105 pounds. She had naturally tanned

---

[15] See, Miami-Dade County State Attorney and Florida Department of Law Enforcement Case No. M97009182

skin and long wavy brunette hair. Lil Jen was athletic and had zero body fat, with curves that accentuated her beauty. Best of all, Lil Jen was a freak. I'd lost my virginity a couple of years prior and I'd been with a few girls in between, but I had no idea what good sex was until I hooked up with Lil Jen.

It was Friday night on Miami Beach when Lil Jen first saw me.

Like any Friday night, members from various street gangs were spread throughout the beach. We always walked in small groups about fifteen to twenty yards apart so that the cops wouldn't have a reason to kick us off the beach. Everyone was looking for the same things: to meet new female companions or to start trouble with rival gangsters.

That night, I along with Torres, most of the Star Creek gang, and several other affiliates of ours slowly combed South Beach. As we walked passed a group of gangsters leaning up against a Cadillac, one of the gangsters stacked and aimed the International Posse (INP) gang sign directly at us. We did not get along with INP due to a brawl at Zipper's Night Club several months prior. In our first encounter with INP, we ended with the upper hand. We knew it was just a matter of time before we ran into them again.

Torres stacked the Star Creek gang sign back at their group and shouted, "Whatcha'll bitch ass niggas wanna do?!"

Torres, Echevarria, Martinez, and I circled the Cadillac. We came to a stop a few feet behind the trunk. Four INP gangsters stood waiting.

One of the INPs said, "Y'all puss ass motherfuckers want to take this shit down to the beach?"

"Is that were you wanna get buried, hoe?" Martinez responded, starring each one of them down in turn.

The INP's question made it obvious how soft these gangsters were. They didn't have the balls to throw-down right there because we could easily be spotted by the Miami Beach Police.

"Ya'll ain't gonna do—"

Before that INP could finish his sentence, I dropped a haymaker on the chin of the one closest to me. A brawl ensued.

As I retracted my fist, the INP's body slivered down the trunk of the Cadillac. His entire structure came to a halting stop when his face impacted with the asphalt in front of him. Torres swung and made contact with the INP who was not allowed to finish his statement. I kept my eyes on the one I hit. Martinez and

Echevarria each picked one of the two remaining INPs. The one I hit attempted to pick himself up off the ground. His first steps were unbalanced. I kept my eye on his face. As soon as he stood up completely straight, I threw a second right-handed haymaker that landed on the exact same spot I initially hit. The INP's body twirled around causing his backside to face me. I simultaneously placed my right foot on his back and shoved his body into a telephone booth. The INP's body smacked the booth and slid down to the ground where it stayed.

I turned around to see Torres dropping blow after blow on the INP curled up against the Cadillac. Torres was about five feet away from me. In the background, Echevarria and Martinez were exchanging blows with the other two INPs.

With no warning, a Miami Beach Police officer appeared, grabbed Torres and pulled him off of the INP. The officer slammed Torres on the ground. I ran as fast I could and rammed my shoulder into the officer's back with all my strength. I knocked him to the ground and kept running. I ran until I found the closest Metro Bus station and jumped on the first bus out of South Beach. I didn't care where it was taking me.

Lil Jen later told me that she'd been at the beach with friends looking for guys just like us, and was only standing a few feet away when the altercation went down. After watching my performance, she did some standard female investigative work to discover my name and whereabouts. A couple days later, she showed up at Star Creek with her lady friends.

Torres and I were posted up outside of Torres' unit when a white new model Nissan Maxima with seventeen inch chrome five-star rims rolled through Star Creek. The car's windows were down and we saw there were four pretty girls inside.

The car slowed and one of the girls called out, "Y'all know Red?"

I responded, "Who wants to know?"

"Lil Jen," she said, smiling. "I'm Jennifer. These are my home girls: Marissa, Michelle, and Rayca."

Torres looked into the car and nodded. "Wassup, Michelle?"

"Why y'all looking for me?" I asked.

"We was in South Beach the other day and I saw you whip some nigga's ass and then knock a cop to the ground so your boy," she pointed at Torres, "could get away." She locked eyes with me. "That was the hottest thing I've ever seen."

"I don't know what you're talking about," I said with a smirk on my face. "Why don't y'all park so it don't look like we're doing a dope deal?"

Lil Jen caught my eye the second she stepped out of the car. She knew what she was doing. She wore provocative spandex shorts with a Nike tank top over a sports bra. Her hair was perfectly straight. Her lip-gloss gleamed in the light of the streetlamps, and she smelled like an angel. Lil Jen was a gangster chick. She spoke like it. She dressed like it. She acted like it. The other girls followed Torres into his unit, but Lil Jen just leaned back against her car.

"You comin' in?" I asked.

"I never seen someone do something like that. You dropped him twice. With only two punches. Then you knocked down the cop so your homie could get away, and you just disappeared." Lil Jen twisted a lock of her waist-length hair around her finger and bit her lip. "I've never been so turned on."

She didn't have to tell me twice. We left Star Creek, picked up beers and blunts and drove back to her house. Our intimacy was dirty and passionate and we connected on a fierce, primal level. And I'll be honest, that's all our relationship was at first, but the more time we spent together, the more I wanted to protect her. Lil Jen was tough as nails, but she had a good heart.

Lil Jen was my first real girlfriend. She met my family. I met hers. We both came from small beginnings, and I always felt as if I could be myself around her. I liked her because she kept it real. Never lied. Never cheated. Never gave me a reason to question her loyalty. It was such a foreign experience to share mutual, unconditional trust. Lil Jen even supported me through my ninety-day incarceration. I faced fifteen years behind bars, yet she never once waivered. Her unrelenting support strengthened my feelings for her. I felt genuinely lucky to have her in my life. After I got out of jail, we spent our first holiday together, and it deepened our connection. I would have done anything for that woman. Even break the law.

I'd always promised her that I would be there for her, just like she'd been there for me while I was incarcerated. One night she took me up on it.

I picked up my ringing phone, "What's going on, mama?"

All I could hear was Lil Jen sobbing on the line. "Are you alright? What's wrong?" I asked.

"It's mom. She ain't getting any better... She is really sick. We had to take her back to the hospital... I don't know what's gonna happen. They won't let me stay overnight with her... And I can't sleep because I keep thinking about her," Lil Jen choked out between sobs.

"Do you want me to come over?" I asked. "I can't stay the night, but I will stay with you until you fall asleep."

"Please, baby. Will you do that for me?"

"I'll be there in thirty minutes. You want me to bring you anything?" I asked.

"No. Just you, baby."

Lil Jen lived on the beach off of the Intracoastal on Collins Avenue and NE 185th Street. Whenever I left her place, I drove north on Collins Avenue toward William Lehman Causeway. The Causeway was the best way to access the mainland. In order to get on the Causeway I needed to make a U-turn on Collins Avenue. The Causeway is located just south of Golden Beach which is an affluent community patrolled by Golden Beach police officers. Between the Causeway and Hallandale Beach Boulevard, the next main road that would give me access to the mainland, was a two mile stretch of road. If I did not make a U-turn before the stretch, I would have to continue north on Collins Avenue through Golden Beach to access Hallandale Beach Blvd. The Golden Beach route was a bad idea because of the number of cops that aggressively patrolled that area; unfortunately, the U-turn was illegal.

It was very late when I left Lil Jen's the night she'd called me crying. Seeing her so upset had rattled me. I just wanted to get home, and I did not want to risk being stopped by Golden Beach police. So, I decided to make the U-turn.

As I turned onto the William Lehman onramp, a marked unit from the Miami-Dade County Police Department quickly pulled up behind my 96 Mazda 626. Like all of my cars, the Mazda was equipped with a set of after-market rims and a sound system. The Mazda was metallic silver with grey leather interior, and it was lowered onto seventeen inch rims. I knew better. Catching a guy driving a flashy car with a suspended license was like shooting fish in a barrel for cops.

The cop's lights flicked on, illuminating my rearview mirror, and regret washed over me. I knew from experience how much cops hated kids with nice cars. The officer instructed me to pull my car off onto the shoulder at the highest point of the Causeway.

We were stopped fifty yards above the Atlantic Ocean in the middle of the night, and I was suddenly very tired. It was the kind of deep exhaustion that comes from fighting the same battle again and again to the same end. I was so sick of the arrests and the jail time and constantly looking over my shoulder, and knowing that I would never be seen as anything but a thug.

As I waited for the cop, I prepared myself for the arrest and to once again be a temporary guest of the Miami-Dade County jail.

I picked up my phone and dialed home.

My mom answered. "David, it's 3:00 a.m. What did you do now?!"

I quickly told her where I was and that I was probably going to jail. I asked her to please send Dad to pick up my car before it was taken to a tow yard.

My mom chewed me out for a good ten seconds before saying, "We're on the way."

As the officer walked up to my Mazda, I hung up the phone and rolled my window down.

The officer approached my driver side window and asked for my driver's license and registration. There was no point in lying. I told him that my license was suspended. He would learn of the suspension as soon as he ran my name, anyway.

The officer peered at me for a moment. "Sir, how much have you had to drink tonight?"

I blinked against his blinding flashlight. "I am not old enough to drink, officer."

"Of course! I'm sure the only law you break is driving with a suspended driver's license!" He had a good chuckle to himself before asking me to step out of the car. I did so.

He looked me up and down and asked why my eyes were glossy. I told him I was tired.

"Son, your breath smells like alcohol."

"Sir, that is impossible," I replied, trying to keep the annoyance out of my tone. "I did not have an alcoholic beverage tonight."

The officer asked me if I would participate in a few field sobriety examinations. I obliged because I hadn't lied. I did not have a single drink that night. I had no doubt I would pass his stupid tests.

Looking back through the eyes of an attorney, there were a few issues with the stop.

First, once the officer learned I was operating a vehicle with a suspended driver's license that should have concluded the stop, unless he had reasonable articulable suspicion of additional criminal activity. Suspicion of criminal activity permits officers to prolong their investigations beyond the purpose of the traffic stop. That requires evidence. Unless the officer who stopped me reasonably detected manifestations of impairment, I should have only been cited for Failure to Obey Traffic Device and arrested for Driving While License Suspended. The law does not permit an officer to prolong traffic stops beyond the amount of time necessary to conclude the process associated with the purpose of the stop.

For example, an officer should only keep you on the side of the road for about 20 minutes on a traffic stop for speeding, unless the officer uncovers evidence of additional criminal activity prior to handing you back your driver license and the speeding citation.

Second, now as an attorney certified in Standardized Field Sobriety Testing, I can state that even if the officer would have been operating under a proper legal basis the results could have been skewed under the circumstances. The manual for the U.S. Department of Transportation and National Highway Traffic and Safety Administration—the folks who designed the field sobriety examination standardized tests—unambiguously state that each of the standardized tests considered independently are only accurate 77%, 68%, and 65% of the time in identifying subjects whose blood alcohol content (BAC) is above the legal limit. Factor in the conditions atop the Causeway in the middle of that night: cars zooming by, wind gusting, bright lights flashing, noise from ships passing, and it would have been nearly impossible to pass those tests sober. Had I known better, I could have challenged the validity and accuracy of each sobriety examination. With a proper motion *in limine*, I would've likely had the charges completely dismissed. Obviously that didn't happen. In hindsight, I never should have complied with the officer's request. No one under suspicion for Driving Under the Influence (DUI) should.

I performed several sobriety examinations after which the officer concluded that I was impaired beyond the capacity to operate a motor vehicle safely. He insisted that I had been drinking even after I followed his finger with my eyes, walked on a straight line for nine steps back and forth without losing my footing, and stood on one leg for what felt like an eternity. The officer placed me under arrest for driving under the influence. I was in complete disbelief. I'd been in handcuffs plenty, but never for something I didn't do. The officer read me my Miranda rights as he walked me back to his marked unit.

Just as the officer settled me into the back seat, my parents pulled up.

My parents got out and asked the officer what was going on. Through the glass, I could just hear the officer tell my parents that I was under arrest for DUI. They asked to speak to me, but the officer refused.

When my mother asked him if they could get the Mazda off the road, he responded, "Too late. Called a tow truck already. Go home. He'll be out in a couple of days."

I hit the window and shook my head at my parents, but they didn't understand. He hadn't called a tow truck yet. My parents left me with looks that reflected the exhaustion I felt.

I rested my head against the seat back in front of me. This had to stop.

When we arrived at the Intracoastal District Station No. 6 of the Miami-Dade police department, another officer administered a Breathalyzer test.

She looked up from the results, a little surprised. "Your blood alcohol content is .000," she said.

I was silent for a moment.

"So I'm not intoxicated," I said.

"Well, according to the result—"

"No," I said. "That wasn't a question. I am not intoxicated. In fact I haven't had a sip of alcohol tonight." I could hear my voice getting louder. I should have stopped talking. I stood up instead. "Where is he?"

"Please sit down," the female officer said.

"Where is he? The cop who brought me in," I said. The other cops were sending looks my way. "I want you to tell that fucking pig who swore my breath smelled like alcohol exactly what those results say."

"I'm sure it was an honest mistake. Please—"

"Honest?!" I flipped over the chair I'd been sitting in. "There's not an honest person in this fucking building. You cops are just as crooked as the people you arrest!"

At that point I had to be restrained. I screamed at the top of my lungs. I yelled profanity after profanity. Every word was dripping with hatred. I was tired of being silent. I was through with just taking whatever they gave me. I wanted them to know that I saw them abusing their power. I saw them hiding behind their badges like cowards.

I wanted them to understand that the province of law enforcement must be trustworthy to all of those who fall under its auspices or else it loses substance. It was simple: Exercise compassion and mercy for those who can be rehabilitated and apply deterrents and punishment to those who commit egregious crimes.

They knew I committed a crime for which I deserved to be punished because I decided to drive with a suspended driver license. But they could not see that what I did was nowhere near as egregious a crime as the one committed by the arresting officer who created a false pretense for a Driving While Intoxicated (DWI) arrest. Unfortunately, more often than not, police officers tend to only be in pursuit of appearances. I made sure they knew I hated each one of them and their unlawful behaviors.

It felt good. But I should have kept my mouth shut.

Once I was restrained, the female officer came back to speak with me. She told me everything was going to be fine if I relaxed and cooperated with her to resolve the problem. She asked me to urinate in a cup just to clear up whether or not I had been drinking.

"If there is no alcohol in your system," she promised, "we will drop the DUI and only charge you with the Suspension."

I was not charged with DUI.

Instead I was charged with DWI. The urine sample detected Tetrahydrocannabinol (THC) (marijuana) in my system. A few days prior to the arrest, Torres and I smoked a couple of blunts. THC remains in the system for several days or even weeks. I was duped yet again.

The Miami-Dade State Attorney's office prosecuted the case against me. I entered a plea of guilty and, in doing so, waived my right to a trial by judge or jury. There would have been no justice, anyway.

The officer's basis for the DWI charge was based on the fabricated suspicion from his DUI investigation. Remember, my "breath smelled like alcohol"? Well, the lab report proved that was not only erroneous but also impossible because my BAC registered at .000. The evidence of the THC was what is known in legal terms as "fruit of the poisonous tree."

It should have been suppressed. But I did not have the assistance of a lawyer who could have argued that the THC evidence should not be admissible at trial because the officer illegally obtained it. The public defender assigned to my case did not even mention the possibility of a motion to suppress evidence, so I was under the impression that I had no choice but to plead guilty. The court ordered my driving privilege to remain suspended for an additional 180 days to run consecutive with the current suspension I was serving. My driver license was ineligible for reinstatement until January of 1998. To protect and to serve and to fill a quota.

10

TWELFTH

APRIL 23, 1997
OPERATING MOTOR VEHICLE WITHOUT LICENSE[16]
GUILTY
TWENTY DAYS INCARCERATED

Ralph Batista was a Boricua who lived in Miami for several years before he moved to New York. He was born and raised in the West Bronx and most of his family was still in the area. Puerto Rican and from New York, Batista never shut up. He was a bona fide hustler, though. Batista was a small guy who stood less than six feet by a large margin and weighed maybe 150 pounds. He wore his black hair in a very short military haircut and kept a thin, perfectly trimmed goatee. He had a New York accent and dressed the part of the hip-hop culture. Each time I spoke with him, I felt as if I was having a conversation with a member of the Wu-Tang Clan.

Batista was a great customer while he was in Miami, and often purchased large amounts of marijuana from us. He also referred a ton of new customers. His loyalty continued even after he returned to his home town. After a few months

---

[16] See, Duval County State Attorney and Florida Department of Law Enforcement Case No. 887135C

of living in New York, he called me and proposed a potentially life-altering business deal.

That night, while Torres and I were drinking and splitting a pizza at his place, I filled him in.

"You aint bullshitting, Red?" Torres said, stopping mid-chew, his mouth full of cheese and dough.

I took a sip of my beer. "He's always been straight up with us. We can trust him."

Torres just stared at me. "Twenty elbows in one lick?"

"We just have to get it to the Bronx."

Rotating his beer can in his hand, he asked. "What's that? A twenty-four hour drive?"

I nodded.

It was a tremendous risk, but twenty pounds in one sale would be our biggest and most profitable transaction to date.

With our John Doe connection we could purchase marijuana at $800 a pound. Each pound sold for $1500 leaving a $700 profit margin. That meant one New York trip could make us a $14,000 profit. If Batista's connection became a consistent customer, our cash flow would see an impressive surge.

"We could go legit, Joey," I said. "If we don't fuck this up, and do it right a few times, we could actually get out of the dope game. Do something completely legal."

"We could be like white people," Torres said laughing.

I could see the plans already forming in his mind. We'd talked about this for the past couple of years, but it always seemed so out of reach.

"I could start my shop," he said.

"I could go back to school," I said.

He took a deep swig of beer and leaned back on the couch.

There was no doubt we were going to New York.

In early March of 1997, we drove to New York for the first time in my Mazda 626. We prepared as if our lives were on the line. We took no chances. Trafficking marijuana across state lines is a federal offense that could get us thrown in the penitentiary for a long time. Our focus was to prevent a police K-9 sniff alert in case we got pulled over on the way to New York. To mitigate the chances of the drugs being found during a police search we had to properly package the dope.

We purchased two medium sized suitcases and beat them up a bit to create the appearance that they have been in use for some time. In order to minimize the marijuana odor, we purchased turkey-roasting bags to wrap the dope and a couple of cans of 3M insulating spray foam to seal the suitcases. We packaged each pound individually inside the turkey-roasting bags. We then grouped and rewrapped ten pounds together. We sprayed the interior of each suitcase with the foam to create a thick layer of insulation. We did not spray the suitcase's interior lid. We only sprayed the container portion of the suitcase. We placed one ten pound package inside each suitcase. When the foam dried, we stuffed the suitcases with clothing to create the illusion that we were traveling to visit Torres' family in New York.

We drove for twenty-four hours straight from Miami to the Bronx Borough. In New York we met Batista in Morris Heights located in West Bronx. Morris Heights was a low-income community. Most of the properties were small, unoccupied brick buildings. The lots adjacent to buildings were mostly vacant. We saw someone pushing a shopping cart topped with various items on every corner. Cars were abandoned throughout the streets. The people gathered on the street corners stared down my Mazda as Torres drove passed.

Off of 16th and Sedgwick Avenue, Batista was standing out in front of a fifteen story beige brick apartment building. I rolled my window down to greet him.

"What's good, dawg?" I asked.

"Welcome to the birthplace of hip-hop!" exclaimed Batista. "Glad you all made it."

"Where should I park?" Torres questioned.

"Throw it right there across the street," answered Batista pointing at an empty parking spot.

Batista and I pulled the suitcases out of the Mazda's trunk while Torres paid for parking. We rolled the suitcases across the street and entered the beige building. A double metal door with large windows opened into the lobby. On the ceiling, several of the lights were burnt out. There were two elevators with metallic doors. One had a sign that read 'out of order.' As we waited in the lobby for the elevator to take us to Batista's fifteenth floor apartment, I wondered whether this was going to end well. The unmistakable odor of marijuana and cocaine assaulted my nostrils.

"Cops don't fuck with ya'll? It fucking reeks in here, homie," I said.

Batista looked at me and said, "Cops don't come crawlin' around Star Creek for a reason, right?"

"True enough."

On the fifteenth floor, we entered into an apartment that was surprisingly well kept and nicely decorated. From the exterior of the building, I would have never imagined the interior of Batista's pad to be as impressive as it was. Batista's balcony overlooked the George Washington Bridge and the Harlem River. Batista explained that the first floor was used for marijuana sales, the second floor was for cocaine sales, and the bosses resided on the fourteenth and fifteenth floors.

According to Batista, they didn't sell anything in large amounts. They bought in bulk and sold in quantity. All of their bulk purchases were broken down and packaged into five and ten dollar baggies. The volume of sales in New York was much higher than in Miami. They were making a killing because they spread their inventory as thin as possible without frustrating their clientele. The demand was constant so the supply was thinned just enough to keep them coming.

Our transaction was easy. The money was in a medium sized brown bag, just like the ones used by liquor stores to package alcoholic beverages. Batista rolled a blunt while we counted the money. After we finished smoking, Batista took us on a tour of the city. We ate lunch in Manhattan. Then Torres and I jumped in the Mazda and headed back to Miami with $30,000 stashed in the trunk under the spare tire.

At $14,000 profit, we repeated the transaction as often as possible. Between early March and late April of 1997, before I was arrested for the twelfth time, Torres and I ran the New York scheme three times. After expenses, Torres and I had nearly $55,000 stashed away. The drive to New York was not very costly. The packaging products were not too expensive. And we never stayed to party or spend the night. We were in and out. It seemed too good to be true. With three successful deliveries notched, we weren't going to say no to a fourth opportunity.

After we dropped the package off with Batista, on the drive back to Miami, Torres started to fatigue and asked me to take over the wheel so that he could rest for a couple of hours.

"I just need like two or three hours and I'll be good," Torres explained.

"Alright, I'll drive. We got to keep going. We ain't stopping with all this money on us."

I knew I sounded paranoid, but if the cops confronted us and they found the money, it would be confiscated and we'd be headed to jail. I did not think a hotel room was safe. I did not think that pulling over at a rest stop was safe. The only safe place I knew was Star Creek. So I got behind the wheel to give Torres a rest. All he needed was a couple of hours.

When I entered Jacksonville in Duval County Florida, a Highway Patrol unit pulled me over for speeding. Or so he said.

I knew my license was suspended. I knew I had $30,000 of ill-gotten gains in my trunk. I knew that speeding would make me an easy target. I would *never* have risked it all by speeding. What actually happened was that a police officer witnessed two young kids driving a brand new Mazda lowered with custom rims on I-95 south at 6:00 a.m. He profiled us.

I probably should have been worried about myself, but all I could think about was that brown liquor bag full of cash in the trunk. I was terrified that if the officer searched the car, or had it towed and searched, they would find the money and keep it.

As the officer approached my window, I kept my voice level and tried to concentrate on anything but the money.

"Do you know why I pulled you over?" asked the trooper.

"No sir, why?" I responded.

"Speeding. You were doing 81 in a 70 mile per hour zone," the trooper said, staring at my hands on the steering wheel.

"I am really sorry about that, officer. I thought I had the cruise control set at the posted speed limit," I explained.

"Nope! License and registration," the trooper demanded.

"Here is the registration. I apologize, but I do not have my driver's license on me because it is suspended. I was only driving because my friend was tired and needed some rest, officer. I am sorry," I said, trying to sound as pathetic as possible.

"Step out of the car, son."

I knew I was going back to jail; that was a given. But I *had* to convince the officer to allow Torres to drive the Mazda home.

"Turn around. Put your hands behind your back."

I complied. The trooper placed his handcuffs on me.

"Is there anything in the car? Drugs? Weapons? Money?" questioned the trooper.

"No sir, just our stuff. Clothes that we took to New York for our visit. That's it," I quickly responded.

"Stay here. Don't move," demanded the trooper.

"Is your license suspended too?" the trooper asked Torres while standing outside of the passenger window.

"No sir. I was just tired from driving the whole time. That's why David was driving," Torres responded, handing the trooper his driver's license.

"Stay in the car. I will be right back," the trooper instructed Torres.

When he returned, he looked between me and Torres.

"Why didn't you get a hotel? You guys smuggling dope?" he asked.

"No sir. We are not drug dealers. We are just broke. We don't have money for a hotel. We only have enough money left for gas and food," I responded.

"Why didn't you pull over at a rest stop?"

"We didn't think it was safe, sir. It's dark out. We don't know the area. We just didn't think it was safe, sir," I said.

The trooper walked me to the back door on the passenger side of his marked unit and made me sit down in the back seat. He came around the back of the vehicle and sat down in the driver seat. The trooper pinned Torres' license on a clipboard. He proceeded to use his walkie-talkie to run a check on the license's validity.

"Looks like your friend's license checks out," the trooper informed me as I heard the same over the dispatch radio.

"Does that mean he can drive home, sir? We can't afford a tow truck, please," I begged.

"Has he been drinking? Or was he really just tired?" questioned the trooper.

"No. He has not been drinking, sir. You can ask him," I responded.

"I'll do that," the trooper said as he stepped out of his vehicle.

The trooper went into the trunk and pulled out a small yellow briefcase. He walked over to the passenger side of the Mazda to talk to Torres. I could see but I could not hear. I saw Torres step out of the Mazda as the officer opened the briefcase. The trooper began to assemble a Breathalyzer. He placed the device in Torres' mouth.

I started to sweat as I waited uncomfortably on the hard plastic seats of the trooper's vehicle. The trooper pulled the Breathalyzer away from Torres' face and examined the results. He seemed to be giving Torres instructions. I could see Torres nodding his head. The trooper handed Torres his driver's license back and Torres walked toward the driver side door of the Mazda. I breathed a quiet prayer of thanks as Torres pulled onto I-95 south.

"Thank you, officer," I said.

The next morning, I went before a magistrate judge who was preparing to issue bail conditions at my first appearance hearing. I obviously didn't want to travel back and forth between Miami and Jacksonville to handle a suspended driver's license case, so being released was not my best option. I wanted to serve enough time to close the case out right away.

"Your Honor, we are here in the interest of the State of Florida versus David Lee Windecher, case number 887135C," started the prosecutor. "The defendant is in custody and has been charged with Operating a Motor Vehicle Without a License and Speeding. The defendant does not have any active warrants. However, he is a habitual offender as his Florida Crime Information Center history indicates that this was his fifth offense on the same charge within the past two years."

The judge raised his eyebrows in my direction. "Son, you just do not get it, do you? If your driving privilege has been suspended you are not to get behind the wheel of any car. Period. There is no reason why you should be driving. None. I should keep you behind bars!" he thundered.

I just dropped my head, trying to appear penitent.

"When is the defendant eligible for reinstatement?" the judge asked the prosecutor as he wrote something down on my case file.

"Judge, according to his Motor Vehicle Report, he will be eligible to reinstate on January 28, 1998," answered the prosecutor.

"I am going to issue bond at $20,000," ordered the judge. "Son, you have nine months before you can reinstate your license. If you come before this court again prior to your reinstatement eligibility date, I will make sure you are not released. Do you understand me?" "Yes sir, I understand. I will not drive again until my license is reinstated," I responded, standing at the podium facing the judge's tribunal. "Your Honor, may I ask a question?" I inquired.

"Go ahead," followed the judge.

"If I wanted to enter a guilty plea in order to accept responsibility today, how much jail time would I get?" I asked.

The judge looked over at the prosecution's table on his right side and asked, "What is the State's sentencing recommendation?"

"Your Honor, the State would ask for ten days to serve, six months probation and a $500 fine on a guilty plea to Operating a Motor Vehicle Without a License. The State will Nolle Pros the Speeding," responded the prosecutor.

The judge looked back over at me and said, "There you have it, son. What will it be?"

"Is there any way I can serve more time so that I don't get any probation?" I followed up.

"Judge, we are willing to recommend twenty days to serve, with 3 months probation terminating early upon payment of the $500 fine," interjected the prosecutor.

"What do you want to do?" the judge asked.

"Okay. So, twenty days in jail and if I pay the fine then there is no probation, no need to report to a probation officer, or to return to court in Jacksonville?" I asked.

"Yes. If you enter a guilty plea, after you serve twenty days in custody and pay your fine, the case will be closed. But you still cannot drive until you reinstate your driver license," answered the judge.

"I understand, sir. I want to plead guilty," I said.

I filled out a plea sheet and a waiver of rights form and signed them both. I read every line to make sure the government or the judge was not screwing me. I was sworn in and subsequently entered an admission of guilt on the charge. The judge sentenced me in accordance to the negotiated plea. A few minutes later, a bailiff escorted me out of the courtroom and back to a holding cell where I waited to be transported to the Duval County Correctional Facility.

I was released from the Duval County Correctional Facility on May 13, 1997. When I walked out of the jail, the sun was setting on the Jacksonville city limits. I stood in the middle of a street staring at the crimson red skyline hiding behind a large grouping of clouds.

I felt worthless, dirty and disgusted with myself. I did not want to look behind me to see the jail at my back. I started to walk in a forward direction until I reached a payphone. I called Torres and asked him to pick me up and bring an extra $500 to pay my fine to close the case out.

Torres was a good five hour drive away. I walked across the street and lay down on my back on a bus bench. Gazing at the sky, my mind wandered until I dosed off.

I woke up to the honking of a car horn and the sound of Torres' voice saying, "You look like a fucking bum. Get up!"

I opened my eyes, turned my head toward the street and noticed Torres' head sticking out of the Mazda's sunroof as he yelled at me.

"You ain't gonna believe it, but this bench is more comfortable than those flea infested cushions in that shit hole I just got out of," I responded, getting to my feet. I climbed into the car next to Torres. "Good to see you, homie. Thanks for coming so fast."

"Naw, it was my bad, dawg. My fault. If I finished the drive you wouldn't have gotten locked up," Torres said.

"No one put a gun to my head, Joey. I knew the risk."

"At least you knew there was a pot of gold waiting for you when you got out."

"Yeah…" I trailed off. I slouched down in my seat as Torres pulled off the curb and back into traffic. "I'm tired of it all, man. I'm tired of police. I'm tired of prosecutors. I'm tired of judges. And I'm really tired of getting locked up," I said.

"This was nothing like Dade-County, man," I went on. "Worse. They shackled us and put us all in the back of a bus to transfer us out to a jail the guards called 'The Farm.' Some God-forsaken shit hole out in the middle of nowhere… Every morning I woke up, and the first thing I thought to myself was 'what is the purpose of my life?'"

"Whatchu mean?" Torres asked.

"I ain't sure. But something has to change. I've been arrested twelve times since January of 1995. That's twenty-seven months and twelve arrests. I've been locked up for four of the last ten months. It is just a matter of time before I get caught up on something that will leave me in there for a long time," I said.

"I need to make some changes. I've got my family to think of."

"Well, we got plenty of dough stacked up, why don't we start a business?"

"Business ain't my thing. I want to go to college, Joey. I've got to become a lawyer. What we go through out here in the streets can't be right. Maybe I can help fix things," I said.

"Whatchu wanna do, be the hood's lawyer or something?" Torres asked.

"I don't know…maybe. I don't even know where to start," I said with a deep sigh. "You're the first person I said this to besides my family."

Torres was quiet for a minute.

"You think you can do it?"

I turned to look at him. "I started havin' this dream lately. It's really weird. I'm in court wearing a suit; not a jumpsuit, a real one with a tie. I am arguing a case or a trial or something. I win, and then I wake up," I explained. "Each time I have the dream, I'm at a different courthouse, with a different judge, a different prosecutor, and a different client. But, I always win. Then I wake up."

"Maybe that's your future, dawg! You know people can do that psychic crystal ball shit. See their life in their dreams and all that," Torres responded.

"You know what's really fucked up about that dream?"

"Huh?"

"I only have it when I'm locked up," I said somberly.

Torres barked out a laugh. "School ain't for me, dawg, but I believe in you, homie. I got your back," he said. "Plus you look white. You could fit right in with the suits. No one will ever know you're from the hood."

I laughed at the mental image of me in a suit. "Yeah, but I can't be in a gang if I want to be a lawyer and I definitely can't sell dope either."

"True," Torres responded. He thought for a minute. "So fuck it. Get out, man. Do what you gotta do."

I nodded, tilted my seat back, and caught a nap while he drove us the rest of the way home.

When we got back to Miami, Torres and I divvied up the earnings from our New York trips. I gave more than half of my portion to my parents, and used the rest to start getting clean. I couldn't do anything drastic right away, but I could do little things. I was determined to slowly wean myself off of gangbanging by hanging out less and less and staying in more often than not. I decided to only sell dope to trusted customers and only enough to maintain cash flow so that my savings would not be depleted. I promised myself that I would no longer drive until my license was reinstated—no exceptions this time. I contacted the clerk of court at each courthouse where I had a pending citation fine and determined the amounts I owed. I made sure that I did not have any active warrants for failing to appear in any of the courthouses. I paid several thousandths of dollars in fine amounts and driver's license reinstatement fees.

It was a relief to not owe anything to anyone. I felt like I was on to something, like a real change was on the horizon.

My Florida driver's license would eventually be reinstated, but not before I was arrested one more time. My final arrest had nothing to do with driving, though. Instead, I would be arrested for walking.

11

THIRTEENTH

MAY 23, 1997
LOITERING[17]
NOLLE PROSEQUI
TEN DAYS INCARCERATED

O n May 23, 1997, only ten days after I was released from the Duval County jail, I was arrested for the thirteenth and final time under the most bush-league-abuse-of-discretion pretenses imaginable. I was charged with misdemeanor Loitering. At my first appearance the judge did not want to hear any arguments on whether I should have been granted pretrial release. The judge denied me bail because I was recently released from jail and had accumulated twelve arrests since January of 1995. The judge ordered me to be held at the Miami-Dade County Pretrial Detention Center. I spent ten days behind bars before the Miami-Dade State Attorney's Office filed a Nolle Prosequi Motion on June 2, 1997.

That was the last time I ever walked out of a jail as a defendant.

On May 18, 1997, a young woman named Nicole Lauren Penrod died in a car accident caused by a drunk driver at the intersection of Ives Dairy Road

---

[17] See, Miami-Dade County State Attorney and Florida Department of Law Enforcement Case No. M97025728

and NE 15th Avenue in North Miami Beach. The intersection was a quarter of a mile away from my parents' home.

Penrod was a passenger in a Toyota Four-Runner with friends Jennifer Ireland (passenger) and Gina Canoniga (driver). Penrod and her friends had been traveling along Ives Dairy Road when drunk driver, Marcel LeDoux, hit them with his pick-up truck. LeDoux fled the scene. The impact catapulted the Four-Runner sideways; the force of impact wrapped the vehicle around a light post. Penrod died almost instantly.

Penrod was only eighteen years old, but everyone knew she was destined to set the world on fire someday. She was an aspiring model and poet who loved the ocean. Her father, Jack Penrod, was a highly respected local entrepreneur who owned restaurants on South Beach and in Fort Lauderdale. Of all his restaurants, the most popular was Penrod's Beach Club located at the southernmost point of South Beach, right on the water. To commemorate his daughter, Jack created a garden next to the ocean for her. Over time Penrod's Beach Club transformed into Nikki Beach, which quickly grew into South Beach's most popular restaurant-lounge location, frequented by celebrities and athletes.

A few days after Penrod's death, Torres and I were walking home from the Amoco gas station located on Ives Dairy Road and NE 15th Avenue where we'd walked to from my parent's house to pick up a couple of blunts. On the way back, we paused in front of the light post—the scene of Penrod's death. The post was damaged from where the car had folded around it, and there were still some debris scattered throughout the immediate area. On the ground next to the light post were flowers, balloons, and notes left by her loved ones. As we walked past the scene, we spotted a wallet lying on the ground. We figured the wallet had either been stolen, its contents removed, and discarded on the side of the road.

Torres grabbed the wallet up off the ground, anyway.

"Check it out," he said opening it up for me to see. "Cash, cards. Nothing's missing."

He handed it over and I flipped through it myself. There was a business card for a high end salon, a Bloomingdale's gift card, an American Express. He was right. Nothing looked out of place. I turned the wallet to get a look at the ID.

A chill slipped down my spine.

I held it up to show Torres.

His face paled.

"Ain't that one of them females from the wreck?" he asked uncomfortably. I nodded. It wasn't Nikki, but it was one of her friends. It was eerie.

Most of us didn't actually know Nikki Penrod, but her death felt personal somehow. It was tragic. Local girl killed by drunk driver. People talked about who she could have become, what she could have accomplished if her life hadn't been cut short. She was highly regarded in Miami, and holding this wallet—even if it wasn't hers—suddenly made her death real and strangely powerful.

"What should we do with it?" Torres asked.

I looked at the photo of the beautiful, smiling girl. "Put it with the rest of it, I guess."

I set the wallet next to the light post with all of the knickknacks, careful not to disturb anything. Torres and I stood at the scene, unsure of what to say or feel. I'd seen plenty of deaths, but none of them had felt like this much of a loss. No one had built a shrine in honor of my friends who'd been stabbed to death or shot in the middle of a fight. When a gangster died, his family, of course, would cry for him, but no one saw his death as the opening of a void. A gangster's death was tragic, yes, but because of what it said about the state of society, not because his individual life was of consequence. The world wasn't being robbed. We weren't mourned for our unfulfilled potential. Our deaths were background noise, side notes in local news stories. Our deaths were statistics.

As Torres and I walked back towards my parents' home, a marked Miami-Dade police vehicle pulled up alongside of us.

Torres muttered a string of unintelligible curses under his breath.

The police officer inside the vehicle lowered his window. "What are you guys doing?"

Without pausing or even looking at him, I stated the painfully obvious, "Walking."

"Well I'm going to need you to stop that."

"Yeah?" I said, eyes straight ahead. "And why's that?"

The officer flicked on his emergency lights in answer. "Do not move. The two of you match a description given of two males brandishing a firearm by the school."

He was referring to Madie Ives Elementary School which was located on Ives Dairy Road and NE 14th Avenue. Torres and I had, in fact, walked through the Madie Ives grass field to get back home. It was a shortcut we always used, but we certainly hadn't been displaying any guns.

The officer stepped out of his car. He explained that someone called 911 because they'd seen two males waving a gun around while digging through a wallet.

"Yeah, we found a wallet over by the light pole," I said nodding back toward the accident scene. "And that's where we left it."

"Then we did walk back through the Madie Ives field, but we don't have any guns," Torres added.

The cop folded his arms across his chest.

"Ah, now that's real interesting," the officer said, looking like he was thinking the whole thing over. He might as well have been tapping his index finger against his chin. I repressed the urge to spit in his condescending face. He looked from me to Torres and back again. "So which one of you has the gun?"

I could feel the heat of my anger creeping up my neck. I shoved my hands deep into my pockets to hide my clenched fists and took a breath to steady my voice.

"There is no gun, sir," I said, attempting civility. "If you go back to 15th, you will see the wallet we are talking about. We didn't take anything. We don't have a gun. Whoever called was mistaken."

"Take your hands out of your pockets and put them where I can see them," asserted the officer.

As I removed my hands out of my pockets, Torres said, "Go on. Go see the wallet. It's still there. It's just like we found it."

The cop looked back in the direction of the light pole for a moment, his face twisted into a faux expression of consideration.

"No, I don't think I will. You see," the cop said, shaking his head, "I'm much more interested in the gun."

We'd been profiled. Again. And this time, we'd done nothing to deserve it. I was finished with jail. I was finished with cops. Police officers were just gang members operating under the protection of the law, hiding their true motives behind the "Serve and Protect" shield. This snide, patronizing cop was enjoying his job at my expense, and I was done being a punching bag for MDPD's glorified night guards with God-complexes.

I glanced at Torres. He had a look in his eye that had put people in hospitals. This conversation had to end.

DAVID LEE WINDECHER

I said to the officer, "Look: we do not have a gun. We're done talking to you because you are now harassing us, *sir*. We are going to walk the twenty yards to my home now. Have a good night."

As I turned around to walk away, the officer—no longer smooth or snarky—drew his weapon, pointed it at us, and exclaimed, "You two are under arrest!"

I spun to face him. "For fucking what?"

The officer paused, glancing around, before saying, "You are under arrest for Loitering. Put your hands on your head." He pulled out his cuffs as he took a step toward me. "You cannot cross the Madie Ives field without permission."

He was taking it from me. Right this second. This cocky pig with something to prove was stealing my life. And I was powerless.

"I thought you were looking for a gun!" I spat. "Search me! Where is it? Where's the fucking gun?"

The officer patted us down. No gun. The officer faltered.

"What's wrong?" I sneered. "Maybe you should check again. Where's the gun?"

In the split second of silence that followed, I actually thought he might admit his mistake and let us go.

He began reading us our Miranda rights instead.

I didn't hear the rest of my rights over my own rage. I was irate. I lost my mind. I can't remember half the things that came out of my mouth but I do remember screaming, "Your motherfucking kids will pay for this shit, you son-of-a-bitch! You hear me?!"

Then the officer slammed my head into the hood of the car.

I just laughed. "You must really hate your little fucking piglets!"

The officer tightened my handcuffs so that my wrists lost circulation and threw both me and Torres into the back of his marked unit.

The officer had no reason to arrest us. Once he realized he could not get us for brandishing a firearm, he used the information we gave him to arrest us for loitering. Telling him that we walked through Madie Ives gave the officer sufficient probable cause to arrest us. Essentially we confessed to committing a crime without realizing it. I guess even the Miami-Dade State Attorney's office thought the arrest was a joke because on June 2, 1997 it declined to prosecute the charge. I still had to serve ten days behind bars before the case reached the prosecuting official's desk.

Something broke inside of me during those last ten days in lock up. I was numb. Everything I'd done, everything I'd seen since I'd come to Miami was playing over and over again like a silent film in my head. When the State Attorney dropped the charges, I felt nothing. When I walked out of my cell, I felt nothing. I could barely breathe, and I wasn't sure I even wanted to. I never wanted to lead a life that would see me become the villain. But I had.

I started to notice what I'd been missing for years. Silver hairs streak my mom's hair. She'd planted a garden with a water fountain in our backyard. When did that happen? My mom used to be my best friend and now I felt so distant from her. The wrinkles on my dad's face made me feel as if I'd lost so much time. As a kid, all I did was watch futbol games with my dad. I could not remember the last time we screamed a gol together. The home that had once been full of laughter was now a place of angry silence and bitter arguments. Christian was peddling and using drugs. He wore baggy gangster clothing. He spoke like a hoodlum. And he was developing the same mentality that repeatedly landed me behind bars. My relationship with Giselle and Karina was nonexistent. They'd grown into teenagers and I barely recognized them.

I was grateful that my mom kept Giselle and Karina away from Christian and me. She'd protected them from falling into my lifestyle, but I felt a tremendous shame. I felt like an outcast.

What had I done to my family?

That's the reason they call it "life in the fast lane," I guess. So much time had disappeared. I felt like an observer in my own life. Going from one drug deal or racket to the next. I kept moving forward, not knowing if the next criminal act would be the one to finally make or break me.

All that time, I'd pushed forward with the justification that I was helping my family out of poverty. I failed to realize that, despite the money I managed to accumulate, my choices were ruining us.

The hood had made me tough and strong. The Star Creek gang had kept me alive, and had taught me more about life than I ever could have gained from a textbook. But look at the price. Look who'd really paid it.

It was time for a change.

PART TWO

"I AM NOT WHAT HAPPENED TO ME, I AM
WHAT I CHOOSE TO BECOME."

CARL GUSTAV JUNG

12

NICHOLE

I was serious in my conviction to change, but as with any addiction, wanting to break free for someone else's sake—even my family's—wasn't enough.

The incident in May was my last arrest, but I remained addicted to hustling. It was the only way I knew how to make money. I started to keep a lower profile, though, because I knew my relationship with the streets had an expiration date. I'd been lucky so far, but I hadn't done nearly enough good to keep karma at bay for long. Someday the streets were going to take something I could never replace. And yet I still craved it.

It was empowering, knowing I could make something out of nothing. The thrill of a joyride was only comparable to its payoff. Moving dope made me a businessman. Winning a fight gave me a powerful confidence that was impossible to create any other way. I had no fear. I looked at every risk as an opportunity to gain. It was gambling with the highest stakes. I was playing roulette with my future, and every time I won, the victory tasted a little sweeter. Even though I wanted out, I didn't know any substitute for my addiction.

In late November of 1997, I met Nichole.

How many times have we heard songs or watched movies or read books that promise "love is the answer"? More than I care to count. But, as naïve as it sounds—Nichole proved it to me.

Her kindness and gentleness softened parts of me I thought weren't even made of flesh anymore, while her ambition and intelligence and self-respect toughened edges of my resolve I'd never flexed. She opened up the world to me. She showed me the trap door in the ceiling of the streets.

The elements of my life didn't change, of course, but Nichole's unconditional love and affection helped me to see it all through a different lens.

In the three years we were together, I learned about college essays and how to treat a sophisticated woman, and I learned that life's just a continuous exercise in letting things go. Not because we don't want them. But because it's right. When I realized that, when I finally accepted that existence is cyclical and every turn that stripped me of something familiar also brought something fresh, I found that loss itself isn't tragic. The only real tragedy in letting things go is never taking the time to properly say goodbye.

One late November night while I was still dating Lil Jen, the two of us drove with Toretto and Rayca, to the D'Lites ice cream parlor in Aventura. Toretto and I went inside to order while Lil Jen and Rayca waited in Toretto's car.

A little bell above the door jingled as I stepped inside the fluorescent-lit parlor with its white tiled floors. The thick smell of sugar was overpowering. Toretto headed for the counter while I scanned the room to see if there was anyone we didn't get along with inside the parlor.

When I looked at the cashier I felt all the air evaporate from my lungs. *Nichole.*

She had long curly dirty blonde hair; her eyes were a beautiful hazel color. Her skin was flawlessly tan, and she had the brightest, most perfect smile.

I'd always been aware of Nichole. I knew she lived in an adjacent neighborhood. She was one academic year behind me, and I remembered seeing her at Greynolds Park Elementary and John F. Kennedy Middle. We'd been orbiting each other all our lives, but somehow I'd never found the right moment to talk to her.

I glanced at Toretto. He was sampling the new flavors.

I looked back out at the large windows toward the car. The lights from the shop made it impossible to see out. I knew Lil Jen had a perfect view of the shop's interior, but it didn't matter.

I'd found my moment.

I was nervous to approach Nichole because she seemed so far out of my league. It was obvious she led a much different lifestyle than mine. I wondered what the two of us could possibly talk about, much less have in common.

I stepped up to the counter anyway.

"Hey," I offered lamely, kicking myself for not thinking of something better to say.

She looked up at me and broke into the most sunny, sincere smile I'd ever seen.

"Hi," she said. "You're David, right?"

And just like that, she had me. It was easy. There were no pretensions, no jagged edges to avoid, no business to talk, we just chatted about people we had in common for a few minutes. For those few, precious minutes I was just David. It didn't matter who I'd acted like for the last seven years. It didn't matter that I had tattoos and dressed like a gangster. She saw past Red, the image I projected, and saw a human person.

I couldn't remember the last time that'd happened.

Nichole had so much energy. She was animated and charming. Her tone was tender. She finished every sentence with a smile or a laugh. Her laughter was adorable. It had this mischievous undertone, like the whole world spun just for her amusement.

I could have kept talking to Nichole all night, but Toretto had finally made up his mind, and I knew Lil Jen was in the car waiting. The last thing I wanted was for her to cause a scene at D'Lites. Lil Jen was, after all, a gangster chick, and nothing turned her on like a good fight. Given the reason our relationship started, you can imagine how much Lil Jen enjoyed starting trouble. For everyone's sake, I started wrapping up our conversation.

Then I heard the tell-tale jingle of a little bell and knew I was too late.

I turned to see Lil Jen standing in the doorway, hands on her hips and one eyebrow raised. In a tone far louder than appropriate, but perhaps necessary to make her point, she said, "Stop flirting with that bitch and let's go, Red."

Lil Jen slammed the door and sauntered back to Toretto's car. Normally, I would have stormed after her or shouted at her to shut her mouth. But those were the dynamics of our particular relationship, and I didn't want to create the wrong impression with Nichole, so I let it go.

I turned sheepishly back to Nichole. "I am so sorry about that. She's having a really bad day. She needs the ice cream to take her meds."

Nichole laughed. "It's okay. Trust me I've gotten worse insults for just forgetting a receipt." She paused for a moment. "Was that your girlfriend?"

This was it.

I liked Lil Jen, I really did. But neither of us was in it for the long haul. We weren't in love. We had a ton of fun and amazing sex, but we were destructive and dysfunctional. So what I said to Nichole might have been wrong, but I had to say it.

"Yes," I said, hardly stopping to breathe for fear of losing my nerve. "And, I know this is going to sound cheesy, but that's only because, until today, I haven't had the chance to get to know you."

Nichole blushed and looked down at the counter.

I emphasized, "I am serious." I tugged a napkin out of the dispenser and wrote my number on it. "Call me sometime? No pressure, or anything—" I looked over my shoulder and then back at Nichole. "Anyway, I better get out of here before she drives the car through your window."

Nichole smiled that sweet sunshine smile. "It was really nice to meet you, David."

I honestly thought there was no chance in Hell that Nichole would call me after how things unfolded that day. My chances were slim even before Lil Jen threw her tantrum. Nichole and I were complete opposites.

Nichole was the person everyone wants his or her child to grow up to be like. I was the person parents shelter their kids from. Nichole had never even tried drugs. I smoked marijuana and drank alcohol like they were an essential part of the food pyramid. Nichole was a good girl. I was in and out of jail. Nichole was extremely popular because she was attractive and genuinely friendly. I was infamous because I used fear and intimidation to get what I wanted. Nichole commanded a room because she was intelligent and a leader within the student body. I commanded a room because I was the mastermind behind every con my network of gangsters executed. Nichole was the girl every dude buzzed about because she was a ten and obviously had a bright future. My girlfriend came onto me because she thought my ability to beat another guy into a pulp was sexy.

True, there were lots of good girls around. Pretentious, judgmental types who did their best to stay aloof of the rest of us. That's what had always made Nichole stand out. She could have done that and no one would have blamed her for it, but she didn't discriminate. She was down with all of the gangsters, as well as friends with all of the nerds. Nichole was pretty nerdy herself, but was too attractive and stylish to be labeled as such. As a matter of fact, Nichole was voted best dressed female during her eighth grade year at John F. Kennedy Middle School. Nichole had it going on.

I turned over everything I knew about Nichole in my mind as I walked out of D'Lites that night. Why on Earth would she want to start something with a person like me?

Only Nichole can tell you why, but she called me the very next day. We spoke on the phone for a long time—for *hours*. I'd never connected with someone so quickly in my life. To that point, I had not spent more than fifteen minutes on the phone with a girl. Nichole and I talked about our backgrounds, heritage, families, or anything that found its way into our conversation. We asked each other every question imaginable to learn about one another—favorite foods, colors, songs, movies, you name it, we covered it. As we learned about each other we started to poke fun at one another. Our conversation was completely different from any other I'd ever had. It was…genuinely happy. We talked until the sun came up.

It was almost December, and my driver's license wasn't up for reinstatement until January. Of all of the consequences I'd suffered for my driving violations, the prospect of not being able to pick Nichole up like the gentleman she deserved was the one that made me feel the most remorse. But I had to see her.

"Listen, Nichole," I said. "This is embarrassing, but I can't drive right now."

"Is your car in the shop?" She asked.

"No… It's my license. It was suspended a while back, and I can't risk driving without it again."

"Well, that sucks, but I'm not sure why that's embarrassing. You're doing the right thing."

I gathered my courage. I wished I was doing this in person.

"It's embarrassing because I should be the one picking you up for our first date."

There was silence on the other end of the phone. Had she hung up? Had I ruined everything?

Then finally: "A date, huh?"

I sighed and smiled. "Well, yeah. I was hoping we could go out next weekend. Maybe dinner and a movie? If you don't mind driving, that is."

The following weekend, Nichole arrived in her brand new 97 white four door Ford Escort, a graduation gift from her parents.

She looked beautiful and I told her so. She blushed, which only made it truer.

"Ready?" she asked.

She moved to open her door, but I jumped to get there first.

Nichole was Italian so I'd made reservations at an Italian restaurant called Il Tartufo off of Las Olas Boulevard in Fort Lauderdale. After dinner, we went to Oakwood Plaza's Regal movie theater to watch *The Devil's Advocate* (what future lawyer didn't want to see this movie?!). Dinner was great. The movie was fantastic. Our chemistry caught fire. It was about midnight when the movie let out, but neither of us was ready to say goodnight.

So, we drove to Fort Lauderdale airport to watch the planes. I never thought I'd want to do something so sappy. We parked her car in a lot right off of I-95 next to the runways. Nichole pulled a blanket out of her trunk and we climbed up on the hood of her car. A plane flew in low overhead, maybe 50 yards above us. It was soothing. And it made me feel hopeful somehow. We lay there side by side, quiet for a moment. I hadn't seen that many stars since Argentina.

After a few minutes, Nichole turned her head to look at me, a long blonde curl falling across her face. "Are you scared to die?" she asked quietly.

I looked up at the inky sky, searching for the right words. I didn't know how to answer that question. There were so many mornings I woke up wondering if my life was worth living. Would the world be better off if I'd died in my sleep?

I let out a long sigh. "My only fear of death is that it won't last," I said. I waited for her to say something, but she was quiet. I turned, searching those kind eyes. "What if I come back reincarnated and have to live through all the same struggles twice?"

She reached over and squeezed my hand.

She didn't have an answer, but her hand in mine was enough.

As the planes came in, we shared our stories, our hopes, and our mistakes. This time we watched the sun come up together.

I learned that Nichole wanted to be an FBI agent. She had a great plan. Nichole wanted to study Criminal Justice while working her way up the ranks as a police officer. I was so impressed by her, and it was perfectly clear that if I wanted to have a future with Nichole, I would have to make some serious personal changes. I'd never met anyone with goals like that *and* a roadmap to get there. We all had dreams in the streets. We all talked about what we'd do when we made it out, but, if I was honest, the future was just a hazy someday.

I told her that I wanted to be a lawyer, and explained my less-than-legal method of earning money for college. I told her about my family, about growing up poor. And I tried to explain how powerless I'd felt for so long, how I controlled the few things that I could. I talked about the anger and how I felt like I had nothing to lose.

"But how long can you live like this, David?" she asked, "Aren't you tired?" I was.

"Honestly, after this last incarceration, I don't really expect to make it to twenty-one unless…" I trailed off, thinking about the kid in the puddle of blood outside Skylake Movie Theater. "Joining a gang was about protection and making some money, but it felt good, you know? Finally having some say in my life, and I got addicted. I've *really* screwed everything up, Nichole. *Everything*. And now I'll never get out."

"What do you mean?" she asked.

"I mean, I have enemies. I have people I've hurt and they would be very happy to see me dead. This isn't some fraternity. I can't just announce that I'm graduating and off to start my career and expect a farewell party." I explained. "If I turn my back on the gang, they're not going to be there when an enemy comes for me."

We were both silent for a moment. Suddenly I felt a pang of shame. "I'm so sorry," I said, "This isn't exactly light first date conversation. You don't need to hear this—" I moved to sit up, certain she would jump at the chance to get away from me.

She grabbed my forearm and sat up next to me. The moonlight shone on her dewy cheeks, and the light December wind tossed her hair. There was an excited spark in her eyes and she was grinning.

"Hey," she said. "Let's make a deal."

"A deal?"

"I think we can help each other. You could teach me things about crime that I could never learn from a professor."

"I guess so, yeah," I said.

"And I can help you get into college," she said.

"What?" I asked, stunned.

"It's perfect!" she said. "But you have to be serious, David. I need you to swear that you're done getting arrested and living like a gangster."

She actually thought I could get into school?

She stuck out her hand in answer to my unspoken question. "Do we have a deal?"

That night, I learned a tremendous amount about the type of person Nichole was. Nichole had an amazing spirit. Her Italian heritage made her feisty. Her desire to become the person she envisioned herself growing into made her passionate. And her unselfish desire to help others revealed her compassion. Nichole was motivated and kind like no one I had ever met.

The sun had started to seep into the night and the stars were fading, but I wasn't tired. I was exhilarated. My body was buzzing and my mind was churning through all the things Nichole had said. I felt like I'd been thirsty my whole life and only now had discovered water.

"The sun's almost up," she said. "I guess we should head home."

She moved to sit up, but in one motion, I tugged her gently down and pulled her against me. Our bodies were beating together, breathing together, our lips were an inch apart. I closed my eyes, but the next thing I felt against my lips was her index and middle finger. My eyes sprang open.

Her eyebrow was cocked. "I am not one of your hoochies, David. You're going to have to earn it."

I cannot begin to tell you how much that act made me respect her character. There was something different about Nichole. As it turned out, she made me wait about a month before I could kiss her. It didn't matter. I would wait as long as it took. I was physically attracted to her, of course, but more than that, I just wanted to be with her.

The very next day, I called Lil Jen and told her that we could no longer see each other. Lil Jen and I remained friends but we never spent time as a couple from that conversation forward.

Nichole and I saw each other almost every day during the month of December, and on New Year's Eve in 1997, she met my family for the first time. I invited her into our small house. Nichole talked to my parents. Met my sisters and brother. She had dinner with us and genuinely enjoyed herself. After dinner, Nichole and I went to the beach to watch the annual fireworks display at Bayside. Something about Nichole made me feel good about myself. She gave me confidence and a sense of hope about existence.

As we stood by the water watching the fireworks, I tucked Nichole under my arm and pulled her close. I saw her smile to herself. Seeing Nichole happy made me happy. I was falling in love.

The hatred in my heart was softened because Nichole showed me a real path to helping my family. She made me feel optimistic for the first time in my life. It was hard to be angry when Nichole brought such overwhelming joy into my life. She didn't care that I came from humble roots or that I'd made mistakes. She saw something in me that even I did not see in myself up until I met her. A future.

After the last firework burst and the sky was gray with smoke, I walked her to her car, same way I had done for the past month. As I opened her door for her to sit down, she turned around, and looked into my eyes.

"I love you," she said.

I blinked. She loved me? I'd never heard those words from someone other than family, and I scarcely dared to hope that someone like Nichole could feel that deeply about someone like me. I took a step closer to her.

"Does that mean I've earned it?"

Nichole laughed, and playfully slapped me on the chest. "Earned what?"

"This," I whispered and I pulled her into my arms for our first kiss.

It was slow. It was passionate. It was love.

I did not let her get back into her car without asking her if she would be my lady. It was the start of a new year and the start of a new life. So, on January 1, 1998 we made it official. Nichole Anne Logiudice and David Lee Windecher were a couple. From that moment on, we spent every day together for three years.

Her promise to help me get into college wasn't an idle one. In February 1998, Nichole helped me enroll at Miami Lakes Technical Institute for the purpose of sitting for the General Education Diploma (GED) examination. Nichole helped me study every day. On March 10, 1998, I passed the GED exam and took my first step toward becoming an attorney.

Nichole supported and encouraged me to find a better life than the one I had been living. Nichole taught me that an educated mind is a dangerous mind. She gave me the tools to fulfill the promises I made to my parents when I dropped out of high school. She taught me that the pen is truly mightier than the sword and how to speak proper English by eliminating the use of such words as 'dawg' and 'my-nigga' when addressing people. Nichole increased my faith in others because I never had to pretend to be someone that I was not when I was with her. Nichole did everything in her control to help me advance and progress. She showed me that the world is not so bad. Toward the end of our relationship Nichole helped me enroll into Miami-Dade Community College.

In turn, I supported and encouraged Nichole while she pursued her Bachelor's Degree. I taught her the street hustle game. I explained to her how drugs where purchased and resold. I taught her how cars were stolen and disposed of through chop shops. I taught her what gang signs and tattoos meant on the streets. I taught her how to read graffiti. I encouraged her to work out and develop the tenacity necessary to get through the police academy rigors. When she secured an internship with the North Miami Beach Police Department, I instructed her on what to look for when pulling someone over. I taught her how to effectively place herself in the street hustler's criminal mind.

But, at the end of the day, while all of the things I taught Nichole were helpful to her career as a law enforcement agent, what she taught me about life far outweighed all of my instruction. Nichole was my stimulus.

Nichole was well on her way to completing a Bachelor's Degree in Criminal Justice when she was hired as an intern by the North Miami Beach Police Department. Yes—the same police department where corrupt officer Wilhite was employed, the same police department who'd hunted me for years.

This worried me.

But it wasn't for myself that I was concerned. What would happen if Nichole's peers discovered she was in a relationship with a person who had been arrested thirteen times, and by their colleagues, no less? It made no sense. Nichole was poised for a family and I was years away from being able to offer her that. It killed me to consider a life without her, but if I truly cared about her, I had to be willing to let her go if that's what was best for her. I loved her for her ambition and intelligence, and I would never forgive myself if I was the reason she didn't fulfill her dreams. I was standing in her way.

On Valentine's Day of 2001, Nichole and I said goodbye.

That night we sat together in my parent's house and cried to each other while we shared memories of the past several years. We made a pact to always remain friends and in the event one of us needed help we would always be there for one another.

Letting go of Nichole was absolutely the hardest thing I had to do up to that point. It hurt unlike any pain I had ever felt in my life. Growing up impoverished was nothing in comparison to losing Nichole. But, it was the right thing for us to do. Our relationship was built on helping each other progress and the decision to split up would eventually help us both grow.

That didn't make it hurt less.

I carried a broken heart for a long time after Nichole and I split up. But it was the best thing that could have happened. It is a testament to the profound and foundational impact she had on me that our breakup didn't send me spiraling back into the streets. Losing her motivated me to become a better man. I vowed to become the best possible version of myself, a person Nichole could be proud of. One day I would have a career as an attorney and raise a beautiful family. I would spend my life with an educated woman of class, character, and positive disposition—just like Nichole.

I had a long way to go, there was no question about that, but now I was facing the world with the most powerful weapon in existence—hope.

13

ACOSTA

Inspiration is like lightning. It's the missing part of our understanding that we can't know we've gone without until its washing over us, electrifying and enlightening. We can court it and pray for it, but it strikes when it will and often in the least likely places: during a conversation with a stranger, reading a book we pick up on a whim, glancing at art hanging in a gallery window, finally understanding a line in a song we've heard a thousand times before. It's that unwieldy, mysterious snap that fuels men on and drives them to challenge and conquer even the most concrete of society's laws.

Before Nichole and I broke up, I enrolled at Miami-Dade Community College. At her behest, I'd sat for the College Placement Test (CPT) which was meant to help academic advisors pinpoint areas in which a prospective student required additional assistance. As it turned out, I was behind in almost all subjects, especially language, math, and computers. The low scores on my CPT meant that I had to pass numerous requisite skill courses before I could even register for classes that counted toward a college degree.

On August 19, 2001, after almost two years' worth of prerequisite courses, I was finally ready to start working toward my Bachelor's.

I spent most summer nights leading up to that fall sitting outside my parent's house, facing west to watch the sun set. I needed the time to think. My mind was swimming with cautious hope and with fear. I missed Nichole.

There was not much that intimidated me, but college did. There was a knot that had wrapped around my insides, and every time I pictured school—the cinder block walls, the shiny floors, the students with their hands raised—the knot tightened so hard I thought it might strangle me. College was unknown territory. I was used to a certain way of getting what I wanted and achieving goals. Intimidation had never failed me, but threats and fear weren't going to get me anywhere but expelled. Intellect was the muscle of college. I would have to earn my peers' respect through admiration or envy of my thoughts and knowledge.

This was an entirely new worldview for me. I hadn't even started and I already felt uncomfortable and out of place. I wasn't even sure I deserved higher education. Maybe there was a reason kids from the hood didn't go to college. We dressed differently. We spoke differently. We were defensive. We were angry. We were poor. There was no way we shared even remotely similar experiences or values with middle-class or world-class kids. How could we learn together? How could an education that catered to people like them also apply to me?

I tried imagining working on a school project with a group of rich kids, taking them back to my parents' house, inviting them to stay for dinner, talking, joking. It was as impossible as picturing myself in their luxurious homes, chatting with their sophisticated parents and eating off of their china. We were from different worlds. I would never make friends with my classmates. They would ostracize me, and I'd deserve it. What was I thinking, trying to fit into their world? I was a poser. I was worse than a wannabe gangster.

And I'd be alone.

I'd have no one to back me and no way to fight against the stigmas and prejudice except out-working them. The idea of beating them out for grades was laughable. I felt so behind, I would be lucky to keep pace with them.

The only thing that scared me more than going to college was the alternative.

I knew that I didn't actually have a choice, though, not if I wanted to steer my future down a constructive path. One way or another, I had to find the strength and confidence to persevere despite the anxieties and fears.

One late July night, I sat out in front of my parent's house, these thoughts spinning and skipping like a worn record on repeat when Anthony Acosta appeared.

He took a seat next to me. "Whatchu doing, dawg?"

I hesitated before answering. Did he really want to know?

Acosta was three years younger than I was, but grew up in the same neighborhood. By 2001, he was deep in the dope game, and I'm the one who taught it to him. Just like Nickson taught me.

I'd introduced Acosta to the gang lifestyle several years back, and he'd bought marijuana from me for years. One day, he asked me how to get in on it. So I opened the door. Acosta was a quick study. He had his own customers and his own connections in no time. Once he was jumped-in, he began moving weight in and out of the state. He loved the traveling because the margins were larger when moving bulk. Plus, he loved the risk; it made him feel like a boss. After the close call on my last trip to New York, I was wary of crossing state lines. Acosta lived for it.

Whatever it took to get paid was what he would do. Jail was an afterthought. Dying was an afterthought. But he was a smart businessman. He took good care of the spokes on his wheels. Acosta even looked out for the families of his mules. He earned respect, and if anyone with beef ever came calling, he had a lot of protection from the older gangsters.

He had the all-consuming, fearless anger that fueled all original gangsters.

I knew that anger. I knew the feeling of invincibility that accompanied the realization that death would find me whether I taunted it or hid from it. I knew the recklessness that followed hopelessness. I knew the pit he lived in. I knew the ache for a better existence. And I knew the paradoxical necessity to ruin any chance of legitimate success just to survive the hood.

I knew Acosta.

And because I knew him, I looked him straight in the eye and told him something I knew he wouldn't understand. Something I hadn't told anyone but my family, Torres, and Nichole.

"I'm going to college, Ant. And I'm quitting the gang."

He stared back at me like he was waiting for the punch line.

"It's not that I don't want to be down anymore," I said. "But I need to see what else is out there, you know?"

There was a moment of thick silence and then Acosta started laughing. "Naw. Get the fuck outta here. You outta yo fucking mind, Red?! You slow? You sound stupid right now."

"I want to see how far I can take my life. Learn something new. Maybe become a lawyer one day. I mean, any coward can sell dope their entire life. What is the point?"

That struck a chord.

Acosta puffed up. "To get paid, nigga. Just like these crackers do. What the fuck you think? We need to feed our families, nigga. Forget a college. Red, look around you. Nigga, you is a gangsta! Always have been. Always will be. It's in our blood to fight and slang. No matter what you do, you will always be a dope boy. Ain't no changing that, motherfucker. Look where we live. You think those rich white folks want us in their bullshit neighborhoods?! Fuck naw. We don't want dem here. And they don't want us there."

Acosta threw his hands in the air, walked a few steps away, his back to me for a minute. He turned. "You trippin, Red. You ain't going to no fucking college. You ain't gettin no real job. You ain't gonna stop making money selling dope. And you sure ain't gonna be no fucking lawyer. You acting a fool because that stuck up bitch left you. Stop tripping, nigga."

I shook my head. "People live, smoke, drink, and die on the same block because they think that's all there is. I want something different. And you're wrong. One day I am going to quit selling dope. I will be a lawyer. And I am quitting the gang. *Right now.*"

Acosta looked genuinely shocked. "Nigga, you crazy. You know what the fucks gonna happen to you now, right?!" His eyes got wide and he took a menacing step forward. "You working with the police, Red?! You working with the fucking pigs!"

I waved him off. "Get the fuck out of here before I make you sorry you ever came, homie. I am just tired of this shit. Time to graduate from the streets. It's my life, and I'll do whatever the fuck I want. So, right now, Ant. It's a wrap. I'm out."

As I expected, Acosta started spreading the news that night. My cell phone blew up for days, but I just let it ring. I was resolved. I was out of the gang, no matter the consequences.

And there would be consequences.

Torres came to my parent's house to find out what was going on. I would have turned anyone else away, but Torres and I were like brothers. I knew he would understand. All Torres and I had discussed while running our shifts at Star Creek was how one day we would never have to sell dope again. We talked about the barbershop Torres wanted to own. We talked about the law firm I'd be a partner in and how I'd help Torres set up his shop. We talked about having beautiful, smart wives and kids who'd grow up never knowing the hell we called home.

We both wanted to believe that there was something bigger out there for us.

So I told Torres everything. I told him about how Nichole helped me with taking the GED, the CPT, and the prerequisite courses. I explained that now I was starting college.

"You're really getting out?"

"It's done," I said. "I'm already out."

He shook his head and scrubbed his chin with his fist. "Everyone thinks you're working with the po-nine."

I rolled my eyes. "You know how much I hate the police. That will never happen. Besides, I gotta keep slanging a while for college money."

"You gonna pay for your classes with dope money?" Torres asked.

"I gotta do whatever I gotta do," I responded.

Neither of us said anything for a while. I was abandoning the family that had kept me alive and fed me for years. I was going to a place that many of them had never imagined and some would never understand. A lot of them would hate me, and none of them would be there for me after this.

Torres finally said, "A'ight, I will smooth this out with everyone. But you do understand that, once word spreads, if anyone comes after you for whatever reason ain't no one gonna want to catch your back."

I nodded. I'd expected as much. "That's fine, as long as you will."

Torres punched me in the shoulder and cocked a smile. "Always my nigga. We brothers. Plus you gonna owe me a barbershop one day!"

A couple of days later, Mom called while I was at the gym to tell me that a gangster named Bones was riding a bike in circles in front of their house. I'd had beef with Bones over drug distribution territories on several occasions, and Bones and I had fought once before. I'd gotten the best of him and his brother when they tried to jump me several years back.

I told my mom to stay inside and lock the doors, I was on my way.

When I pulled up, Bones was sitting on his bike smoking a cigarette, cocky as anything.

I slammed the car door and walked toward him. "What the fuck you doing here in front of my people's crib!?"

I stood about a foot away from Bones, staring him straight in his eyes.

Bones flicked his cigarette onto my parents' driveway and stood, his face inches from mine. "I heard you ain't down with your boys no more."

I fought the reflex to put him on his back right then.

"You heard what you heard, but that don't mean I won't drop you right here, right now."

Bones smirked and moved to shove me.

I immediately swung a right-handed haymaker that caught him at the lower portion of his left jaw. Bones hit the ground and looked up at me.

"You remember that feeling, right? What the fuck do you want from me?!"

Bones said, crawling to his feet. "Don't worry. You'll find out tonight."

As he rode off on his bike, I flipped open my phone and made a call I'd made a thousand times before.

"Joey?" I said when he answered. "I'm gonna need that help sooner than I thought."

I knew Torres and I could take a good number of Bones' gang, but I had no idea what to expect. Bones had suffered a lot of humiliation at my hand. This was his chance to finally redeem himself. For all I knew, he might bring an army. And this wasn't just about me.

As soon as my dad got home from work, I laid it all out for him and Christian.

"It could be bad this time, Pa. Bones has been waiting for this."

"Don't worry. God always takes care of us," my dad said, placing a hand on my shoulder. "I'm proud of you for quitting the gang, David."

My Dad, Christian, Torres, and I prepared as best as we could.

We parked the cars inside the yard to use as barricades in case a shootout ensued. We placed baseball bats and tire irons in various places throughout the yard. We loaded all of our guns and prepared extra clips. We changed into lightweight clothing so we could move around comfortably and quietly. We strapped on our best sneakers to ensure we had good traction. We had my mom and sisters stay in the room furthest from the front door. And then we waited.

Finally, around 10:30 p.m., we heard the sound of loud exhaust mufflers coming from down the street. We jumped up and shut off all of the house lights, just as a Chevy Caprice crawled up to my parent's house, its headlights off.

We were temporarily blind as our eyes adjusted to the dark. But I had no trouble hearing a door slam and Bones' voice calling, "Red, where you at, bitch ass nigga? Come on out!"

I stood up, but didn't leave the porch. "I'm right here. You coming here to my parent's house! You making a big fucking mistake."

"Come on down, Red. We got some business, you and me."

"Y'all got guns? I hope you ain't trying to use guns because we strapped and ready to die, motherfucker!"

Bones was silent for a moment. I could just see his shadowy outline. "Naw. No guns. Straight fade. You and me. Then you and anyone of these niggas with me until you fall."

I jumped off the porch and hit Bones at a run. He was ready though, probably aided by cocaine, because he did not go down as he usually would. I landed several hard hits but he stayed on his feet.

Then I was staring at the sky from the ground. I'd been blindsided. But I was still conscious.

From the ground I heard my father shout, "You like that, you son of a bitch?!"

I rolled onto my stomach to see my dad throwing blows, landing one after the other, against two former rival gangsters: Lesley (aka 18-Wheeler) and Zahler. I could see Torres was also fighting and winning against someone I didn't recognize. My vision swam as I stood, but I could see Christian swinging at Bones and another gangster named Chip.

That was my target. I ran full speed toward Chip, wound back a fully closed right fisted haymaker, and drove it into Chip's right temple. I'd never hit someone that hard in my life. Chip was out cold before he hit the ground. When his body landed, the impact made a hollow thumping sound that turned my stomach, but I didn't have time to investigate.

My brother could handle Bones, so I ran toward my father. My gut told me it was 18-Wheeler, the biggest person in Bones' gang, who'd blindsided me.

My dad had 18-Wheeler in a headlock, so I stomped Zahler on his lower back to get him off of my dad. Zahler turned and we started to exchange blows. Zahler was much smaller than I was and I backed him up a few feet with just a couple of punches to the face. Twenty seconds in, Zahler stopped defending himself, and took off running instead.

I turned around to see that my father still had 18-Wheeler in a headlock, but 18-Wheeler had something in his hand I hadn't seen before.

"Pa!"

But it was too late. 18-Wheeler swung the arm holding a rock at my dad's head. My father clutched his face and blood poured out between his fingers.

I was paralyzed.

I could feel the wind blowing against my face as 18-Wheeler stood up and my father dropped to the ground. I felt tears drop from my eyes down my cheeks. I felt my lips form words, but I couldn't hear the sound.

This is my fault. Everything is my fault.

Suddenly the world went black. When reality caught up to my mind, I had 18-Wheeler pinned on the street, my shins driving his shoulders into the crumbling asphalt, his face bloody between my knees. He was scared, and I was glad. I wanted to kill him. He closed his eyes and I swung again and again while he tried to slide out from under me.

He kicked his legs up and down, trying to buck me off, so I wrapped my hands around his thick, sweaty neck and squeezed with all I had, tears still slipping down my face.

When his legs stilled, I released my grip and slid sideways so I could place my knee on his throat. Blinded with tears, I dropped haymakers onto his face as hard and as fast as I could.

Suddenly, I was being yanked away, my arms pinned behind me. "That's it, that's enough, David, calm down," my dad whispered. I froze instantly and Dad let me go. I turned to see him.

He was alive.

He was fine.

I felt my body deflate as I turned in a slow circle.

Bones was on the ground. Chip was on the ground. 18-Wheeler was on the ground. Zahler was gone. The unknown driver was begging for peace with Torres.

We'd won.

I wiped the tears against my shoulder.

One by one, we peeled Bones' gang off the ground and shoved them back in their Chevy. We'd won. But as they drove off, I started counting off all the other Bones out there. How many more nights would we have like this? How long would I have to live with one eye on my six?

I do not regret joining a gang. I do not regret quitting a gang. I've made plenty of poor decisions in my life. I do not regret any of them.

I risked my life in ways no one ever should and for reasons that made no sense, but by the fall of 2001, my new challenge was to see how far I could take my life. If I was going to continue to take risks, they would be to reach a purpose. I wanted to live a life of substance. I wanted to lead a life worth remembering. I knew that in any breakthrough, the first guy through the wall usually comes out bloody. But it would be worth it. I was willing to risk it all for a real chance at a real life. I would accomplish my goals and fulfill my promise to my parents, or I would literally go down fighting.

I memorized the words Acosta said to me that night in front of my parent's house. Those words resonated so deeply that I cannot hope to properly explain what they meant to me, but here's my attempt: I needed to be told that I couldn't do it. I needed to hear my own fears and self-doubts come out of the mouth of a kid who was just like me. Acosta's words gave me courage, momentum, and the determination to change the hood's perception of itself.

The hood was a self-imposed cycle, a self-fulfilling prophesy. We believed that we couldn't obtain—and worse, didn't deserve—the American Dream, and so we crippled ourselves. We acted out against the stigma in the most destructive ways possible. We adopted a "the world screwed me over, so screw the world" mentality and lived accordingly. The thing about sticking it to society is that we were the only one's hurt by our hatred and anger. Nothing we did proved anything other than that society was right.

I saw that. Thanks to Acosta.

The sweetest irony is this: Back then, when Acosta told me I'd never get off the streets and I'd never be a lawyer, he couldn't have imagined that a little over a decade later, his freedom would be in my hands. But on November 22, 2011, Acosta was charged with Possession of thirty pounds of Cannabis with Intent to Distribute by the Broward County State Attorney's office.

Guess who he called to help him with his legal battle against the government.

14

GOD

Even now, I'm not what you'd call religious. I don't go to church every Sunday and I don't fold my hands and bow my head over every meal. For most of my early years, I believed in nothing at all. Agnostic, I guess, is what they call it. I think cynicism is a more apt description of my relationship with God in my teens. I wanted to believe it, but I doubted everything. It was hard for me to digest the idea of an all-powerful God who loved me and had his hand on every world event. Everything we went through was part of his grand cosmic plans for us? Our struggles meant something? Our pain was for a higher purpose?

Wasn't it more likely that God was just the desperate creation of the human imagination? Wasn't it more plausible that people need so badly to feel like we have purpose—that existence isn't just a random series of events—that we created a God to control everything we couldn't understand? And if God was real, then why was he punishing me? What had I done to deserve my life? Why was he punishing my family? Why did he let my brother and sisters struggle when they were so clearly meant to achieve great things? I wanted to find higher ground, but to me, the concept of faith was a farce.

I've experienced many emotionally low moments. A life without faith is a very dark, lonely road. I always found a way to shut the emotions down and push forward, but I knew that suppression was a temporary fix. Self-destruction was the only end to that unhealthy coping mechanism.

On my twenty-third birthday, October 16, 2001, the clock struck twelve on my darkest hour. I went to bed that night, feeling panicked and depressed, unable to calm my heart rate or clear my closing throat. My thoughts were wild and I couldn't rein them in.

Everything was beyond my control. I watched my father work seventy hours per week, but his $25,000 salary was barely enough to allow us to survive check-to-check. The money I earned from selling drugs gave my family temporary relief, but I knew the risks were too high, and not just from a legal standpoint. I was ruining my younger siblings' lives. Christian was selling drugs and carrying guns, and I didn't know if there was anything I could do to steer him off that path. Where had he learned it, but from me? Giselle and Karina were dressing and behaving like gangster females. They were becoming more like Lil Jen than like Nichole. They were hanging out with boys that I knew were trouble because they used to be my boys.

I was destroying my family.

How could I save them from turning out just like me? I wanted to lead by example, but for so many years I'd set the wrong one. I wanted to believe that if they would follow me down the destructive path then they would also follow me down the constructive one.

I hated myself for it, but I could barely focus on my family. My heart was still aching from the tremendous void Nichole had left. She was the one who would have talked me through all of this. She would have made me feel brave and strong and smart. But she was gone. No one could ever love me like she had. And how could I ever love someone else as much as I had loved her? I shared my whole self with her. She taught me to be complete; she taught me to love selflessly, and now all I felt was a deep brokenness.

To top it off, now that I was out of the gang, I was constantly on alert. I couldn't afford to lower my guard. I had to look over my shoulder every moment. And school—the great beacon I was supposed to be following—was alienating.

No one was proud of how far I'd come; they were just judgmental of where I'd come from.

These thoughts weighed heavily on my mind every second of every day, but that night especially they whirred around me in a great, hot wind.

I woke up, drenched in sweat.

I was overcome with sadness and hopelessness and I started to cry. I lay in bed involuntarily shaking. To this day, those were the worst hours of my life. I thought I was going to die. I could barely breathe. I needed help. I wanted God so badly to exist so he could make this, make everything, stop. I needed to believe that there was a reason for my personal circumstances and that my life had a purpose. Otherwise, why keep fighting?

When the sun came up and the panic subsided, I went to church.

I needed to have a talk with God, and he couldn't avoid me if I was banging on his door. I was angry and scared, but I was ashamed too. I had no idea how to speak to God. I'd never once prayed. I had no clue what to do.

Annunciation, the church I wanted to attend, was usually empty—at least the parking lot was. So I figured that was the best place to learn. No one could judge my ignorance if no one was there.

As I'd hoped, when I pulled into the Annunciation parking lot, there were no other cars parked. I walked up to the front entrance and pulled on the double doors. They were open. Inside, the church was dimly lit. It was quiet. I took a step inside. The scent of anointing oil was pungent. My skin was warm. My mind was relaxed. My eyes were wide open. And I could hear my breaths. My anger had melted away and left me feeling weightless. Directly in front of me were two long galleries of old wooden benches about five yards apart. Between them was a walkway that led to a stage where a large figure of Jesus Christ on the cross was hanging.

At the edge of the first row of benches was a bowl filled with what I assumed was holy water. I dipped my index and middle fingers into the cup. With the holy water dripping from my fingers, I touched my forehead then my heart and then each shoulder, left first, and then right. I had no idea what I was doing or what it meant, but I remembered seeing people do it before. And it felt right. I then bowed my head and walked toward the stage. I sat down in one of the benches closest to the front. I picked up a Hymnal from the back of the bench in front of me and started to read one of the hymns.

It meant nothing to me. It was a jumble of *thees* and footnotes and it only made me feel stupid. So I slid to my knees and tried to talk to God.

I cleared my throat.

"God?" My voice came out louder than I expected and echoed back to me. I lowered it to a hushed whisper. "God. I...Well, I don't know the right words. I'm not even sure what I'm doing here. I've never done this before... But if what people say is true, you probably know all of the things I've done, right? I've done a lot, I know, and I came here because... Well, I'm sorry," I heard my voice break. "I'm so sorry. I probably don't even have a right to ask this. But I want to change. For the better. I'm scared, I'm so scared, that I can't do it alone. And I can't fail, God. That's what you do, isn't it? You change people? I need you to do that for me. I need you to help me make my wrongs right. I don't want to be remembered as a drug dealer or a gangster. Please just give me a chance to prove that I can do better than I have in the past.

Everything just seems so dark. I don't want to feel this way anymore. My family and I, we need you. Things are so bad right now. Christian is so lost, and I'm scared for my sisters. And my parents...God, I'd give you anything to let them rest.

I guess I need your guidance and strength. I'm asking for a lot, but I don't have much to work with on my own. Just help me stay focused, give me will power to do the right things, and remove temptations. Don't let me go back to where I came from, please. There are a lot of people who hate me. And I'm all alone. There's no one to look out for my family if I'm dead, God. What will happen to them if I'm dead? So if you can't do anything else, can you protect my family?"

I took a haggard breath. "God," I went on, "I don't even know if you exist. I want to. I want to believe, but... Can you give me a sign? You did that in the Bible, didn't you? Just show me you're real." I suddenly realized I had no idea how to end. "So... Thanks for listening."

I sat there with my eyes closed waiting to feel something. I thought I might feel stronger or more at peace or some kind of angelic tingle. But nothing.

When I opened my eyes, I rose to my feet and noticed a woman quietly sitting in the gallery next to me.

The woman smiled gently. "How are you doing?"

With tears in my eyes I confessed, "I am a little confused. This is my first time, you know, praying. My family really needs help, and I am not sure I know how to pray the right way."

"What kind of help do you need?"

"I just…I feel so lost. Everything depends on me. Everything. And I'm scared."

The woman asked me to follow her outside. Together we walked out of a door behind the stage and into a patio on the side of the church. The woman led me to a statue of Mary and asked me if I knew who she was.

"That is Jesus' mother."

"She is the mother of us all, including you."

The woman then handed me a rosary and said it was mine to keep. She told me to always keep it by my side because it would protect me. The woman then recited a rosary prayer with me. I told her that I might forget some of those words. So, she taught me a prayer she said would be easier. The woman told me to reach for my rosary and recite the following prayer any time I needed His strength:

"Our Father, who art in Heaven, hallowed be Thy name; Thy Kingdom come, Thy will be done on earth as it is in Heaven. Give us this day our daily bread; and forgive us our trespasses as we forgive those who trespass against us; and lead us not into temptation, but deliver us from evil. Amen."

I didn't know it then, but it was the Lord's Prayer. The one Jesus taught his disciples when they asked how to pray.

She said to memorize the prayer so that whenever I needed God's strength all I had to do was recite it, and He'd be there.

Before I left Annunciation, the woman handed me a folded up piece of paper and told me to read it later.

She patted my shoulder. "You are always welcome here," she said.

As I walked back to my car, I repeated the prayer continuously in my mind. I hung the rosary from my rearview mirror and held the cross in the palm of my hands as I stared at it for a few seconds. I'd been afraid that even if God existed, he would never understand or accept me because of the things I had done. Something inside of me told me that could change if I spent more time talking to Him.

When I got back to my house, I pulled out the folded up piece of paper the woman gave me. It was a poem by Blaine M. Yorgason entitled *The Monument*. It read as follows:

God,
before he sent his children to earth,
gave each of them,
a very carefully selected package of problems.

These,
he promised, smiling, are yours alone.
No one else may have the blessings,
these problems will bring you.

And only you,
have the special talents and abilities that will be needed,
to make these problems your servants.

Now, go down to your birth,
and to your forgetfulness.
Know that I love you beyond measure.
These problems that I give you are a symbol of that love.

The monument that you make of your life,
with the help of your problems,
will be the symbol of your love for me.

Your Father

I affixed the piece of paper to the mirror in my bedroom. I read it every day before I left the house. *The Monument* showed me that God freely gives us the wisdom we need to conquer our challenges. But we have to ask for this wisdom and for the strength necessary to carry out what has been preordained for each and every one of us. *The Monument* ignited the development of my faith.

From that day forward, I have prayed almost every day. Each time, I thank God for my health, my life, the opportunities He gave me, and my family. I started my prayers by asking God to grant me composure to accept the circumstances I couldn't immediately change, such as poverty. I then asked Him to give me the strength I needed to take advantage of the opportunities within my control, such as obtaining an education and becoming a lawyer. And most importantly, I asked God to bless me with intuition to make decisions that would help me lead a life of purpose, the purpose He chose for me.

Two days later, God provided me with the sign I asked Him for.

I was driving home from school. It was an ugly day out. It was pouring down rain, and I could barely see through my windshield. As I was crossing through an intersection, a tourist from France driving a rented Ford Aerostar van ran a red light at eighty-five miles per hour.

I did not see the van until it was about ten yards away from the right side of my car. By the time I did, it was too late.

I threw my car into a lower gear and stepped on the gas in a desperate attempt to get out of the line of impact, but there was no time. The van made perpendicular contact with my car on the center portion of the passenger side.

I could hear the crunching sound of twisting metal. My passenger side windows shattered and glass went flying in all directions. But it seemed as if it was happening in slow motion. I could see the small particles of glass floating in the air. A million thoughts ran through my mind. *This is the end of my life*, I thought. *This is how it all ends.* I did not have time to shed a tear or say goodbye to my parents and tell my brother to take care of the family and that I loved them all. I was going to die and there was nothing I could do about it.

The van was traveling so fast it catapulted my car into a median on my left side. My car hit the median so fast it caused the car to spin and then skid forward. My car only stopped when it flew head-on into a pole.

Just before impact, I saw something swing. The rosary, illuminated. In that instant, I made God a thousand wordless promises. Then the light exploded until it was all I could see.

The next thing I remember was coming to. Everything was washed in a coat of shiny red. The passenger seat in my car was on top of me. I felt hot liquid trickling from my face. I tried to assess the damage to my body, but everything felt hazy. I felt for my legs. They seemed to be intact. My arms were smeared in blood, but they were mobile. I looked up at the rearview mirror and I saw my face had a large laceration from the impact. That explained the blood. But the rosary was no longer hanging from the rearview mirror. I tried the door, but it was not budging and I was trapped by my seatbelt.

I don't know how long I was there. It could have been an hour, it could have been seconds. I kept fading in and out. But suddenly, there was a man at my window helping me out of the car. He laid me down on a patch of grass. I caught a glimpse of my car and almost vomited. I could not believe I was alive. Then I lost consciousness.

The next time I woke up, I was in a hospital bed with tubes in my nose, an IV in my arm, and bandages on my face. My mom was stroking my hand talking to me with tears in her eyes. The rest of my family was crowded into the room too. I looked up at my mom.

"I'm alive?" I croaked.

She started to cry all out and pressed her lips to my hand. "Thank God," she said.

It was a miracle, she told me. I had no serious injuries, broken bones, or anything that would prevent a full recovery. She told me I needed stitches on my face and that was the worst thing that happened. All of sudden I remembered everything, especially my conversation with God. I struggled to sit up in my bed.

"My rosary! Where is my rosary?"

"David, you need to calm down," she said. She whispered to Karina to go get a nurse.

I ripped the IV out of my arm and yanked the tube from my nose. I was going to go get my rosary and nothing was going to stop me. The nurse appeared and tried to coax me back into bed. I stormed out of the room with nothing but the hospital gown on.

After a heated discussion with the hospital administrators, I signed a release form and went home still in my gown. When I got home, I quickly changed and asked my dad to take me to wherever my car was.

My car had been towed to a junkyard in Opa-Locka. It was the middle of the night, but my dad drove me to the tow yard where my car was being kept anyway. It was closed. I could see my car from the outside of the fence.

I viewed the rosary as a token of change. Change I promised God I would make if He gave me an opportunity to survive that horrific car accident. I was not breaking my promise.

I climbed the fence and jumped over into the tow yard. I ran to my car and pried the driver side door open. It could have flown anywhere. I dug through the heap, until I stuck my hand under the driver's seat and felt the beads in a pile of shattered glass.

I heard a dog barking in the distance. I looked up and saw two Dobermans about twenty-five yards away.

My dad was yelling at the dogs from outside the fence to try to divert them. But those Dobermans were trained well. They came right at me. I jumped on the hood of my car and leaped from bumper to hood until I reached the fence. I got there just before the Dobermans caught up. I climbed back over and landed on the street. My heart was racing, but I had my rosary.

From the date of my accident, that veil of hopelessness lifted. I was no longer impeded by fear or sadness or anger or bitterness. I was grateful God had given me an opportunity to atone for my sins and to make the most of the rest of my life. I was going to make things right no matter how hard the obstacles became. It was not a matter of me against the world anymore because God had my back. I believed in Him. And I knew He believed in me. My newfound relationship with God would eventually make me the man I am today. This wasn't just some phase that I used as a crutch to get through the tough stuff. I developed a strong faith in God that has lasted my whole life since.

It no longer mattered what others thought of me or where I came from because I finally realized that my life was in God's hands. I knew it in my bones that the struggles I endured were engineered by God. I learned to be a part of the world without being broken by it.

All I'd wanted was a purpose. And I started to feel as if I had one. My purpose was to inspire those who grew up with similar circumstances to live their lives with enthusiasm and ambition every day. I wholeheartedly believed that I was going to help others and make the world a better place. I was finally starting to understand who I was, what I was meant to do, and where I wanted to go when it was all said and done.

15

TORRES

From the day I developed my faith in God, I didn't miss a day of college. I felt empowered by my faith. I became enthusiastic about the possibilities. I started to enjoy learning. I was an academic sponge. I absorbed everything. I read all of the material associated with the courses I took. I treated being a college student like a job. In some ways it felt just like hustling; it was a race to see who became the most intelligent. I was intent on expanding my intellectual capacity. I kept my head low and worked hard. When I started seeing results, my confidence grew.

I developed strong convictions about my faith. From time-to-time I would return to Annunciation to pray, but I mostly prayed at home. My prayers were usually the same. I always thanked God for my family, my health and my opportunities, and always asked Him to help me lead a life of purpose.

In August of 2003, once I obtained enough credits for an Associate's Degree, I transferred from Miami-Dade Community College to American Intercontinental University to pursue a Bachelor's Degree with a major in Business Administration.

AIU sold me on their program. The student-teacher ratio was ideal because there were about twenty students per class, which allowed for more interaction with professors. The University was located inside a brand new five-story office building. The campus was fully equipped with advanced technology; wireless domains, wireless printers, digital libraries, flat screen digital monitors in every classrooms, online portals to submit assignments, online student forums to communicate with classmates, and all new students received an IBM laptop. Near the campus there were various coffee shops for study group gatherings as well as restaurants that served breakfast, lunch, and dinner. Sawgrass Mall was five minutes north and Fort Lauderdale beach was ten minutes east. The AIU campus was a significant upgrade compared to the MDCC North campus. It felt like a new start. It was exciting. I applied, was accepted and set to start that fall.

But, my excitement was checked by reality only a few months in.

On November 28, 2001, Torres was arrested and charged with Robbery with a Deadly Weapon.

Torres and I had remained best friends even after I started college at MDCC. We always kept in contact. I visited him and his mom, and he came by once every two weeks to cut my hair. But Torres and I were on different paths. Torres became a father for the first time on December 24, 2000 when his son, Anthony Jose Torres, was born. On May 27, 2001, I became little Anthony's God Father. Torres became a father for the second time when Alicia Teresa Torres was born on July 9, 2002.

Even as a parent, Torres was heavy in the dope game. I was still hustling enough to just get by. Torres' risks were much higher than mine because he hustled harder and in a higher frequency to take care of his family.

The night of the incident, Torres was involved in a drug transaction gone wrong. Someone tried to rob him. They didn't know that Torres was strapped. A fight ensued and someone alerted the authorities. After Torres fled the scene, the Broward County Sheriff's Office apprehended him with a semiautomatic handgun in his possession.

Torres faced punishment under Florida's 10-20-Life statute, the slogan for which is "Use a gun and you're done." The Broward County State Attorney offered Torres five years to serve in custody in exchange for a guilty plea on the charges. Torres declined and invoked his right to a trial by jury. Torres believed he could beat the case.

On January 7, 2003, a jury returned a verdict of guilty and Torres was sentenced to fifteen years to serve in custody. His release date is November 23, 2018.[18]

I lost my best friend to the hood and to the legal system.

Torres' imprisonment left a void in my life. He was a good person with no prior convictions. He didn't deserve such a lengthy sentence. I had been to jail plenty, but a fifteen year bid seemed impossible to survive. It seemed too harsh.

But it scared me straight.

The day Torres was convicted was the day I quit the dope game.

I graduated from AIU on June 5, 2005. A few days before the graduation ceremony, I visited Torres in prison. He asked me to make him a promise.

"I need you to walk Anthony on stage with you when they call your name," Torres said. "I want him to grow up to be like you, Red. I can't... I can't believe I am in here for fifteen years," Torres said with tears in his eyes. "I failed them. They are going to forget about me. But I want Anthony to remember what you did. I need him to believe that he can do it too."

"He's gonna to do it," I responded immediately. "I'm always going to be there for him. No matter what. Just like I'm gonna be there for you, waiting to open up your barbershop, soon as you get out of here. You have my word. Anthony will be on that stage with me. We gonna graduate together."

Torres gave a little half smile through his tears. "I wish I could see the two of you. My son and my brother. Walking across that stage."

I graduated second in my class with a 3.97 GPA.

I was the first Windecher to graduate from college. My family was out in the audience of the Broward County Convention Center, waiting to watch me receive a Bachelor's Degree. My emotions were out of whack.

The happiness on my parents' faces was a visual that I wanted to spend the rest of my life replicating. This is what doing something right felt like. For a change, I'd finally made my parents proud. Yes, the celebration was for me. But

---

[18] See, Broward County State Attorney and Florida Department of Law Enforcement Case No. 0319854; Also, view Torres' Florida Department of Corrections Inmate Detail using DC number L55795 at http://www.dc.state.fl.us

it was also for them. I couldn't have done it without them. This moment was also for my brother and sisters because I wanted to inspire them.

It took every bit of composure I had to contain my tears of joy. I didn't want to cry because I wanted to show my family how serious I was about finishing strong. I was disciplined, and this was just one more step in the right direction. I had a long way to go.

But still, I had done it. I had taken a monumental step toward becoming a lawyer.

Walking across the stage with Anthony holding my hand as my family looked on from the crowd, was the proudest moment of my life to date.

Before I took any real steps toward law school, I needed to tip the scales a little further in my favor. Yes, I'd turned my life around, but my professional resume was still pathetic. Any law school I applied to would question my character based on my criminal history, and I figured a strong record of earning legitimate income would help admissions officers at least consider me before tossing out my application. I needed to establish an employment history.

Growing up in the hood, before they lose hope, kids dream about two occupations: being rappers and playing professional sports. Football players talked like us, dressed like us, understood us, some of them had even come from our neighborhoods, but they'd made it. They were the epitome of success. My love of football had never waned, and I followed the National Football League closely. So when positions opened up in September of 2004 while I was still in college, I applied for an internship with the Miami Dolphins. On December 15, 2004, the human resources department rejected my application stating, "Unfortunately, we do not have any positions available at the present time... Best of luck in your career pursuits."

Their response only motivated me to work harder. I wanted that job. I wanted them to want me. So I devised a plan to prevent the Miami Dolphins from denying me an opportunity to work in the National Football League. I needed to show that I was a worthy candidate for employment opportunities with the team.

After I graduated from AIU, I incorporated a start-up business: PC Clique, Inc. The corporate purpose of PC Clique was to render network administration services to small and medium sized businesses in the Miami-Dade County area. I partnered with my friend, Delano Muthra. I met Muthra, an information technology major, while I was in college. He handled the servicing networks side of the business; I handled the sales side of the business.

I went door-to-door to offer network troubleshooting services and maintenance contracts. Muthra then came in and repaired, upgraded or maintained the business' network infrastructure. Within a few months we established several contracts. We did well enough to launch a website, design company uniforms, employ a technician, and purchase a 2006 Scion TC as the company vehicle. We wrapped the Scion with the PC Clique logo and contact information. For the first time in my life, I was earning legitimate income for my family and myself.

Muthra took over PC Clique after I was offered a position with the Miami Dolphins. Muthra bought me out of my half of the business, changed the name of the company, and continued to execute the service and maintenance contracts we secured while working together.

On Friday, December 29, 2006, after establishing one and a half years of employment history as Sales Director for PC Clique, I updated my resume, filled out an employment application for the Miami Dolphins, and submitted both to the human resources department. I knew that this was not going to be enough. I knew that saying in my cover letter that I was "extremely interested," "determined," and "a hard worker," wasn't going to cut it. I needed to *show* them.

So, that Friday I did a little research. With very little effort, I found the name of the organization's hiring coordinator: Liza Fandino. With equally little effort, I was able to obtain Fandino's email address, phone number, and fax number. I immediately reached out to her.

Her phone rang through to voicemail, so I left a message.

"Hello, Miss Fandino. My name is David Lee Windecher. On Friday, December 29, 2006, I submitted an employment application, along with my resume and cover letter, for the opening in the Sales and Marketing department. I am calling you to request an interview because I believe that with my sales experience I will be an asset to your organization. Please call me back at your earliest convenience. I would like to be a Miami Dolphin's employee as soon as possible. The best way to reach me is on my mobile phone. That number is: (305) XXX-XXXX. Thank you."

After the New Year holiday, I left the same voicemail, emailed the same message, and faxed the same letter of interest to Fandino every day for two weeks straight. I also hand wrote and mailed a letter to Fandino every day for those same two weeks.

Before I could fire off my daily email on Monday morning of week three, my phone rang.

"David, sweetheart, please stop. You're killing the rain forest with your letters. We get it: You really want to work here."

It was Fandino. I recognized her voice from her answering machine.

I smiled. "Thanks for calling me back, Miss Fandino," I said. "I'm so sorry for my…uh, persistence, but I'd really love to sit down with you. I have some great ideas that I think you'll want to hear."

I could almost hear her rolling her eyes. But she sounded amused when she sarcastically said, "I'm afraid to say no thinking about what you might do to get my attention. Why don't you come in for an interview tomorrow?"

I, of course, responded in the affirmative. On Tuesday, I met with Fandino for about an hour and a half. We hit it off. Fandino asked me to come back the following day to meet with Eric LaPointe, the organization's Director of Sales and Marketing.

On Wednesday, LaPointe told me that he heard about what I did to secure an interview and that that type of creativity and dedication was what the Miami Dolphins wanted. He hired me on the spot.

A few months after I started as a Public Relations Coordinator in the Sales and Marketing department with the Miami Dolphins, I began to take initiative. I wanted to make a name for myself. The Internet and social media fascinated me. I learned a lot about both while running PC Clique. They seemed like such untapped resources. I started brainstorming ways to help the organization generate income by selling tickets online.

The Miami Dolphins' official website was complicated and hard to maneuver. Ticket purchase prospects had to click through a labyrinth of links before reaching the section displaying available tickets. Not to mention, finding the link to the virtual tour of the stadium's seating was nearly impossible. Back in 2007, MySpace was the most popular online social media platform. So I started a MySpace page with a domain of *myspace.com/finstix*. (It's still there, by the way.) I used the *finstix* subdomain name because the Miami Dolphins' official ticket box office advertised the toll free number 888-FINS-TIX.

I enhanced the MySpace profile page with images of the team, stadium, players, and anything that would draw a fan in. I added redirection links to the Miami Dolphins official website to make it authentic. Most importantly, on the main profile page I included images of the team's schedule with an easily visible link to the virtual tour of the stadium's seating chart.

Fans could quickly review which game tickets were available for sale, learn how much the tickets cost, and then browse through a virtual tour of the available seating before deciding to make a purchase. I added the 888-FINS-TIX number to the top of the page so that prospective buyers could call the ticket box office when they were ready to make their selection. If prospects preferred shopping online, I gave them the option to purchase tickets directly from *myspace.com/finstix*.

Miami locals started to friend request the *myspace.com/finstix* profile in unimaginable frequency. When I showed LaPointe what I'd done, he was taken aback. LaPointe asked me to join the weekly "meeting of the minds," a round table discussion with the team's executives.

LaPointe and I walked into a large conference room together. In the center of the room was a rectangular mahogany table about twenty feet long and six feet wide. There were two black leather chairs at each end of the table with more of the same along each side of the table. Team posters hung from the peanut butter colored walls. Autographed helmets, footballs, and assorted team memorabilia were displayed throughout the room. About twenty executives in suits sat around the table chatting and waiting for the meeting to start. I definitely stood out in my white Miami Dolphins polo and slacks. I grabbed a seat next to LaPointe.

The round table discussion started when Harvey Greene, the team's Senior Vice President of Media Relations, stood up from one of the chairs at the far end of the table to address the group. It seemed like this was his show. He opened up by communicating his excitement about the newly hired head coach, Cam Cameron. After about a minute of waxing on, Greene abruptly stopped, his eyes narrowed in my direction. He slid his gaze to LaPointe.

"Who's this?"

LaPointe cleared his throat, "Well, Mr. Greene, this is David Windecher. He's a new hire, a Public Relations Coordinator in my department."

Greene crossed his arms, eyes back on me. "And what is David Windecher doing here, Eric?"

"He has some great ideas. I think we might really benefit from his perspective. He started a MySpace page aimed at selling individual game and season ticket packages online."

"A what?"

"MySpace page, it's a social networking site. It looks fantastic. It's way easier to use than our website. And there's been a spike in sales since the profile went live." LaPointe turned to me. "David, do you mind briefly explaining?"

I described the MySpace page and the features I included. I explained that the goal of the profile was to interact with fans online, generate product awareness via the internet, and, most importantly, increase season ticket sales.

Greene cut me off. "The way we are going to increase season tickets sales is by putting a winning product on the field and showing fans what the Miami Dolphins tradition is all about."

A few execs nodded. A couple whispered. Some just stared at me.

Greene continued, "We do things around here the old fashioned way. Over my dead body will we use some space page or whatever you kids call it to increase ticket sales!"

At that point, I probably should have kept my mouth shut. This clearly wasn't an audience that was open to change, and I clearly didn't have enough clout to change their minds. But, hey, when was I ever going to have this shot again?

"This is 2007. The Internet is not going anywhere. If we don't use it, we'll get left behind. No one wants a dead body, Mr. Greene, but with all due respect, I can bring in a noose tomorrow." There were audible gasps. Mouths were agape. Eyebrows two inches higher than they should have been. I pushed on. "People are pissed at the Dolphins, you know that? First the Culpepper over Brees signing. Then the Saban debacle. The team has not made the playoffs since the '01 season and sales are down because we finished 6 – 10 last year. We need to reestablish the fans' interest in our team. We need to meet them where they are. And trust me, they're on MySpace."

When I stopped talking, my heart was pounding in my ears. Had I actually just chastised an executive of the Miami Dolphins in front of his peers? Worse—had I just offered to bring him a noose?

I was so fired.

Greene blinked. "I have been doing this for a very long time, young man. And you'd be wise to watch your tone."

"What's your name, again?" A voice said.

I looked around the table for the source. It was Joseph A. Bailey III, the team's CEO. My body felt so heavy, I thought I was going to sink through the floor.

"David, sir."

Bailey nodded, tapping his knuckles on the table twice. "I like the way you think, kid. See me in my office after this meeting."

"We need to live the 'out with the old, in with the new' policy. Tradition is fine, but not if it suffocates us," Bailey said back in his corner office.

"Yes, sir," I nodded.

He leaned up against his elegant mahogany wood desk and motioned for me to have a seat on the buttoned black leather couch next to his small bar. He had a large screen used for video display from a projector hanging from the ceiling covering the wall across from his desk. Degrees, certifications, and family photos covered the walls. Most noticeably, he had an intricate model of Dolphin Stadium with the new architectural designs and upgrades that were scheduled for implementation during the offseason.

He offered me a drink, which I declined. He poured himself a glass of water with lemon.

We chatted for a bit about my work experience, my education, and my online initiatives. After a few minutes, Bailey said, "Listen, David, I want you to work with the marketing team to come up with some ideas to generate online interest."

"I'd love to, sir."

"Good," he replied. "Then get to work. I look forward to hearing about what you come up with."

I was thrilled to have his backing, and I was already strategizing on the walk back to my desk.

The rest of the executives weren't so supportive. Most were disdainful of my assertiveness. I was totally blackballed. No one took my ideas seriously. No one wanted change. They liked the routine. They wanted to work without innovation. They liked collecting a check for showing up and answering emails. It's all well and good to have the go-ahead from the big guy, but there was only so much I could do with the lower-level execs throwing up roadblocks at every turn.

So I decided to take matters into my own hands. I contacted AT&T and registered 877-FINS-TIX. I removed the team's number from the MySpace page and replaced it with the new one. I then had the number routed directly to my cell phone. In just a matter of days, my cell phone started to ring like a F.E.M.A. line after a hurricane. I started to sell season tickets right from my cell phone in quantities that the Miami Dolphins could not believe.

One day, I walked into the ticket box office, erased the total number of season tickets sold from the white board, and increased it by a package of fifty. Brett Annis, Director of Ticket Operations, pulled me aside and demanded an explanation. I told him exactly what I'd done.

The next day when I got to the stadium, several of the executives were waiting. I was asked to join a meeting with Annis, Eric LaPointe, Brentton Jones, and one other executive whose name I cannot recall. LaPointe and Jones were people I worked with on a regular basis. They loved what I had done. The others... not so much.

I was informed that because of the similarity or likeness between the numbers, 877-FINS-TIX and 888-FINS-TIX, I must turn my AT&T number over to team officials. They indicated that they appreciated my efforts, but explained that, as a loyal employee, I should turn the number over. I was told that it was a serious conflict of interest for me to own or control it.

I explained that my efforts were never aimed at creating a conflict, nor were my intentions ever to damage the organization in any shape or form.

My plan was to increase season ticket sales through the use of social media. That was it. I never stopped to think about what would happen if it actually worked. I wanted to be a part of the team by contributing to the organization's bottom line. I was shocked at the negative response I received for making the organization money. The toll free number was available for purchase in the public domain. So why should I be chastised for doing something constructive? It was not my fault no one else thought of it. I took offense to the organization's stance.

"I pay forty dollars per month for the number—out of my own pocket—as an employee," I said, "and all I wanted to do was demonstrate the profitability and effectiveness of an online presence. I was doing this to prove a point, which I've obviously done."

The meeting concluded with the organization being adamant about my turning over the 877-FINS-TIX number along with access to the *myspace.com/finstix* page.

I refused.

My gut instinct told me that the organization was trying to work me over. If the use of social media was producing results, then why not delve deeper into the idea? If they didn't care about implementing social media to generate season ticket sales, then why was I being strong-armed into relinquishing my resources? I would have gladly turned over the number and the page if the organization had approached me in a different manner.

I countered that if they wanted me to relinquish the number and page, then I wanted $50,000 in exchange. They laughed at me. So, I resigned.

My phone continued to ring.

Within two weeks, I received an offer from a local ticket broker named Robert "Breeze" Brown. I'd contacted Breeze because he owned a ticket sales boutique in Fort Lauderdale and a website, *premierseats.com*, which he used to sell individual Miami Dolphin game tickets. I offered Breeze the same deal I'd made the Dolphins: the number and the *myspace.com/finstix* page for $50,000. He wasn't interested in the MySpace page, since he was already running a profitable site; but he offered me $25,000 for the number. Breeze wanted to advertise on billboards and compete against the Miami Dolphin's ticket box office.

After the Dolphins declined to beat Breeze's offer, I accepted. To this day, Breeze still uses the 877-FINS-TIX number. And I took my twenty-five grand and used it to prepare to for the Law School Admission Test (LSAT).

I contacted Kaplan Test Prep and, for about $1,500, purchased an LSAT preparation course. The course was held at the Florida International University north campus. The course instructor was an attorney who was considered an expert in all of the tricks that could boost one's LSAT score. Kaplan provided me with all of the necessary textbooks, copies of all the previous LSAT questions, answers and explanations, practice exams, and online access to additional study materials. I also invested in additional textbooks and study guides because I wanted to prepare in advance of the LSAT course. I lived off of my 877-FINS-TIX earnings so that I could channel all of my energy in the direction of the LSAT.

On December 6, 2008, I sat for the LSAT at the Broward County Community College north campus. On December 29, 2008, I learned that I'd scored high enough on the LSAT to begin submitting applications to prospective law schools.

A spiritual friend of mine taught me a valuable lesson that has become a rule I apply to everything I do. In order to uplift and support other people, you have to be on higher ground. There's only so much you can do for others if you're standing on their level. For that reason, I decided to move away from Miami to pursue my legal education.

Regardless of my being a college graduate, people in Miami still recognized me as Red the drug-dealing gangster. No matter what I did, the stigma followed.

Kids from the hood may not have many advantages, but we understand what it takes to adapt to situations and evolve to meet the challenges of change. If I was going to make a new life, I needed it to all be new. I needed to be somewhere where I had no friendly faces and no condemning past.

PART THREE

"THE FUTURE BELONGS TO THOSE WHO BELIEVE
IN THE BEAUTY OF THEIR DREAMS."

ELEANOR ROOSEVELT

16

ACCEPTANCE

To attend law school, like any institution of higher learning, one must submit certain credentials. Specifically, evidence of a Bachelor's Degree with a decent GPA from an accredited university, an acceptable LSAT score, and a letter of intent submitted with an enrollment application.

I'd been preparing to meet these requirements from the day I started college. The average LSAT score is about 150, but applicants need to score well over 160 to get into one of the top twenty-five law schools. Mine was 151, which wasn't great, but it was offset by my undergraduate GPA of 3.97. The letter of intent was easy. It was my life. I'd been dreaming of becoming an attorney since my dad lost his civil trial back in California.

My main concern was, as you might expect, my criminal history. Law school applications require disclosure of any and all personal history, including arrests. I wasn't ashamed, and I would never hide where I came from or what I experienced during my climb. I knew that my past would make me a more relevant, more compassionate, more humble attorney. The difficulty was in getting an admissions committee to recognize that.

Legal ethics are—for obvious reasons—significant to any Bar Association. With a RAP sheet as long as mine, even if I was admitted into law school, even if I graduated at the top of my class, there was no guarantee that I would be allowed to sit for the bar examination. That was a huge gamble. Not just for me, but for any school who took me on. I needed to find a program that believed in me and would fight for me. Whether that existed, though, I wasn't sure.

Because I wanted to attend law school outside of Florida, but remain close to my family, I narrowed my attention to the Georgia law schools: Emory, University of Georgia, Mercer, Georgia State University, and John Marshall. I figured that the higher ranked institutions would automatically disqualify me, so I focused on schools that were considered "opportunity institutions." So, even though I submitted applications to both, I knew there was no way in hell I'd get into Emory or the University of Georgia. I was denied as expected. Mercer also denied my application, but Georgia State University and John Marshall sent requests to learn more about my character.

On February 9, 2009, I had a phone conversation with Georgia State University Director of Admissions, Cheryl Jester-George, about visiting the school's campus to discuss my enrollment application. Jester-George scheduled me for a visit on February 20, 2009 at 11:00 a.m. I was thrilled. Georgia State was a public university and the cost of tuition was drastically less than that of any private institution. On February 20, I took a tour of the campus before meeting with Jester-George. I was intrigued. The university was in the heart of Atlanta.

I'd landed at Hartsfield-Jackson Atlanta International, the world's busiest airport, and was immediately impressed. Hartsfield-Jackson had a much more contemporary architectural design than the Fort Lauderdale-Hollywood and Miami airports. A passenger train looped the entire airport to carry departing travelers to their designated gates and arriving travelers to baggage claim. Information desks with friendly staff were positioned throughout the airport. Flat screens with flight information and directories were everywhere. The public transit trains called MARTA (Metropolitan Atlanta Rapid Transit Authority) were accessible inside of the airport and could help travelers commute to and from anywhere in Atlanta. A parking deck garage larger than a football stadium was adjacent to the airport for those who preferred to drive themselves and park at the airport. Shuttle vans transported travelers to rental vehicle companies or to their parked cars. It felt like I'd traveled into the future.

The first thing I noticed when I walked out of Hartsfield-Jackson was that February was much colder in Atlanta than Miami. The temperature was in the

20s. When the wind blew it chilled my bones and sent shivers down my spine. My face froze. My lips chapped. And my ears burned. Atlanta's climate would take some getting used to. But I liked it. It felt brand new to me.

As I drove my rental into the city on the interstate, the first familiar thing I noticed was Jermaine Dupri's So So Def Record's infamous "Welcome to Atlanta" billboard. I knew what it was from listening to hip-hop growing up. Then I saw Turner Field, home of the Atlanta Braves. The stadium was located next to the interstate, and it felt as if it was on top of me as I drove by. After I passed Turner Field, the interstate transformed into eight lanes that fed into various highways and different portions of the Atlanta Metropolitan area. The interstate ran right through downtown Atlanta. Side-by-side skyscrapers towered to the left and the right of the interstate.

The GSU campus was nicer than anything I had seen in south Florida. The school was built-in to the downtown area of Atlanta in Fulton County. Students and professionals shared the city. From Decatur Street SE and Jesse Hill Jr. Drive SE to Edgewood Avenue NE and Pryor Street, the area was checkered with academic institutions and professional office buildings.

I parked the rental in the student parking deck closest to the College of Law campus. I walked into the office of admissions and signed in for the pre-interview tour. The tour of the law school made me feel as if I was on campus in a television sitcom. It was squeaky clean. The walls were decorated with the institution's credentials and awards. Sharply dressed individuals traversed the halls. The classrooms were auditorium style with rows of seats on an inclined plane. The professor's podium area was designed like a stage starting at the bottom of the last row of seats. Behind the podiums were large white boards and projection screens.

The law library was a beautiful two-story building with individual and group study areas. Computers with Internet access were set-up individually in cubicles. Modern couches and seats were grouped together around wooden coffee tables for group discussions. Everyone I encountered was pleasant.

And when I finally sat down to discuss my criminal history with Jester-George, things could not have gone any better.

Jester-George, an African American woman who smiled a lot, was very pleasant. She was probably in her thirties, had long hair, dark eyes, and perfect teeth.

I sank into a very comfortable chair directly across from Jester-George's chair behind her cherry wood desk. A degree from Clark Atlanta University hung on the wall. She logged into the computer to call up my application.

While her computer was booting, we made small talk. As it turned out, there was common ground and we really hit it off. Jester-George mentioned that she was related to an NFL player, so I told her all about my work with the Miami Dolphins.

When I got into my past and the things I'd learned from it, Jester-George was very receptive. I swore that I would work harder than any other student to become an exemplary lawyer and community leader. I would make Georgia State proud.

Before the meeting was over, Jester-George scrolled through my enrollment application. Looking over her screen, she said, "Well, it looks like we have yet to make a decision on your application, but I am encouraged by your visit. I will touch base with you in the next couple of days regarding our decision."

I walked out of her office picturing myself as a Georgia State law student. On the way back out to my rental car, I checked my phone. I had a couple of missed calls from my mom. I called her back and barely gave her time to say "hello" before I exploded with my news. I told her that if everything stayed on track, there was a definite chance that I could be moving to Georgia to start law school in the fall of 2009.

My mom excitedly told me that a letter from the Georgia State University's office of admissions had arrived earlier in the day.

"Could this be your acceptance?"

I paused, suddenly uneasy. Surely Jester-George would have given me the news in person if they'd accepted me. Had I forgotten to send something in? I mentally worked my way down the checklist, but came up with nothing.

"This lady didn't say anything about a letter," I said "Can you read it to me?"

I opened the door to my rental as my mom tore open the letter. She cleared her throat.

"'Your application as a beginning student has been carefully reviewed and evaluated. I am sorry...' she faltered. "Oh, David..."

"Finish it, Ma," I said, trying to keep my voice light.

We both knew how that apology ended; I'd read the same line three times already, but I needed to hear it.

"'I am sorry to inform you that we are unable to offer you admission to the College of Law.'"[19]

OFFICE OF ADMISSIONS
College of Law
PO Box 4049
Atlanta, GA 30302-4049
Phone: 404/413-9200
Fax: 404/413-9203

GEORGIA STATE **LAW**
UNIVERSITY

February 11, 2009

David Windecher
21311 NE, 13th Place
North Miami Beach, FL 33179

Dear Mr. Windecher:

Thank you for applying to Georgia State University College of Law. The Admission Committee appreciates your interest in the College of Law and the time you took to apply.

Your application as a beginning student has been carefully reviewed and evaluated. I am sorry to inform you that we are unable to offer you admission to the College of Law. The College of Law has received a number of applications and must necessarily decline admission to many worthy applicants.

We thank you again for applying to the College of Law and wish you every success in your future endeavors.

Sincerely,

Cheryl Jester-George, Ed.D.
Director of Admissions

CG/mgl

I nodded to myself, standing in the parking lot with my car door wide open, feeling like the biggest idiot in the world.

"David?" she asked gently.

"When was it dated, Ma? Who signed it?"

She was quiet for a moment, searching for the information or just trying to delay upsetting me.

"It was signed by Cheryl Jester-George, Director of Admissions, on February 11."

"Nine days ago? That doesn't make any sense. What date is on the postage stamp?"

"Hold on..." my mom paused. "February 17. Three days ago."

I turned around and looked at the building I'd just left. I searched the building for Jester-George's window.

"David, don't you think this could be a mistake? Could you talk to her?"

---

[19] See, Georgia State University Office Of Admissions letter dated 2/11/09

A clerical error? That was a nice fantasy.

But it wasn't a mistake, and I knew it.

I turned away from GSU and stepped into the car, shutting the door gently, careful not to slam it. I was furious, but my mom didn't need my anger.

"Everything will be okay. I'll call you later," I said and I dropped my phone into the passenger seat. I slammed my fist into the steering wheel.

The woman lied to me. She lied!

I couldn't believe it. She looked me in the eyes, smiled, and told me she was "encouraged" by our conversation! She did that, knowing perfectly well that just a few days prior she'd personally signed and mailed the end to any hope I'd had of attending GSU.

Why had she bothered to take a meeting with me? Did she think I was an absolute moron? Did she think that I wouldn't notice the date stamp on the letter?

I sat for a few minutes turning it all over in my mind.

I was not going to Georgia State.

This was a blow, but it certainly wasn't the end. I still had options. There were schools further north in the Carolinas and west in Alabama. I turned the key in the ignition and felt the engine turn over.

I gritted my teeth at the thought of that woman and her pleasant tones and smiles.

I *would* go to law school and I'd make it my goal every day to make Jester-George sorry she couldn't claim me as an alumnus.

I pulled out of the lot and drove straight to John Marshall to meet with the Director of Admissions, Shannon Keef.

By the time I arrived at John Marshall, I'd pulled myself together. I was ready for this. I'd played it too safe before. I'd tried to present myself as a normal guy who had a dark past he'd give anything to make up for. But I wasn't a normal guy. I'd lived through things they couldn't imagine. I'd seen people die. I'd spent nearly seven months behind bars. I'd lived on nothing and came from nothing. And I'd survived.

I learned three things about John Marshall during the application submission process.

One: It was ranked fifth among the five law schools in Georgia.

Two: Despite its low ranking, John Marshall was a private institution with the second highest tuition cost in the state.

Three: Less than 70% of John Marshall students passed the bar examination on their first attempt.

Those discoveries left a sour taste in my mouth. It made me feel as if John Marshall was an opportunistic institution that charged a high premium because it knew that its prospective students—like me—would not get accepted by the other local programs. There was no doubt I was a special needs student. The cost weighed heavily on my mind, but I didn't really have a choice. I needed an institution to take a chance on me despite my criminal history, even if that meant paying dearly for it.

The John Marshall campus paled in comparison to GSU. It consisted of a single building. The exterior looked more like a correctional facility than a higher learning institution. The parking deck was decrepit with a narrow roadway and tiny parking spaces. The campus was very clean but extremely outdated. The front entrance led to a security desk located in a small reception area. The elevators looked like they belonged in a Section 8 apartment complex. They squeaked the entire time up to the office of admissions.

My hopes were not high.

Keef stepped out of her office to greet me as I signed my name in the visitation log. She was a tall Caucasian woman with dirty blonde hair and light hazel green eyes. Keef sported an animated, friendly demeanor and immediately made me feel surprisingly welcome. She asked about my day, my flight, and wanted to know what I thought about Atlanta. As I sat down, I noticed Keef's walls were covered with portraits of family or friends and a frame with a degree from Central Michigan University.

Keef and I discussed the reasons I would be a good fit for the school. Keef, as expected, expressed her concerns about my criminal history. Her primary concern was the stringent and exhaustive character fitness portion of any state's bar examination. A fancy diploma with the words "Juris Doctor" printed on it in old fashioned font did not guarantee me an opportunity to sit for the bar examination. It was nothing I hadn't expected.

I leaned forward in my seat.

"I need you to hear me," I said. "I know that there is a lot of bad in my past. But this isn't some whim for me. I know that there are people out there who can't change. They're not strong enough. But I am. I will never be able to explain to you what it took to get off the streets. I risked my life to leave the streets—I risked my family's lives. So believe me when I say that I will take every measure necessary to prove to you and the Board of Bar Examiners that I am fully rehabilitated."

"Mr. Windecher—" she began.

"I'll get internships and externships. I'll lead volunteer days. I will work harder than any student who's ever walked these halls. This is my dream. This is what my life has been leading up to. This—"

Keef raised a hand to stop me. I shut my mouth.

"Well," she chuckled, "you're certainly passionate enough," Keef said, leaning back in her chair and looking me over. She pursed her lips and tapped her finger tips together.

I had a thousand other things to tell her, but I just focused on keeping quiet.

"Let's go meet the Dean of Students, shall we?" Keef asked.

I left John Marshall feeling sick.

I'd sat down with Michael Mears. He'd nodded at my promises to work hard and he'd tilted his head thoughtfully when I described my determination. In the end, he'd promised me nothing but that he'd consult the board of directors. When he shook my hand, I did my best to keep the desperation out of my eyes.

What if they denied me?

I was not at all confident that an hour of face time had been enough to overshadow a past that, on paper, looked like the history of a career criminal.

But what did I know? Just a few hours back, I was ready to buy a Georgia State sweatshirt and change my ringtone to their fight song.

I was emotionally exhausted. I felt ragged and sucked dry. So I prayed. And I told myself that whatever happened was in God's hands. Then I headed back to Miami to patiently wait for the phone call that would determine so much of my life.

On February 28, 2009, my dad's birthday, the family was piled into the living room and Giselle and I were in the kitchen. My mom always made our birthday cakes. This time she'd made her version of Tiramisu—my dad's favorite—with vanilla ladyfingers, French press coffee, and crushed English walnuts covered in whip cream. Giselle and I were spreading the whip cream icing when my cell phone rang.

When I reached for it, Giselle snatched it with a raised eyebrow.

"This is family time, big brother," she said.

I held out my hand. "That could be John Marshall."

"You've been glued to that phone ever since you got back from Georgia." She tucked it behind her back and adopted a mask of mock concern. "Is this how it's going to be? Your family always second to your career?"

It had already rung twice. "Seriously, give me the phone."

She shook her head. "I'm sorry, but I just can't do that."

It rang again and she started to back out of the kitchen, a mischievous grin on her lips.

"Don't test me, G," I said, trying to sound serious.

She took another step backwards, and I sprang into action. I had her in a headlock and the phone in my hand before it finished the fourth ring.

Giselle squirmed under my arm as I answered.

"Hello?"

She elbowed me hard in the gut, knocking the wind clean out of me. I let her go with a gentle shove.

"David?"

"Yes," I coughed, trying to catch my breath. "Yes, this is David."

"This is Shannon Keef," the voice said. I froze, my wide eyes locking with Giselle's. I turned the mic away and mouthed *John Marshall.* She ran over and pushed her ear up next to mine.

"Yes, ma'am. How are you?"

Giselle rolled her eyes at me.

"I'm doing well, David. I just called to personally congratulate you. We want to give you a chance to join the John Marshall family."

Giselle let out a little squeak of excitement and ran out into the living room.

"You're serious?" I said.

Keef laughed. "Very. And you'll want to get ready. Your first semester of law school starts on August 18."

"Thank you. Thank you so much, Ms. Keef! You won't regret this. And please thank Dean Mears for me too."

"I will, David. We'll see you in August."

I was in a daze as I walked into the living room.

I was going to fulfill the promise I made to my parents on the night I told them I was dropping out of high school.

My family looked up at me, nervous, careful smiles on their faces. Maybe the American dream could be more than a fantasy. For all of us. Maybe all of that stuff about working hard and fighting for your passions was true. Maybe the hood didn't define me. Maybe I defined me.

I broke out into the goofiest grin I've ever worn.

"I'm going to law school!"

17

WILDFIRE

I've never felt more out of place than during my first semester at law school. On the first day of orientation I arrived early, very excited and slightly anxious. I wore a black suit with a white shirt and purple paisley tie. My hair was neatly combed and my beard perfectly trimmed.

There must have been at least 200 1Ls (first year law students). As we filed in, administrators greeted us with a bag of study supplies and snacks. Then we were directed to an auditorium that was walking distance from the campus. There, we sat through a code of student responsibility presentation conducted by two John Marshall alumni. The alums spoke to us about what type of conduct was expected from us, how we should strategize over the next three years, and which steps we should take when transitioning from student to practitioner. After the presentation, we were directed back to the campus for a simulated class.

I met a few people during the intermission, but I mostly kept to myself. I said very little and listened intently. I didn't want to appear overeager or cold, so I just said hello after hello and moved on. I wanted to observe who was who and what was what without opening up too much. I wanted to see how students interacted with each other and with the professors.

The simulated class was held inside a conventional classroom. There were thirty desks inside a square room with a large whiteboard. The professor standing behind the podium started class by directing a torts question at one of the students, Brad Griffin. The professor proceeded to probe Griffin for the entire hour and a half of class. Griffin remained standing the entire time and answered question after question after question. This was just a taste of what was to come.

A few weeks into the process, I realized that law student life was not exactly how I'd imagined it. I assumed that there would be differences between me and the other students, but, honestly, I was expecting gaps that I could aspire to close.

I was surrounded by a bunch of pampered pansies. All those students did was complain. I heard it all; from, "I cannot believe my parents are paying my tuition but not my parking costs. It's completely unfair! I am *not* spending my money on that crappy parking deck," to, "I'm only here because my parents want me to go to law school. I just want to get this over with," to, "John Marshall is an embarrassment of a law school; we're all doomed."

That was the refrain I heard over and over—John Marshall was a tier five institution, so none of us would be good lawyers or get decent jobs. Those idiots perpetuated that garbage and spread it to everyone they encountered. Some students even started blogs and made social media posts about how terrible John Marshall was compared to the other law schools. I was horrified and humiliated for them. I'd never imagined that ingratitude existed like that.

Despite first impressions, I thought the school was fantastic. The professors were friendly, knowledgeable, and for the most part all had great experience as practitioners, which I believed the students should appreciate. Maybe John Marshall didn't have Harvard quality facilities or professors with pedigrees tracing back to the Founding Fathers, but the students at Harvard were studying the same Constitution that the students at John Marshall studied. Our text books used the same cases. The words were not different. The laws weren't inferior.

The difference was the attitude. The kids at Harvard knew they were the best; so they worked like it, carried themselves like it, and expected to be treated like it.

John Marshall students wanted something they hadn't earned and weren't willing to work for.

Every time one of these idiots whined, I wanted to punch them in the throat. It's not like any of them were Emory material and had been unjustly relegated to John Marshall. There was a reason why we were there. I had a ridiculous criminal history. A lot of them hadn't worked hard enough in undergrad or had bombed the LSAT.

But why couldn't they understand that we had been given a chance to succeed, despite our histories? This law school was a blank slate, and they could become the greatest attorneys of their time if they made that their goal. Nothing was standing in their way but their own negativity.

This was the hood all over. They saw themselves as inferior, so they were.

My disappointment in my fellow students didn't end with their attitudes. I'd always imagined moving away from the hood would mean leaving the world of drugs behind me forever.

How wrong I was.

There were more, and higher end, drugs being used in the law student/attorney social circles than there ever were in the hood.

At this point in my life, I'd been drug free for several years and I had no intention of looking back. But it seemed like I was alone in that choice.

Drugs were integral to law school culture. And I'm not just talking about John Marshall. Students from John Marshall hung out with students from Emory, GSU, UGA, and Mercer, and they all fed on each other's excuses and enabled each other.

The daily consumption started with a heavy dose of Attention Deficit Disorder medication: Adderall or Vyvanse. A lot of students had a prescription. Those that didn't, purchased it from other students. Or they would barter; Adderall or Vyvanse in exchange for marijuana or cocaine. You could always spot a kid who was abusing his ADD meds. People who'd once been decent humans acted like arrogant pricks, and they walked around with these vacant, dead eyes.

Once the Adderall or Vyvanse wore off, the students needed a little cocaine pick-me-up. Are you shocked? I was. Even back in Miami, I didn't mix with coke addicts. Those who consumed cocaine regularly were psychologically unstable, untrustworthy, and a danger to themselves and to everyone around them. I cannot count how many times I walked in to discover someone sniffing cocaine in the bathroom stalls. I never saw it with my own eyes, but I heard it. Students would pretend to be using the facilities, and then flush the toilet to deafen the sound of them inhaling a bump or a line of cocaine. But I could always hear it.

Finally, after classes adjourned for the day, students from all of the local law schools hit the bars to get intoxicated beyond what the average person can imagine. They learned to get fraternity drunk in undergrad and perfected it on daddy's dime in law school. This was a daily occurrence at its worst and a weekly one at best. Even the kids who didn't abuse the rest of the drugs were out at the bars getting wasted to forget their "tough" lives. It wasn't atypical to hear a kid bragging about blowing five-hundred bucks on an evening out in Buckhead. On top of everything, it was a pissing contest. Who would buy the most shots? Who would pay for the cab?

To justify their habits, students told each other that "being a law student is so stressful we need to drink to unwind," or, "this is what lawyers do." If the students managed to avoid getting black out drunk, then one of the students would host a marijuana smoking party to cap off the evening.

For the most part, I continued my habit of quietly observing my surroundings and kept to myself during my first semester at John Marshall. I was there for one reason and one reason alone. From day one, all I thought about was crossing the finish line. I was strong enough to stay focused. I was never afraid that I might slip into their habits. But I needed to figure out how to separate myself from the crowd more than just socially.

I wanted to be the best law student to ever graduate from John Marshall. I don't mean just keeping my nose clean and getting a 4.0 GPA. It would have to be more than that. I wanted to wear the shoes everyone else wanted to walk in. Then I wanted to go out into the real world and accomplish things that would inspire others.

Law school is such a challenging and competitive environment. I could already feel my way of thinking shifting. I had to constantly play offense. Getting in was just the beginning. There were a thousand opportunities to enhance my resume and a million ways to combine those opportunities. But I had to chase those doors down. Even though more than half of the students were on drugs, they still had experiences I did not. This was their world. They'd been raised thinking about careers and networking and job fairs and suits and table etiquette. Some of these students really were brilliant. They just happened to also be assholes. Some of them had financial resources that ensured success, or they had parents who would just give them a job after graduation.

But I had something none of them had. I'd graduated from the streets. No one had the heart or balls I had. There was not a single student who could out hustle me. I would outsmart everyone. And if I couldn't outsmart them, I would out work them. And if that wasn't enough, then I would intimidate them in a language they understood.

I implemented a psychological technique that is best known by the catch-phrase, "Fake it till you make it." Before law school started, I used some of the money from the sale of 877-FINS-TIX and put a down payment on a brand new Lexus IS 250, purchased several nice suits, a briefcase and all of the high-end gadgets that lawyers use to perform their duties. The idea was to go through the law school routine by appearing as if I was just as capable of obtaining a professional's resources with my finances, just like any of them. Despite the fact that was not true, I did this to create the perception that I came from an afforded background. I kept them guessing. Intimidation and fear all over again.

Law school was just the streets with a high-class makeover. Attorneys are cutthroats. Law students are baby-cutthroats. All of them are used to getting what they want, and they don't let the rules get in the way.

During the first year of law school, students were required to complete a legal writing course. At the end of the first year at John Marshall, the top four performers from each of the legal writing courses were invited to join the institution's Moot Court team. The Moot Court team simulates in-court activity such as arguing motions or presenting oral arguments in competitions against other schools in national tournaments. Being on the Moot Court team provides the closest thing to practical experience, and it looks fantastic on a resume.

At John Marshall, the legal writing students were required to present oral arguments to volunteer judges to decide the top four. The competition's judges were comprised of actual state or superior court judges, John Marshall alumni, or experienced upperclassmen. The judges gauged the best performers based on their knowledge of the law, deference to the court, and their ability to improvise when asked an unprecedented question. Before the competition started, our legal writing professor, Andrea Doneff, addressed the students about the conditions of entering the competition.

"Moot Court is not for everyone," Professor Doneff said. "Not all of you need this for your specialty. If being on the Moot Court team is not something you really want, please do not enter. You could be taking an opportunity from someone who truly wants it."

I knew I really wanted it. Working a courtroom, talking to a jury—that was all me.

Out in the hall, I started running through procedure in my mind. I did have a funny kind of advantage. I'd seen plenty of courtrooms in action, and a lot of these people's only frame of reference was *My Cousin Vinnie*.

"But you want to do entertainment law," the student behind me said. "Moot Court would be a waste of time for you."

I looked behind me to see another guy shrug.

"I'd definitely turn down an invitation if I got it, but I think the competition will be a great experience."

I bit my tongue and forced my fists into my pockets. It wasn't right. But a lot of things about the law weren't right.

The competition was held in one of the school's mock trial courtrooms. Inside the room was an elevated stage with a three-judge mahogany wood tribunal. The panel of judges wore black robes and were chatting quietly before the competition ensued. In front of the tribunal was a matching mahogany wood podium with a microphone. Behind the podium, to the left and to the right, were counsel tables. Behind counsel tables was a gallery of rows for spectators. Sitting in the gallery observing the oral arguments were current Moot Court team members, upperclassmen peer mentors, professors, as well as parents and friends of the competitors.

Professor Doneff came out into the hall and called in the student competitors one at a time. My turn was called second to last. I walked in, greeted the judges, and proceeded to argue my position. As I exited the mock trial courtroom, the student who indicated that he would "definitely turn down an invitation" walked in.

That student came in fourth and received the invitation, and, as it turned out, didn't accept it.

Guess who came in fifth.

But everything happened the way God planned it.

One of the spectators, George Pearl Dean, was assigned by John Marshall administration as my upperclassman peer mentor. He was in his second year, otherwise known as 2L. After the oral argument competition, Dean invited me to interview for an internship position at a private firm. Dean said he was impressed by my presence and explained that, while I finished fifth, he thought I had the most potential. Dean believed I would be a great fit as an intern at the criminal defense law firm of Arora & LaScala.

Dean and I developed a friendship that will last a lifetime. And Dean introduced me to an attorney named Manny Arora who hired me as an intern. Come to find out, Arora & LaScala was a boutique law firm which specialized in the representation of high profile clients.

Prior to launching the Arora & LaScala partnership, Arora was a Judge Advocate General (JAG) and Lieutenant Colonel in the Air Force. He simultaneously held the position of Senior Assistant District Attorney in the Fulton County Major Felonies Division. Arora is distinguished because of his Super Lawyer rating and recognized as one of the best legal minds in the United States with the highest AV rating by Martindale-Hubbell (the nationwide lawyer rating system).

Michael LaScala is a DUI specialist. LaScala is a National Highway Traffic Safety Administration DUI Detection and Standardized Field Sobriety Testing expert. He is the king of DUI defense in Atlanta. And like Arora, he is also distinguished as a Super Lawyer.

Between the two, Arora & LaScala developed a reputation as being the criminal defense secret weapon for the Atlanta Falcons; various NFL, NCAA, NHL, NBA, and MLB players; WWE wrestlers; renowned rappers; public officials and politicians. If you're facing criminal charges, Arora & LaScala is the firm you want to represent you.

During the summer between my 1L and 2L year, rather than spending my days inside a classroom with the John Marshall Moot Court team, I invested my time into learning how to defend criminal charges at the highest level. After a couple of months of shadowing Arora, I was given my first real legal assignment.

Arora represented Patricia Reid who was accused of running a Criminal Enterprise and Public Corruption. She was charged with Racketeering and Bribery. Reid was brought up on charges after a Dekalb County Grand Jury reviewed a 721 page indictment in less than one-hour. The District Attorney, Gwendolyn

Keyes Fleming, used a Power Point presentation to explain the indictment. Arora wanted to make sure the Grand Jury clearly understood the lengthy and unique indictment. If the Grand Jury did not understand the indictment, then there would be a legal basis to file a motion to quash (dismiss). My assignment was to knock on the Grand Jurors doors and ask a few procedural questions.

On June 20, 2010, a former agent with the United States Department of Justice Drug Enforcement Agency, Michael Nealon, Arora's Private Investigator, drove me and another intern, to visit the Grand Jurors at their homes. We asked if they understood the case; how long the process took; whether they asked questions; how many witnesses testified; whether they were given a copy of the indictment; and whether they read the indictment. A couple of the Grand Jurors were not very excited about our unannounced visit and contacted the District Attorney to complain.

Within a couple of hours, and for several days after, we were all over the local news stations. The District Attorney filed a temporary protective order requesting that we stay away from the Grand Jurors. Arora held a press conference to inform the Atlanta community that there was neither statutory nor case law which prevented us from inquiring about procedural matters with the Grand Jury.

The news spread like wildfire through the John Marshall campus. And just like that, I established my new brand of notoriety.

18

THE AMERICAN DREAM

O n April 1, 2011, I contacted Jill Polster, the Senior Assistant District
Attorney and hiring coordinator at the Dekalb County District
Attorney's office. Arora believed that my best shot at the bar examination hinged on obtaining an externship with the D.A.'s office. If the government
was willing to take a chance on me, the State Bar might be inclined to follow suit.

All history aside, my resume was in pretty good shape. During my 1L
year, I was voted into the position of President of John Marshall's Sports and
Entertainment Law Society. As President, I coordinated student volunteer
groups that worked alongside the Atlanta Falcons through the National Football
League's Play 60 program to teach kids how to play sports at local Atlanta elementary schools.

As a 2L, I registered for John Marshall's Peer Mentor program and was
assigned four 1L mentees. I was in charge of mentoring the 1L mentees on how
to adjust to life as a first-year law student. Midway through my second year of
law school, I was awarded the Kaplan PMBR Head Representative position at
John Marshall. This position made me the student in charge of coordinating
the bar preparation courses for my entire graduating class.

And most persuasive was the internship with Arora I had under my belt. A recommendation from Arora was sure to weigh in my favor; he and Polster had known each other for quite some time. Plus, it helps that he's one of the most highly respected attorneys in the United States.

Polster invited me to interview on April 8, 2011, for an externship under the Third Year Practice Act, which allows law students to obtain practical trial experience by volunteering for the government while in law school. Under the Third Year Practice Act, I would be permitted to adjudicate criminal matters for the Georgia government.

I walked into the Dekalb County courthouse thirty minutes earlier than the scheduled interview. I walked through the building to inspect the courtrooms and various offices and noticed that certain areas were under construction, apparently the District Attorney's office was being remodeled. I took the elevator to the fourth floor where the DA's office was being housed during the remodeling process and checked in with the receptionist.

A few minutes later, Polster stepped out from behind a double door that required a security passkey to enter. She was a fair skinned Caucasian woman. She stood about five foot five, had short black hair tied back in a ponytail, and wore a striking dark grey skirt suit with a white blouse and black heels. A shiny silver government badge dangled from the lanyard around her neck.

"Hey kid. You sure you want to be here?" she asked. "This place can sometimes feel like Hell on Earth."

"A recent unofficial study showed that gingers don't have souls. So that is neither here nor there for me," I responded.

"I like you already," said Polster with a laugh.

We walked back through the double doors toward her office. The construction had taken a serious toll on the office arrangement. The makeshift office had carpet that was so worn it looked as if a 5K had been run on it every day for a decade. The investigator's offices were located closest to the entrance. They were very small, did not have windows, and were painted a depressing yellow color.

Paralegals were spread out haphazardly, their workstations shoved into any spot that would accommodate a small desk.

The assistant district attorneys were all grouped together in a large room toward the corner of the office. Open-air cubicles separated their work areas. Each cubicle had a Dell computer that looked as if it were the brand's first generation product. None of the attorneys' desk chairs matched and all looked as if they were picked up from garage sales and Goodwill. Files were all over the place in each attorney's cubicle; on top of desks; in crates on the floor; everywhere I looked, there were files.

I was starting to get the "Hell on Earth" bit.

Polster's office was a seven by six open-air cubicle. Inside was a metal desk with a wooden top that barely fit into the small area. There were three chairs, one for her, and two on the opposite side of the desk. Pinned to one of the cubicle walls was an enlarged evidence exhibit from a recent murder trial. The exhibit was a letter written by a defendant and mailed to a friend while he sat in jail awaiting trial.

The letter clearly read: *Yeah I shot that fucking bitch. And I will do it again if they let me out this motherfucker. I'm a cop killer and proud of it. Fuck the police. Fuck the DA. I'll kill em all if I could.*

"Why do you keep that up there?" I asked.

"It's a reminder that if I don't do everything I can to investigate and prose-cute my cases diligently, someone that doesn't care about hurting people could be released into our community," Polster replied.

We discussed law school, my experiences working with Arora, and how the Third Year Practice Act can benefit future trial attorneys.

Before we wrapped up the interview, Polster asked me, "Have you ever been in trouble?"

I shook my head. "I have been in so much trouble, you wouldn't believe me if I told you. It would literally take the entire afternoon."

Polster laughed. "I think you'll fit in well with us." She turned to her trial partner, Oto Ukpong. "What do you think, little O? Should we hire this guy?"

"He is cute. Sort of like a better looking version of Chuck Norris," answered Ukpong.

"In all seriousness," I said, "If I were hired I would be a hero to my family. To my entire neighborhood back home. There are a lot of people monitoring my progress. Some don't think it's possible to rise out of the same small beginnings. This means a lot to me. Not only because it is what I want to do, but because if I do it, I will help inspire a lot of people who don't have a lot in the way of hope."

Polster hired me on the spot.

That same day, I gave Arora notice so that he could begin to interview another law student to assume the law clerk position with his firm. Arora hired Alison Smock from the University of Tennessee College of Law. I stayed on through April to finish the assignments I was given, and on May 17, 2011, my first day at the Dekalb County District Attorney's Office, the Honorable Chief Judge Michael E. Hancock swore me in under the Third Year Practice Act.

The courtroom was completely empty when I arrived. A single deputy stood inside the double door entrance to prevent anyone from entering. I sat in the jury box waiting for Judge Hancock to take the bench. I could hear the swishing sound of the air conditioning coming through the vents above. The courtroom was brightly lit with embedded ceiling lighting. The floors were covered with thin gray carpet. The walls were painted with white eggshell paint. The ceiling's molding and wall trim were made of red Spanish cedar wood. The jury box, podium, gallery, counsel tables, court reporter desk, witness stand and judge's bench were all made with the same matching wood.

Twelve thick black leather chairs were bolted to the ground inside the jury box. Directly behind the judge's chair, on the wall above, hung a circular Dekalb County Georgia state seal. Standing tall behind the judge's chair, to the left and to the right, draped from golden poles, were the Georgia and American flags. The courtroom was super hi-tech. Microphones mounted throughout the courtroom captured every word spoken. Cameras installed in the ceiling captured every move. The judge, prosecutor, and defense attorney each had a Dell desktop computer. The computers were synchronized with the court's projector screen to broadcast media to the jury.

Judge Hancock entered the courtroom from a door located directly behind his bench. He was an elderly, heavyset African American man who stood about six feet tall. He sported a very short military-style haircut and a pencil-thin mustache, and a pair of reading glasses perched precariously on his nose. A royal blue shirt and yellow tie peeked out from under his robes.

Hancock left an indelible mark on the Dekalb County legal system long before I ever met him. He was an Emory graduate who worked as an investigator with the Dekalb County Juvenile Court prior to attending law school. In 1979, he was the county's first African-American public defender. In 1983, he became the county's first African-American full time chief judge in the Dekalb County Recorder's Court. He served there until 1991, at which point he once again made history by becoming the first African-American appointed to the Dekalb County Superior Court bench. There were many firsts in Hancock's lifetime. I wondered if I would be the first person Hancock would swear into the Georgia courts to assist prosecuting attorneys in criminal proceedings with my type of criminal history.

Hancock calmly greeted us with a wave of his hand as he sat down in his chair.

To this day, I get goose bumps just thinking about that moment. If I've ever felt anything that can be compared to an out-of-body experience, this was it. I kept thinking back to the times when I'd felt so angry and trapped; all the nights I'd gotten up for a glass of water and found my mom mending clothes at the kitchen table; the day I'd stolen the bike pegs, the day Ortiz jumped me in, all the times I'd been beaten by the cops; learning to sell dope just to make money to help my family survive. That was the past. This moment changed all of that.

I'd reached the moment I'd worked toward since the day in 1997 when I looked in the mirror and said, "Enough is enough."

I could finally see the finish line.

The one other person in that courtroom who knew what that moment truly meant was the girl sitting next to me in the jury box. I was sworn in side-by-side with one of my best friends from law school, Holly Waltman. Waltman understood because she knew my life story and she had one of her own. Her father's health was ailing, and his time was running short. But she was strong for him. Both of us were living to uplift our families. We encouraged each other to keep fighting during the difficult times of the law school process. Waltman was Arora's other intern who knocked on the Grand Juror's doors along with Nealon and me. We became each other's sidekick. I nicknamed her Clutch because she always came through for me when it was absolutely necessary. She was my wing woman. During the holidays that I could not travel to be with my family because of the law school schedule, Holly's family took me in as their own.

Standing there with my right hand raised, my mind popped with the names of all the people who'd helped me or hurt me along the way. *Wilhite, Torres, Christian, the Dolphins, Jester-George, Manny, Nichole.*

Nichole.

I hoped she'd be proud of me. I felt my throat constrict, but I was giving my first official testimony on record, and there was no way I'd stand there with tears in my eyes.

I held my head high, stuck my chest out and repeated after the Judge in my strongest voice. Each word I spoke entrusted me with the burden of upholding truth and justice, of leading by moral example, and becoming a part of a system that could do great good. I was humbled. I was entrusted with the duty to prosecute criminal cases, which also meant that I could use my discretion to help rehabilitate defendants who had the potential to do better, just like me. I had a voice and a duty to use it on behalf of the American people—people like my father—who could not speak for themselves.

I called my mom, my rock, first.

She'd been there. She'd seen it all, cried with me through it all, and gave me tough love through it all. She was the reason I was so disciplined in my studies and professional endeavors. She taught me focus and determination. She helped me succeed in all the ways she had power: she made sure we were ready for school every day; she always made sure that even if I was wearing the same shirt all week and my lunch was a cheese sandwich, the shirt was clean and the sandwich was made. She devoted her evenings to helping us with our homework and cooking us dinner. We would all eat and laugh and talk every night together as a family. My mom worked tirelessly to make sure every night was special. When I got a little older, she listened to all of my crazy ideas and supported me through failures. My mom never wavered. She always believed in each of us. My mom never doubted I would get to this point, but made me promise to earn it the right way.

I dialed my dad next. When he answered, I wasn't able to utter a single word. The emotions finally reached a tipping point. I choked up. I just sat there crying on the phone. My dad listened quietly for a while.

"Es okay," he said, his voice thick. "Es okay. I know, David. I know."

I caught my breath, and managed a shaky, "Thank you!" But that was it.

"You deserve it, because you made it happen. You deserve it," he said, "I'm proud to be your father, David. It is a pleasure. I am very proud of you."

I felt an old, sharp burden fall away.

My dad was proud. My father has always been the world's strongest man in my eyes. He never let life get the best of him. He never quit at anything. He didn't know how. He sacrificed day-in-day-out for the good of our family. If it wasn't for his lifelong investment into his family I would never have had a chance.

When I was home from law school during the winter break of 2010, his best friend, Brent, had called my parents' house and I'd answered the phone. We spoke for a few minutes about his work and my school.

Brent was excited to hear about law school. "You know, David, when your father and I worked together I would always invite him to lunch with me. Every time, he'd tell me he couldn't. 'I need the money for my kids,' he'd say. He always told me you were meant for something great. I guess he was right."

I'd had to pass the phone on quickly to keep from breaking down on the phone with Brent.

That was the man who raised me. The kind of man who sacrificed for his kids in every aspect of his life. Lunch out was a small thing. None of us would have blamed him for taking a tiny bit of what he earned to spend with his friends. We probably never would have known. But that wasn't who he was.

He spent his present on our futures.

"One day, Papi," I told him now, "you won't have to work so hard for us. I'm going to take care of you. You and mom. It won't be long now. I promise."

Although he didn't say anything, I could almost hear him smiling through the phone.

The next day, we were in the middle of an Armed Robbery trial when Dekalb County Chief Investigator, Craig Scott, walked into the courtroom.

He placed a hand on my shoulder, leaned in, and whispered, "Mr. Windecher, will you come with me? I need to discuss an important matter with you."

I left the courtroom with Chief Scott, curious stares following us, and a pit of dread growing in my stomach. Scott opened the door to an interrogation room where Polster was waiting, looking like she'd been punched in the gut.

She glanced up at me and managed a weak smile and a nod toward the cracking leather chair across from her. "David, sit down."

I did.

"Listen, I am sorry but…" She threw a desperate look at Chief Scott. He just shifted uncomfortably and examined his watch. "David, we have to let you go."

I felt like I'd been struck by lightning.

Polster stared down at her desk. "You cannot work for the government. Not in any capacity. Your record…"

I sat there in awe for a few seconds. *Let me go.* That made it sound like I was a caught fish being mercifully released to the sea, like a prisoner getting his charges dropped. What could I say? Of course I had a record. She knew that, didn't she? Just a month prior, I'd sat down with Polster and explained my life story and how much this meant to my entire family. And didn't they run a background check?

But none of these thoughts came out of my mouth. I just sat there waiting for it to make sense.

"David, you've spent time behind bars. You will *never* be permitted to work for any government agency."

"Never," I repeated.

Polster shook her head, "I'm so sorry David."

"My last arrest was fourteen years ago. I was a kid."

"Please don't take this personally. You're going to be a great attorney in the private sector."

I was still too stunned to make a sensible reply.

Polster stood; Scott opened the door. Obviously this conversation was one sided and finished.

"Now," she said, "don't you go get your license with the intention of coming back to Dekalb and kicking our butt day-in and day-out." She smiled. It was meant to be kind, encouraging. It felt patronizing. "This is not the end for you. I know it."

It felt like the end.

"But," I said, trying to kick my brain into gear, "don't I deserve an opportunity to prove myself?"

"I'm afraid that's out of the question."

"Really? In a judicial system that purports to act as a rehabilitative agent? So many things have changed since my last arrest—*I've* changed. I'm not an actor playing some role that will eventually end. This is real. Look at the rest of my record. I've flipped my failures into success." I searched her face, looking for a sign of empathy or of wavering. I found neither. "I *will not* have my career condemned because of mistakes that stemmed from circumstances I did not choose."

Polster just shook her head, looking, again, to Scott for help. He was checking his phone this time.

"Let me speak with the District Attorney, then."

Polster smiled pleadingly, "Mr. James will dismiss the matter as trivial. As I've said, there are no exceptions in this arena. You need to let this one go, David."

That phrase again.

At that moment, every bit of the adolescent anger and bitterness I'd so successfully kept at bay, welled up again. I could never forgive the government for this type of treatment. Not again. Not this time. I felt defeated. Insulted. Embarrassed. And heartbroken.

Investigator Mike Davis escorted me out of the building like the criminal they'd profiled me as. Davis was the embodiment of every horrible cop I'd ever met. A moron made self-important by a badge and gun. He walked me out of that building, every moment making it clear that I was a second rate citizen.

By the time I reached my car, I was livid.

I hadn't felt this much acidic anger since the streets. Since I'd been screwed over, profiled, beaten up and left for dead.

How could the judicial system do this to someone who'd worked so hard to complete the rehabilitation circle? How was I supposed to explain this to my family who, just a day ago, learned of my tremendous accomplishment? They believed I was given a chance to put away real bad guys while helping to rehabilitate those who, like me, had the capacity to make good of their lives.

There was no way I was going to tell anyone back home until I figured this out. The next day I sent Polster an email asking her to reconsider allowing me to speak to the District Attorney.[20]

David Windecher <david.windecher@gmail.com>

RE:

3 messages

David Windecher <david.windecher@gmail.com>   Thu, May 19, 2011 at 8:38 AM

To: "Polster, Jill G." <jgpolster@dekalbcountyga.gov>

Good morning Jill,

Yesterday was quite the humbling experience. I did not sleep very well. I am in a very poor position academically because of the result and the worse will unfold over the next few days. I am trying hard to mitigate on my end, however some things are out of my control, and I am very worried.

I want to ask you to please fight for me, please fight to get me five minutes in front of Mr. Robert James, please. After hearing Mr. James' message to the interns on Tuesday, I feel that if he got to know who I am, and knew my life story, that he would have a good perspective on me, sufficient to allow him to make a decision on whether to make an exception.

Please help me Jill.

Sincerely,

David L. Windecher

Polster, Jill G. <jgpolster@dekalbcountyga.gov>   Thu, May 19, 2011 at 2:42 PM

To: david.windecher@gmail.com, "Scott, Craig S." <csscott@dekalbcountyga.gov>

David,

Chief Scott will be in touch with you. Mr. James is aware of the situation and, I believe, may want to speak with you.

I've copied Chief Scott on this email so he'll have your contact information.

Thank you,

Jill

1 of 2   12/3/14, 3:24 PM

---

[20] See, email to Dekalb County Assistant District Attorney Jill Polster dated 5/19/11

It may have been because she realized I wasn't riding off into the sunset without my guns blazing, but, more likely, it was that I may have had a valid action against Dekalb County for a violation of my Due Process rights. Since I'd quit my job with Arora, I had standing. They'd essentially told me: "Hey kid, congrats! You're hired. Go ahead and quit your other job now. Oops! Wait a second; we forgot to do a background check before we brought you on. So, um. Our bad."

Either way, Polster forwarded my email to Chief Scott. Chief Scott called me on the morning of Friday, May 20, 2011 and informed me that the District Attorney wanted to meet with me on the following Monday to discuss my situation.

After I hung up with Chief Scott, I panicked for a moment. How was I supposed to prepare for the single most important moment of my life to date? If I didn't get this job, my chances at being allowed to sit for the bar were going to be on life support. What would I do without my license? Be a paralegal? I didn't come this far to fall that short.

But wasn't my entire life preparation enough?

I knew when Polster fired me that if I could somehow get in front of Mr. James I could regain control over my destiny. I did not need to prepare an ice-breaker, or sympathetic story lines, or resumes, or anything. I was going to walk into his office and be myself. I would talk to him man-to-man, mano-a-mano. I felt a twinge of fear. I could use some faith.

I walked over to my refrigerator and read *The Monument*, reminding myself that no matter what happened on Monday, God had my back.

My dream would not die like this.

Robert James turned out to be one of my favorite of all the people I've ever met, and certainly one of the most compassionate. We spoke for a couple of hours that Monday. As it turned out, James endured many challenges to reach the level where he stood. We came from different backgrounds, but the stories we shared about dead, addicted, and incarcerated childhood friends were nearly identical.

"I don't think you're here by chance, David," he said, "I think you were sent for a greater cause."

James called me the truest form of the "American dream" - the resilient kid who grew up impoverished, was raised in the hood, became a statistic of the penal system numerous times, and somehow fought his way onto the straight and narrow.

James gave me my job back.

Better than that, he assigned me to the District Attorney's Juvenile division where I could use my experiences to help kids who were growing up just like I did. I was allowed to adjudicate cases in four separate juvenile courtrooms. He gave me an office with a phone, a computer, a printer, and my own personalized email account. A *government* email account at that.

James kept calling me the "American dream" and said that one day I would be a change agent. He said he believed I would bring about change because I could lead by example.

I promised him that I would always do good by him and that he could always expect my full backing.

The fact that he is one of the most prominent figures in Georgia gives me hope. He is a progressive thinker with the ability and the will to change people's lives for the better. I will be forever indebted to him. His decision—his risk—in allowing me to work for the government essentially sealed my fate with the Georgia Board of Bar Examiners.

At the end of the meeting, we recited a prayer and he said, "We'll see you at work on Wednesday. Go and make history, David."

The finish line that had blurred when I was fired suddenly lit up like a star.

He was right; I was the AmerIcan Dream.

19

QUESTION
TWENTY-ONE

O n January 12, 2012, I filed my application with the Supreme Court
of Georgia to determine my fitness to sit for Georgia's bar examination. On February 8, 2012, the Board of Bar Examiners responded
to my application stating that my responses to "Question 21" required further
explanation.

Question 21 referred to my criminal history.

On February 13, 2012, I responded to the Board's request with the following letter:

Dear Marcia Huls,

The only thing in life one can never get back is time. Time is the
most valuable asset anyone owns. Thank you for taking yours to
review my application. Below is my response to the two respective
matters I was asked to address.

I. **A written statement of your past and current use of drugs, including how often you might have used drugs (past/present), types and under what circumstances.**

I do not use any drugs at all. I have first-hand experience with the consequences of using illicit substances. I was raised in an environment where drugs were all around me. I knew what marijuana, cocaine, and alcohol were before I was thirteen years old. Please don't misinterpret that statement to mean that the household I grew up in may have exposed me to those substances. That was not the case. On the contrary, my parents did everything in their power to keep me out of trouble. What I am referring to is growing up in a lower socio-economic environment. I grew up in what you'd call the hood; that is where I learned about drugs. Just think about the ghettos you see in movies or in some television shows; that is the environment I grew up in. I started smoking marijuana at an early age. That turned out to be a blessing in disguise because I realized the detriments of using drugs early too. That is why I am drug free today.

My parents did not have much money and we lived in lower socio-economic neighborhoods throughout my adolescent years. I lived in the type of neighborhood where you either chose to be in a gang and run the streets or become a statistic. I had to rise above all the pressures of drug peddlers, addicts, thieves, thugs, and gang affiliation to reach the point where I am today. For a short while I succumbed to this environment.

My parents were barely making ends meet. Smoking marijuana with my friends in the streets who endured the same or similar challenges was all I had. I didn't know how else to escape the nightmare of growing up poor and surrounded with pain. I realize that claiming to suffer from debilitating poverty while having the funds to purchase marijuana may seem contradictory. But there is an element to growing up in the hood that a person can only understand if he or she experienced it. You do not need money to smoke marijuana.

Through those years of my life, I saw lots of ups and downs. Those experiences helped me to appreciate the little things that most people overlook. I may have grown up poor, but I realized that I was rich because I have a great family. My family stuck by my side through thick and thin. I am the oldest of four. It was that birth order that was one of the catalysts for change in my life. I have one younger brother and two younger sisters that I would give life and limb for. When I was running the streets, living angry, and carrying a bitter disposition which led to reckless behavior, I started noticing that my younger siblings where taking on my persona. They began to falter and head down the same path I was traveling. When I realized that I had such an influence on them I decided to change. There was no way I would let my brother or sisters fall victim to being gang members or using drugs. I knew that I had to change.

I always believed I was smart enough to accomplish anything I wanted to reach for, but growing up in the hood made me feel as if progressing was impossible. The odds were stacked. It was my faith, my family, and my strong desire to do things right that helped me mature enough so that I could lead by example. I eventually decided to make a change and rise above the expectations society places on people from the hood. I do not know of an-other person who attended North Miami Beach High School scheduled to graduate in 1996 that has had the privilege to attend law school.

Given where I come from, I understand that if I were to use any drugs I could not be a good example or role model for others who have to endure some of the same struggles and challenges that I have overcome. While I am proud to have risen above all of those challenges and reached the levels that I have, I am aware that I have a checkered past. If I came across an individual with all of my marks, and I was assessing their fitness to practice law, I too would want them to prove to me that they have changed. So I understand why I am being questioned about this issue. The only way I can prove my character in this sense is through my actions. I am used to that, and I welcome it. It has been an uphill battle, and I hold myself accountable for every poor decision I have ever made. However, it has been those trials that have helped mold me into the man I am today, and I cannot apologize for those mistakes. Apologies seem like excuses, and I do not like excuses; I like solutions.

I also believe that a person should be judged from beginning to end; not just for a portion of his or her life, but by the totality of their existence. I am thirty-three years old now. I have not been arrested since I was eighteen. And since then I have done everything in my power to rise above being anointed another thug from the hood. I want to help rehabilitate those who are facing the same obstacles I have defeated. In order to accomplish such a feat one must set strict standards and lead by example. That is why I do not use any drugs. I cannot even remember the last time I used marijuana, which is the only drug I have ever used. I understand words are just words, and even though I hold true to what I say, to prove that I am drug free, I will consent to a screening at any point in time.

II. A statement of your rehabilitation in light of <u>In Re: Cason 249 Ga. 806 (1982)</u>.

For bar fitness purposes, rehabilitation is the reestablishment of the reputation of a person, by his or her restoration to a useful and constructive place in society. <u>In Re: Cason, 249 Ga. 806 (1982)</u>. Positive action showing rehabilitation may be evidenced by such things as a person's occupation, religion, or community service. <u>Id. at 809</u>.

A. <u>Occupation</u>.

One must occupy that which they believe is truest to their purpose. I hold the occupation of leader. I look at myself as a leader because I believe that my experiences in life can encourage someone who grew up in a similar situation to overcome adversity. As a leader I understand that I should never ask something of someone that I am not willing to do myself. I also understand that to create a new beginning one must take the initiative in doing things right and leading by example.

I currently hold an externship position with the Dekalb County District Attorney's Office in the Juvenile Division. I am well equipped for this position because I understand what those teenagers are going through. I have been there. And, against all odds, I have fought my way out of those circumstances. I cannot think of a better way to repay the world for the opportunities that I have been given than by fighting now for those teenagers' rehabilitation. With my position I can actually make a difference by implementing change. My experiences as a teenager were harsh. I have seen people shot and killed before my own eyes. I have lost friends because of gang affiliations and drug smuggling. I have lost friends to addiction. And I lost my best friend, Joey Torres, to the penal system. The streets broke my heart day-in and day-out. There was so much pain in growing up impoverished, looked down upon, and oppressed in so many ways. I thrived on misery because it felt as if there was no way out. That temperament led to reckless behavior and repetitive mistakes. So, I understand those teenagers' realities, and when I speak with them, they know I understand. I can see it in their eyes. On several occasions I have been asked how they can get to where I am. There is no better feeling than believing that you can make a difference in a child's life.

I plan on making a difference for children the rest of my life. I do not plan on working in the Juvenile Division of the Dekalb County District Attorney's Office for an entire lifetime, but I have a few plans that I will see through. Currently, I am working with Assistant District Attorney Diana Kovach and the Multi-Bar Leadership Council on forming an education outreach program. Our goal is to find attorneys that have inspiring stories to speak at metro-area schools.

I am also writing a book about my life story with hopes that it will circulate through the juvenile system. I want to motivate troubled teenagers to overcome the challenges of growing up in the hood. My goal is to assign the book as reading material for juveniles that are incarcerated or on probation. I want them to read it so they can understand that I was just like them, troubled and challenged by similar circumstances, but I found a way out. I want them to believe that if they fight hard enough they too can find a way out. I have started the book and have about 50 pages written. I have a ways to go but the book is completely outlined. I just need more time to finish it. I plan on finishing the book after law school. I have a couple of sponsors that want to endorse the book and help me promote it. Once the book is complete, I want to establish a non-profit organization, or work with one, to raise funds that will be used to help rehabilitate juveniles with criminal records.

In the end, my occupation as a legal practitioner will elevate my ability to lead by example. I will be able to implement change through my craft. I will be able to provide hope and inspire troubled teenagers to believe that no matter the circumstance one is born into they can place themselves on higher ground through diligent effort.

B. Religion.

"But by the grace of God I am what I am; and his grace which was bestowed upon me was not in vain; but I laboured more abundantly than they all; yet not I, but the grace of God which was with me." 1 Corinthians 15:10.

I live my life by 1 Corinthians 15:10. I have no regrets for any of the things I have endured in my life because I believe all of my challenges and all of my successes have been preordained. However, I hold myself 100% accountable for the poor decisions that I made. I understand that I have been given free will to choose, but I do not regret my poor decisions because had it not been for those experiences there is no chance that I could be the man I am today. If I were to take anything back it would be the pain I caused my family on the numerous times I was arrested. The disappointment in their faces hurt so much. That disappointment, plus a relentless desire to be a better person, coupled with my strong faith in God causing me to believe that those experiences were necessary, is what lead me into the position I am in today. A long time ago I read a poem titled "The Monument" by Blaine M. Yorgason. This poem is magnetized to my refrigerator, and I read it every day because it serves as inspiration. It reads as follows:

> God,
> before he sent his children to earth,
> gave each of them,
> a very carefully selected package of problems.
>
> These,
> he promised, smiling, are yours alone.
> No one else may have the blessings,
> these problems will bring you.
>
> And only you,
> have the special talents and abilities that will be needed,
> to make these problems your servants.
>
> Now, go down to your birth,
> and to your forgetfulness.
> Know that I love you beyond measure.
> These problems that I give you are a symbol of that love.
>
> The monument that you make of your life,
> with the help of your problems,
> will be the symbol of your love for me.
>
> Your Father

I am not religious in the sense that I go to church every Sunday and sing along with all the others who want to repent for their weekly sins. I believe—as I've said—that apologies are excuses and that actions speak louder. I simply choose not to sin. And so, I do not need to repent on a weekly basis. I do not lie, I do not cheat, I do not steal, I do not use drugs, and I do not hurt others.

I am not perfect, nor will I ever be, but I live a righteous life because I chose to change many years ago. My home is my sanctuary. I pray every single night. The only thing I fear is God. I put my life in God's hands a long time ago. Nowadays I thrive on faith, wisdom, and family oriented values. And I strive to help those who are still drinking from the bitter cup I poured as an adolescent because of my circumstances.

To me, being religious consists of having strong family values and having a life of purpose. It also means doing good by your fellow men, even if they are not your family, and even if they may not do the same by you. It also means sharing your gifts with others. Because to reach the position I am in today, others shared with me, and believed in me regardless of my past.

My plan with religion is to help persons find a way to the righteous path. If I can save just one person it will have been worth it. I know what it means to struggle and so I want persons to experience the same gratification inherent in hard work and perseverance that I have been able to attain. However, I will never try to convince someone that they should believe in God because I truly feel that this is a personal virtue that one must be ready to receive when the time is right for them. But, if they ask me how I got to where I am today, I will explain to them why my faith is an essential element of my growth.

A   Community Service.

Service to one's community is an implied obligation of members of the bar. Cason, at 809. By admitting a person to the practice of law, the bar holds that person out to the public as worthy of patronage and confidence. <u>Penobscot Bar v. Kimball, 64 Me. 140 (1875)</u>.

Legal practitioners are leaders amongst their community. Legal practitioners within the community are perceived to be persons with the ability to make a difference and further people's best interest. Given such an important responsibility, one in the position to practice law should never lose sight of the desires our Founding Fathers expressed in the Constitution with regard to "forming a more perfect union." One person can make a difference. And, each legal practitioner should strive to uplift those in disadvantaged positions.

Personally, in order to carry momentum going forward, I have taken measures to ensure that I started doing my part before I obtained a Juris Doctorate degree. I know what it means to come from behind. My experiences have instilled within me a strong desire to give back to our community. I have already taken several initiatives and I have several plans for the future. They are as follows:

> First, during my first year of law school I started volunteering with the Atlanta Falcons in administering the NFL's Play 60 program. This program's prerogative is to motivate kids to go outside and play rather than sit inside in front of a computer. This was important to me because I believe there is a strong correlation between sports and keeping kids off drugs and out of trouble. And, from a health perspective, it is imperative that we do our part in fighting illnesses that start with the lack of physical activity, such as obesity. This is personal to me because I am very athletic. While I was growing up, the one thing that would keep me off the streets were sports. I wanted to get involved with the Falcons because I knew it was something I would be very passionate about. At the beginning of my first year in law school I ran for President of the Sports and Entertainment Society and I was voted into the position. Being President I was able to change the

bylaws and make decisions on how John Marshall students could get involved in the community through sports. I contacted Kendyl Moss, the Community Outreach Coordinator for the Falcons, and coordinated with her to have our students volunteer for community events. The relationship developed quickly and John Marshall students have since been involved in numerous events with the Falcons. I am no longer the President of the Sports and Entertainment club because I wanted to do something else during my second year of law school.

Second, during the summer between my first and second year in law school I enrolled in John Marshall's peer mentor program. My goal was to help the incoming class understand how to cope with the anxiety and pressure of being a first year law student. I strongly believe in leaving every situation I encounter better than I found it. The first year of law school is a grind and it can intimidate and frustrate the strongest minded individuals. This was my chance to help some students adapt to their quickly moving environment. I was assigned four mentees. By the end of my second year of law school, which was the end of my mentee's first year of law school, it was discovered that two of my four mentees finished ranked first and second in their respective class. Michael Baron and Trinity Best both transferred to Emory University. The administrators at John Marshall joked with me that I would no longer be allowed to be a peer mentor because they were losing money. I countered by stating that the first and second place rankings were guaranteed the Solomon Scholarship, meaning they would receive a full credit for their second year tuitions, so why not let these guys pursue what they thought was best. To this day I have a great relationship and friendship with Michael Baron and Trinity Best. They often call to thank me. I just tell them that I was doing right by my fellow men and that they should pay it forward when given the opportunity. It was a pleasure for me to get to know both of them. Before the following year's class of incoming students was announced, John Marshall recognized its peer mentors in an award ceremony. Out of 50 candidates I was awarded Peer Mentor of the Year in 2011. I was humbled and honored. I treasure the award because after everything I have been through it feels great to get some recognition for doing something that felt so good doing. I have never been the guy who needs a pat on the back, but this one I enjoyed. Along time ago I realized that this life is not just about me. It is about helping others along the journey. This award was a blessing.

Third, rewinding back to the summer between my first and second year of law school, Dean Sheryl Harrison asked me to greet the entire incoming class of first year students during the upcoming fall semester. Dean Harrison asked me to discuss the code of student responsibility. I was asked to be in a position where I could make a difference in the lives of incoming students by helping them understand what it means to develop and preserve an admirable reputation. I took this very seriously. I was grateful for the opportunity given where I came from, the streets. This was something I felt proud of because it meant the collective thought amongst John Marshall administrators was that I was the type of person with the kind of character the institution wanted to convey to their incoming class. I was given a platform to speak to a group of about 150 students, with a microphone, for one hour, about how they need to prepare themselves for the future. It was an honor to do that. I enjoyed helping others understand how to develop the reputation to go out into the job market and obtain a position in the legal industry. To date I have introduced the code of student responsibility two consecutive years. Now think about what that means; it means that I have been given an opportunity to show people that it is not about how your life starts but about what you do along the way. I am very lucky. I do not take this for granted for a single moment.

Fourth, after my second year of law school I sought after a coveted position in being the Head Representative of Kaplan PMBR. I wanted this position because I knew that I would be at the forefront of delivering the information and materials that would be essential in every law student's success on the bar exam. I love helping others. I took this opportunity seriously because I know that the dissemination of information and preparation resources are essential tools requisite in building a student's confidence in knowing they can pass the bar exam. I wanted to be in that position because I knew how much it would mean to me to help others achieve their goals and aspirations. It is hard to predict what the results will be, but I am working hard to help John Marshall students achieve the highest bar passage rate in the university's 79-year history. I understand some of these things are out of my control but I am doing the best I can to put students in a position to succeed.

Lastly, as mentioned above, I plan on publishing a book about my life. The book will be titled "The American Dream – HisStory In The Making." The book will detail what happens when a life on the streets meets a legal education. A portion of the proceeds will be distributed as set forth above. My goal is to create opportunities for people who are facing the same challenges and obstacles that I have been fighting through all of my life. And I will produce as much success as I possibly can with the book because I really want to help those who are in the same position I was in. No one wants to remain impoverished, nor does anyone want to live in the hood forever. I know those challenges are very hard to overcome; especially when one feels as if they are a victim of circumstances they cannot change. I will change the attitude about growing up impoverished and disadvantaged because in the end it turned into an advantage for me. It will take me some time, but I will make it happen.

III. Conclusion.

I want to close this letter out by saying that I knew this day was coming. I have been preparing for it my entire life. I knew just as much when I applied to law school. That is why on February 20, 2009, before being accepted into John Marshall School of Law, I personally visited with Shannon Keef, the admissions coordinator, to discuss my life. I knew it would make all the difference in the world because a phone call or letter would not be enough to justify such a troubled past. I knew that my record would be an issue during the character fitness portion of the bar examination process. For that reason I would like to respectfully ask for an opportunity of having the Board's audience in a formal hearing to discuss who I am as a person, what I plan on doing here on earth, and what I want to leave behind before I go to Heaven.

Given that I was arrested so many times as an adolescent, I understand the burden I carry with regard to my criminal history. I want the Board to understand that I do not look at that burden as something I must overcome just for the character fitness portion of this process. The burden will be an ongoing procedure for the rest of my life because it is my duty to show that persons can change, not just for a short period of time, but also for the long haul. Everyone makes mistakes, but it is about what one can learn from those mistakes. The goal should be turning a negative into a positive. I do not want to be condemned for my mistakes as much as I do not want to be given all the credit for the things I have accomplished. I have been fortunate to be given some extraordinary opportunities. None of my opportunities would have been possible without people believing that my moral compass was intact.

I believe I have established clear and convincing proof that I am rehabilitated. As a matter of fact, I belief I have established that I am rehabilitated beyond any reasonable doubt. I hold a constructive place in society. My actions speak louder than any words written in this response. It has been a long journey. Looking back, it is humbling to see that because I stuck to my plan I am so close to accomplishing what at one point seemed impossible. I cannot make any sense of all the mistakes I made growing up. But I know that I am a changed man in comparison to who I was when I was 18 years old. I would ask the Board contact Mr. Manny Arora, who I clerked for and has become my mentor, or Mr. Robert James, the District Attorney who personally afforded me the opportunity to be an extern for the state, and ask them if they believe that I "have the character to withstand the temptations... [of handling] other people's money and affairs." I have always been willing to work hard for my opportunities. I do not have an entitled disposition about myself. I believe in people and I hope they believe in me. Nowadays it's almost impossible to do anything without a good supporting cast. I truly feel that the world has more good than bad and we just have to continue to do the right thing even when adversity challenges us. I plan on being a very powerful figure of constructive force. And I am willing to earn that position. But I cannot do it without your help. I respectfully ask the Board to certify me fit to practice law. I look forward to your response. Thank you!

Cordially,
David Lee Windecher

You might think that I would have been anxiously waiting for their response, perhaps pacing or losing sleep, but I was calm. I know people have little faith in the justice system, and I'll be the first to name its faults, but I knew in my soul that the Board couldn't let my story end there.

And they didn't.

On May 10, 2012, I received a letter from the Supreme Court of Georgia Office of Bar Admissions issuing me a Certification of Fitness to Practice Law.

Nine days later, I graduated from law school. That was perhaps the greatest day of my life. I sat with the W's in the rows of graduates, and I couldn't help but feel like I was part of something greater than I'd even dared to hope. I watched with surprising pride as student after student crossed the stage, shook hands, and accepted his or her Juris Doctor Degree.

Yes, a lot of my classmates were spoiled pansies I hoped never to encounter professionally, but so many others were hardworking, wise, and dedicated individuals who inspired me, and who I was proud to call my peers. Brad Griffin could become a distinguished property law practitioner. Thomas Lyman and Miguel Castro could become the faces of civil practice in Atlanta. Holly Waltman was a phenom-criminal defense trial attorney in the making. Zach French's entrepreneurial mind could pioneer the next big movement.

I was sitting in a sea of success, an ocean of potential, and I belonged. I saw, instead of the vast, black void that had been Red's future, an endless horizon. I had beaten down the darkness in me, the drugs, the streets, the statistics. My future was my own. And I could change more than just my own life.

When my name was called, I walked across the stage, pointed at my family with my left hand, brought it back to tap the center of my chest, and then, I pointed at the sky with my right hand.

Because that's how I made it; with the love of my family and the strength of my God.

Life is often equated to a series of battles within a war, and, in my experience, that's a fair metaphor. There are certainly moments of reprieve, of hope, and of success in combat, but there will always be another enemy troop on the march, or wounds to tend, or an attack to plan. The battles only cease when the war does and the war can only end when you have nothing left to fight for.

The magnitude of the day I graduated was deep and resonating. A major battle had certainly been won, and another was in my near future: the Georgia Bar Examination.

I'd planned ahead as best I could. I was set up to study from home with all of the supplies I needed. I'd worked for Kaplan PMBR, so I had all the strategies in place.

But, as will happen in war, I ran out of money.

I was no longer taking classes so I did not qualify for any additional Federal Department of Education student loan disbursements. My position with the DA's office had been unpaid, so I had no savings, and I had to study for the bar from May through July while somehow covering three months' worth of living expenses.

My main problem was paying for my mortgage. I moved up to Georgia months in advance of starting law school and financed my place in Marietta with HSBC. I thought of the purchase as an investment given the amount of time I knew I would spend living in Georgia. But the market tanked. The mortgage was underwater. And I was unable to refinance the property to a lower payment because I was unemployed and did not qualify for any of the Federal principle balance reduction programs. My options were limited. It was only a matter of time before it sank.

When I received my final loan disbursement from the Federal Department of Education in January of 2012, I contacted HSBC about applying for a shortsale. A shortsale is the sale of real estate in which the selling price of the property falls short of the balance owed on the mortgage. A shortsale is the alternative to a foreclosure. The primary difference is that, in a shortsale, any deficiency between the property sale price and the balance owed on the mortgage is discharged. Both result in a negative credit report inquiry, however a shortsale would mitigate some of the residual impact on my credit score. Credit worthiness is one of the sticking points on the bar examination application.

I owed $100,000 on my HSBC mortgage note. The property would not appraise over $40,000. I was in the hole $60,000. Knowing I would not be able to obtain the funds to pay on the mortgage past April, along with the fact the property was so far upside down, made a strategic shortsale my best option.

According to HSBC, I needed to be in forty-five days of continuous default on the mortgage before I could apply for a shortsale. I used the money from the final Federal disbursement to pay my mortgage through April 2012. This way I would have enough time to complete the application process with the State Bar before my credit reflected a shortsale.

I had faith that it would all work out, and I didn't want to let it bother me—especially not during my graduation celebration—but I was still worried.

We threw a massive graduation party. My friend and law school compadre, Zach French, his fiancée Alex Imerman and Zach's mom, Brooke French, planned a party for the ages. French and Imerman lived on a ten acre property in the heart of Buckhead with a three-thousand square foot vintage style barn that was decorated like a museum. Antiques and paintings were placed conspicuously throughout the barn. A driveway fifty yards long was lit up all the way to the back of the property where the barn stood. Gas lamps lit up the entire property. In the distance you could see the horses walking around in their paddocks. A stage was placed in an open field next to the barn where a band played live music for our guests. Open bars were located inside and outside the barn. The catered food was world class. And a couple of hundred people showed up to celebrate with our families.

Giselle pulled me aside.

"What's up, Dave?" she asked.

"I couldn't be happier," I told her, and it was true. Almost.

She appraised me for a moment, looking past the smile and seeing the tired eyes.

"This wasn't easy for you."

I shook my head with a smile. "No, but I'd do it all again."

She nodded. "So now what?"

I blew a long breath out from my mouth. What *was* next? "I guess I've got to get a job or sell my car or take out another loan."

She narrowed her eyes. "You're having money problems?"

"It's not that I didn't see it coming. I've got most of it under control, I just, you know, can't afford to eat for the next three months. Really," I went on, "it's nothing to worry about. Let me get you another drink?"

I tried to take her glass, but she held on. "Let me help."

"What?" I asked, completely surprised. "No, I'm not taking money from you, G. You're my little sister. I take care of you."

"We're family. It's a two way street, and I'm helping whether you want it or not. It'll be fun. I'll come up to Atlanta—"

"You can't just move up—"

"And I'll work and pay all the bills while you study. It'll be perfect."

I opened my mouth to argue and she cut me off again.

"No. It's decided. I'll go home to pack and be back in a few days."

She walked away without another word.

True to her word, Giselle went back to Miami, picked up all her clothes, and drove up to Atlanta to help me finish strong.

Shortly before my graduation, I hired John Hollingsworth, a shortsale attorney, and commenced the shortsale process by missing my first ever mortgage payment in May 2012. The shortsale was set to take place sometime in September 2012. He made sure I missed the least possible number of payments. Hollingsworth was worth his salt.

But Giselle was my real hero that summer. Giselle saved me. She paid for all of the bills and let me just focus on the bar prep materials. We had a blast that summer, despite my painful study schedule. She picked up a job at my friend, and fellow law student, Kevin Haviv's family business, H & A International Jewelry. I made breakfast every morning because I was up early studying. We would eat and shoot the breeze until Giselle had to leave for work. I studied all day. Then, when Giselle got home, we'd head to the gym, which kept me sane. Giselle would make dinner while I recapped the day's studies, we'd eat, and she'd watch a movie that I would fall asleep five minutes into.

On July 24 and 25 of 2012, I sat for the State of Georgia Bar Examination at the Georgia International Convention Center.

Securing an opportunity to sit for the bar examination was a drawn out process that started long before the scheduled test date. There was the application process. Then there was a prerequisite exam before the bar exam. That exam is called the MPRE – Multistate Professional Responsibility Exam. The MPRE gauges ethical capacity. Scores range from 50 (low) to 150 (high). A passing score varies depending on the jurisdiction. Georgia requires a 75. Florida requires an 80. If you don't pass the MPRE, your bar examination scores are irrelevant because you will not be issued a bar number. I took the MPRE exam in March of 2012 and scored an 87.

Georgia's bar examination consists of three sections: (1), two multistate performance tests which require applicants to draft a motion, brief, or some type of legal document such as a last will and testament; (2), four essay questions which require applicants to identify legal issues and provide answers based on a lengthy fact pattern; and (3), 200 multiple-choice questions which require applicants to possess extensive knowledge of constitutional law, contract law, real property law, tort law, evidentiary rules and procedure. The writing portions are scheduled for day one and the multiple-choice portion for the second. Applicants are required to check-in to the examination room no later than 8:00 a.m. The exam is split into two three hour sessions starting at 9:30 a.m. and running through 5:00 p.m. with a lunch break between 12:30 p.m. and 2:00 p.m.

The bar exam is a beast. It requires every ounce of focus and determination one can conger up. For most people, passing the bar examination is the finish line they must cross at the end of an eight-year marathon. Without crossing the finish line you don't get a bar number. Without a bar number you cannot practice law. And it is easy to get caught up in the emotional roller coaster associated with the process because the statistics will make you over think. Of 1162 applicants that sat for the bar in July of 2011, only 78.2% passed. Even worse, of 114 John Marshall applicants, only 65.7% passed.[21] Numbers do not lie. The pressure was real.

The question became, was I going to run from the bar exam rigors or was I going to run toward it with enthusiasm? I wanted to punch the bar exam in the mouth. All of my dreams. All of my aspirations. The promise I made to my parents. The promise I made to God. All wrapped up in a two-day gauntlet.

My mind was set by the day of the exam. I was hitting on all cylinders. That summer I simulated the two-day examination at least four times during bar review. I knew I was my only competition. And nothing was going to stop me from passing. I had it down.

This was the moment of truth for me. I had more clarity than ever before in my life. I was in a zone. I was excited. I wanted the challenge.

When I arrived at the GICC there were students milling around the convention center. Some had concentrated looks on their faces. Others had the deer in headlights look. I steered clear of any communication. I did not speak to a single person for those two days.

---

[21] See, https://www.gabaradmissions.org/georgia-bar-examination-statistics#0711

We stepped into a room the size of a football field. At the back of the room was a large stage where members of the Board waited to deliver instructions. Next to the stage was a digital clock with large red numbers that could be clearly seen from the entrance fifty yards away. Rows of fold up picnic tables and chairs were lined up from the front of the room all the way to the back. The tables listed applicants in alphabetical order. I found my table near the back of the room. As I walked up, I noticed an exam booklet upside down on the bottom right corner of the table.

I sat down and closed my eyes. I started to inhale and exhale slowly. I thought about my mom, my dad, my sisters and my brother. I thought about how hard I worked to be there in that moment. I prayed to thank God for the opportunity and to ask Him for His strength.

As soon as I was done praying, Sallie Lockwood, Director of the Office of Bar Admissions of the Supreme Court of Georgia, started giving instructions. I firmly inserted my ear buds and tuned her out. I was ready. My eyes were keyed in on the big timer next to the stage. I knew exactly what to do when it started counting down the first 3-hour session.

When the timer started, I turned the exam booklet over, flipped it open to the first page and read, "State of Franklin v. Soper." Excitement came over me because anytime the issue involved the "State," it meant it was a criminal law question. I kept my emotions in check but couldn't help to be pumped to start the bar examination with a criminal question. I had over two years of experience with Arora and the Dekalb District Attorney's Office combined. I had written hundreds of criminally related motions. I started with so much momentum that by the time we reached the first day's lunch break, I didn't feel tired or hungry or stressed at all. I was fired up and wanted to keep going.

We returned from lunch and there was another exam booklet in the same place I found the first one. The process repeated itself. When I turned the booklet over, I read through the first question and realized that the question was also about criminal law. Ironically, it was about a drug dealer and a career criminal involved in a drug transaction. This was the life I actually lived. And now I was being tested on something I had experience in. The excitement that ran through my body as I typed my responses cannot be explained with words. By the time day one came to a close, I was unfazed by the past. My mind and eyes were on

217

the future. I knew that if I finished day two strong, it was only a matter of time before I had a bar number.

I arrived at the GICC the next morning having barely slept. I stayed up late reviewing the multiple choice question flash cards I prepared during bar review. By the time I finished studying, it was late and I was still wide-awake. I laid there and waited for the most important day of my life to start. Even though I hadn't slept, I was buzzing with energy. The process to start day two was identical to day one. The day was broken up into 100 multiple-choice questions in the morning and 100 multiple-choice questions in the afternoon. I finished the first 100 questions with twenty minutes to spare. I took that time to observe my surroundings. I sat back in my chair and watched as other students finished their exam. I wondered what their life story was like. I wondered how much they went through to get to that point. I wondered how much that moment meant to them and their families. I kept thinking about how thankful I was. I was just three hours away from accomplishing a goal that was fifteen years in the making.

I finished the next set of 100 questions and walked out of the GICC feeling fulfilled. I left it all in that room. I had no regrets. I was proud of the man I'd become.

I had to wait another three months until the bar results were released on October 26, 2012 and I could practice law. So in mid-August Giselle and I headed home to Miami to stay at my parents' house in the same neighborhood where this journey began.

Being back in Miami-Dade County felt as if I had taken a step backwards. It seemed as if nothing changed but me. And that made me feel bad. The city was still saturated with angry gangster wannabes, con artists and corrupt cops. The majority of the people I grew up with were still doing the same thing. It felt as if time stood still in Miami. No one grew. No one changed for the better. Everyone I knew complained about one thing or another. I did not feel comfortable speaking of my progress because I felt guilty for having success. I did not want to rub it in anyone's face because I still cared about all of those people back home. I still wanted the best for the community, and I felt ashamed that

I'd found a way out and everyone else was living the exact same life. I knew I would not stay in Miami long.

On September 26, 2012, HSBC approved the shortsale and discharged my debt. I owed $100,000 on the property. The shortsale was approved at $40,000. This messed up my credit pretty bad. There was nothing I could do about it, but I do remember thinking that I'd better have passed that exam.

Finally, October 26 came. There were two ways to learn of one's bar examination results. First, was when the mail arrived. Second, at 4:30 p.m. EST when the mass online alphabetical listing went live on the State's website. That morning I got up early and went to the gym for nearly three hours. The mail arrived at my mom's house at 11:45 a.m., and I'd be a liar if I said I wasn't standing outside waiting.

When the mail carrier arrived, I flicked through each piece of mail. Nothing from Georgia. I tried to keep from panicking. I was on edge, so Christian took me to grab lunch and kill time. We went to the Yard House at the Gulf Stream Park venue in Hallandale Beach. The Yard House was a brand new restaurant that was built while I was away at law school. Frankly, I didn't care where we went. I wanted to do anything to kill time. I was on edge. I wanted to know badly.

Just as we sat down, I got a text message from my law school friend Boris Milter that read, "Dude!!"

I responded, "'Dude'? What does that mean!?"

Milter replied, "You did it bro!"

Apparently, the pass list had leaked and several students and administrators had access to it, but none of that mattered.

I was an attorney.

I lost my mind. I started jumping up and down like a crazy man inside the Yard House, but my joy was too big for the restaurant. I ran outside at full speed. I literally ran in circles. I jumped up and down like a lunatic, throwing my fist in the air. And the rest was a blur. I know I called my parents to tell them, and I know my phone didn't stop ringing for the rest of the evening.

I did it.

I freaking did it.

I reached my American dream. Against nearly all odds, I became an attorney in the United States of America.

20

THE BATTLE
FOR FLORIDA

O ne night near the end of my visit to Miami, I bumped into Acosta at
a gas station on Ives Dairy Road next to I-95. We had some catching up to do.

A few years back, on November 22, 2011, Acosta was arrested by the
Hallandale Beach Police Department on third-degree felony charges for Possession
of thirty pounds of Cannabis with Intent to Distribute.[22]

Acosta faced a mandatory minimum sentence of three years imprisonment
and a $25,000 fine. After Acosta was arrested, he asked Christian to call me
because he'd heard I'd proved him wrong and wanted to know if I could help
him. At that time, I was still an extern at the DeKalb County District Attorney's
office, so I referred the case to Arora. Arora flew down to Miami and met with
Acosta. Arora discovered a Fourth Amendment Constitutional issue with how
law enforcement agents had obtained the evidence being used against Acosta.

---

[22] See, State of Florida vs. Anthony Acosta – Broward County Case No. 12005620CF10A

Arora offered to handle the case along with local counsel, John Priovolos, for $50,000 plus travel expenses. Acosta hired them on the spot.

On April 10, 2012, the Broward County State Attorney's office offered Acosta twenty-five days in jail or nine months' probation, with zero fines, to resolve the case. The government realized it might lose the entire case based on Arora's proposed Fourth Amendment motion to suppress the evidence against Acosta. The offer was something Acosta was in no position to refuse. He chose the twenty-five days in jail because he wanted to put the case behind him as quickly as possible. So in the end, for Possession of thirty pounds of Cannabis, Acosta served twenty-five days in jail. That result was like winning the criminal case resolution lottery. That is the norm for Arora and Priovolos.

Acosta raised a hand from across the gas station.

I nodded hello.

After he finished fueling up, he walked over and shook my hand, a look of awe and disbelief on his face. "So you really did it, homie," he said. "You a lawyer."

I nodded.

"I never woulda thought…Red: a suit. Turned out good for me, though. I woulda been locked up if not for you and your boys," he said. "I was in real deep. You came through for me."

"I'm just glad everything worked out, Ant. What's fair is fair. The cops made a huge mistake and Manny and John exposed them. Somebody has to hold the government accountable," I said.

"Yeah, well, thank you. My family… They appreciate what y'all did. I appreciate it."

I paused for a second. "I should thank you too."

"For what?"

"Do you remember that day in front of my house? You remember what you said to me?" I asked. He looked confused, so I told him: "You said I couldn't get out. You said I'd never be a lawyer. That lit a fire in me, Ant, and it carried me all the way through. So thank you."

Anthony laughed. "You the oddest dude, man. But, I'm glad you jumped out. Ain't nothing changed out here, you know that. You lucky, Red," said Acosta. "Now get back to Atlanta, dawg. Ain't nothing out here."

"Don't worry. I'm not ready to call this place home again," I said. "Not sure if I ever will be."

Even as I spoke those words, I realized that there was one last thing I had to finish in the state that had been my home for so long. For the second time, a conversation with Acosta led to a decision.

I needed to close the circle. I felt a duty to my childhood self to lay my past to rest. I had the chance to become a positive force in the darkest, most corrupt system I knew. I needed to show my friends and my enemies that life is not about what happens to you, but about what you make happen.

Even though I was the poster child of rehabilitation, it was going to be difficult with Florida; there was no doubt about that. The Florida Board of Bar Examiners was going to place me under the microscope. Not only for my criminal record, but because now I would show a shortsale on my credit history report.

But, as I drove out of that gas station and watched in my rearview as Acosta drove back to his same, unchanged life, I knew: I would become a licensed attorney in Florida. Even if it killed me.

On November 16, 2012, I filed a bar application with the Supreme Court of Florida to sit for the Florida bar examination on February 26 and 27 of 2013. The application for the Florida bar examination cost me $1,000. Thankfully, I was able to cover this cost because John Marshall had an incentive program that paid a $1,500 stipend to graduates who passed the bar exam on their first attempt. I registered for the Kaplan PMBR Florida bar review, a $3,000 prep course, which I was able to get on credit.

Unlike Georgia, the Florida Board will accept applications and register applicants to sit for the bar prior to finding them fit to practice law. On November 26, 2012, the Board accepted my application and mailed me a ticket of admission for the 2013 February bar examination. I was given file number 38300.

On February 5, 2013, I received a letter from the Board, indicating that the financial affidavit I submitted was unacceptable, as it did not show employment and income while I attended law school. The Board requested an amended affidavit to explain how I met my financial obligations while I was enrolled at John Marshall—i.e. mortgage, car payment, credit cards, utilities, and the like—with an average monthly net income of $0. The financial affidavit I submitted was not incorrect.

I, in fact, did not secure any income during the entire time I was enrolled at John Marshall. My net monthly income really was $0. But this is not unheard of or even surprising, for law students. We have a long list of practically mandatory resume-building extracurricular activities on top of classes and hundreds of pages of dense casebook reading per week. And—if we want any hope of getting a job after graduation—we *must* get internships or externships starting our 1L summer through our 3L year. So taking on a part-time job is basically out of the question. Some students are offered summer associate positions with large law firms and generous paychecks to help pay for tuition, but the government's externs were unpaid.

I'd saved every penny possible before law school and was financially careful throughout the process. I drafted a letter to the Board indicating such.

On February 21, 2013, the Board delivered a letter acknowledging receipt of my response to the financial affidavit issue and permitted me to sit for the bar on February 26 and 27 of 2013 at the Tampa Bay Convention Center in Florida.

In the meantime, I'd accepted a position as an associate attorney at Arora LaScala and moved into my friend Kevin Haviv's house because he'd offered me a place to live while we were studying for the bar together.

I love the Havivs. Kevin Haviv was of Jewish decent. His wife, Mauri, is a Georgia peach with roots in Milledgeville, Georgia. They're great people individually, but together, Haviv and Mauri are delightful. They laugh constantly and never miss an opportunity to gently poke fun at one another, and they are very loyal to their friends. The world would be a better place with more folks like them in it.

Haviv and I met in law school and became friends. We were in the same cohort so we had almost every class together. Over the years, we spent a lot of hours studying and quizzing each other. After we graduated, Haviv applied to sit for the Georgia Bar exam in February on the same days I was scheduled to take the Florida Bar exam. Even though we were studying for different exams, we easily fell into a study schedule and routine just like we had in law school.

I had to be laser focused. I was practicing law full time and studying for the bar full time. Sheer determination and will, along with Haviv's encouragement, is what got me through those months.

The Florida bar was completely different than the Georgia bar exam in both format and substance. Format wise, Florida had 300 multiple-choice questions and four essays while Georgia was 200 multiple-choice questions, four essays, and two performance tests. Substance wise, Florida and Georgia laws varied significantly in several subjects; the policies were different; the defenses were different; and the Florida Constitution had provisions that were not written into Georgia's.

Just like me, Haviv had special motivation that drove him.

Before I moved in with the Haviv's in November of 2012, Haviv called me in late October to give me the news that he and Mauri were going to have identical twin boys—Elijah and Ezra Haviv. I was thrilled. I was going to be Uncle Dave.

But the joy only lasted a short while.

When Mauri was fourteen weeks pregnant, the twins were diagnosed with chronic twin-to-twin transfusion syndrome (TTTS). TTTS is a rare condition that affects twins sharing a single placenta. At sixteen weeks pregnant, Mauri was informed that due to the rapid progression of the TTTS she would lose the pregnancy within the week without surgical intervention. Haviv and Mauri spent New Year's Eve in the hospital while Mauri recovered from the surgery. At only seventeen weeks pregnant, due to complications from the surgery, Mauri's water broke. Elijah was given a 10% chance of survival. Ezra received 0%. Miraculously, Mauri remained pregnant for another eleven weeks while on bed rest at Northside Hospital.

Through that unspeakably terrible time in Haviv's life, he and I became brothers.

On February 26 and 27, Haviv and I sat for the Georgia and Florida bar examinations.

On March 25, 2013, at twenty-eight weeks and six days pregnant, Mauri caught an infection, went into labor, and gave birth to Ezra Haviv, weighing 2 lbs. 11 oz., and Elijah Haviv, weighing 1 lb. 3 oz.

Both required ventilators. Both required medical procedures. Elijah had open-heart surgery. Ezra underwent brain surgery due to hemorrhaging. The boys were hospitalized indefinitely.

On April 15, 2013, I was at the Haviv's waiting for the mail truck that carried the results of my bar exam. I'd just moved to my new place in Buckhead, but the Board still had the Haviv's address on file.

Haviv and I were talking about the boys while he got ready to head to the hospital to see them. The mail arrived just before Haviv left. It was hard to get worked up about the results when some of my dearest friends were in so much pain, but my heart still jumped when I heard the mail truck out front.

I walked back into the house from grabbing the mail as Haviv came down the stairs.

"We could use some good news around here. Open it up," said Haviv.

I tore the envelope apart. My eyes flitted around the page for a moment, unable to focus, failing to process the gibberish that was English. Finally a line materialized: *successfully sat for the Florida Bar Examination.*

I passed the Florida bar!!

I looked up at Kevin and he was smiling so hard it looked like he might strain a cheek muscle.

"Dude! Congratulations. Man, you deserve it," he said, slapping me on the shoulder. "So now what? When do you swear-in?"

"Hold on, let me finish reading this thing..."

I skipped ahead along the page, before stopping suddenly. I could feel my smile fading as I read on in silence.

It felt like my stomach had bottomed out. I sank onto the couch to read.

The letter stated that, while I had passed the Florida Bar examination, I was not authorized to take the Oath of Attorney. The letter further indicated that processing of my application could take up to anywhere between six to eight months from November 16, 2012, the date on which I submitted my Florida Bar examination application. The letter did not explain why I was not allowed to take the Oath of Attorney, but it did inform me that my application would become stale if I was not admitted to the Florida Bar by November 16, 2015.

"David?" Kevin asked timidly.

I wanted to scream. I wanted to punch a wall. But I did not want to make a big deal of my problems. What he was going through far outweighed anything I had on my plate.

I shrugged and offered a half smile. "Florida, strikes again." I got to my feet. "It says that I am not ready to swear-in because my application hasn't been completely processed yet. I'm going to get going. Call me later and let me know how the boys are doing, okay?"

I was already dialing the Board as I shut the front door behind me.

As the line rang in my ear, I forcibly regulated my breath.

Someone finally answered.

"Yes, I need to speak with someone about the status of my application."

During the excruciating conversation that followed, I was told that I had no choice but to wait the required six to eight months while the Board investigated my character to determine my fitness to practice law. What happened to the United States Constitution's Full Faith and Credit Clause? I was already a licensed attorney in good standing in the state of Georgia.

Unfortunately, I had no choice but to play their game. So I had to be patient. On the short-end I had to wait until May 16, 2013. On the long-end I had to wait until July 16, 2013.

Or so I thought.

On April 23, baby Elijah passed away from intestinal complications. Haviv and Mauri were holding him while he passed.

The next few months were all about waiting: The Havivs waited for Ezra to be released from the hospital, Haviv waited for his bar results, and I waited to hear from Florida about my application's status.

Defying the odds of a 0% chance of survival, Ezra would eventually grow healthy enough to be released from Northside Hospital. Haviv would eventually be notified that he'd successfully sat for the Georgia Bar examination.

But I kept waiting. For nearly an entire year.

May 16, 2013 came and went without any notice about my status. On June 4, 2013, I drafted an inquiry which I delivered via overnight service to the Board. On June 5, 2013, the Board responded by stating: "Your file has been processing for a little over six months. With normal processing being six to eight months, there has not been sufficient time to complete the investigation."

So I waited.

6/19/13:	I received letter requesting a certificate of Good Standing from the Georgia Supreme Court, a copy of my HSBC mortgage application, and an amended financial affidavit with an emphasis on the "Average Monthly Net Income."
6/24/13:	I submitted all of the requested documentation.
7/2/13:	I received notification that the Board received all of the requested documentation.
7/16/13:	I contacted the Board and inquired about the grievance process. I was told to research the rules of law as applied. I found the following:

> **3-40.2 Dissatisfied with Length of Board's Investigation.** Any applicant or registrant whose character and fitness investigation is not finished within 9 months from the date of submission of a completed Bar Application or Registrant Bar Application may petition the Supreme Court of Florida for an order directing the Board to conclude its investigation. If not inconsistent with these rules, the Florida Rules of Appellate Procedure are applicable to all proceedings filed in the Supreme Court of Florida. A copy of the petition must be served on the executive director of the Board. The Board will have 30 days after the service of the petition to serve a response. The applicant may serve a reply within 30 days after the service of the Board's response.

I did *not* want to file a motion with the Supreme Court. If I did, I would turn the dogfight with the Board into a street brawl. I'd fought the Florida system enough as a kid to last a lifetime, but I'd certainly use my rights as leverage.

Strategy was key. After the nine months noted in Florida Rule 3-40.2 expired, I drafted a letter indicating knowledge of the law permitting me to petition the Supreme Court for an order directing the Board to conclude its investigation.

8/19/13:   The Board responded by stating, "It is anticipated that your file will be placed before the Board by no later than the Board's October meeting and that you will be notified of the results by no later than late October 2013."

Finally. I would have to wait nearly another two months but at least now I knew when to expect an answer. Maybe I should have just petitioned the Florida Supreme Court because shortly after the August 19, 2013 letter I received a troubling inquiry from the Board.

8/28/13:   The Board asked me to amend my Florida bar application by disclosing Notices to Appear for each of my arrests.

Let me clarify. Notices to appear are the documents mailed by the clerk of court notifying defendants when his or her court date has been scheduled. Asking me to produce these was absurd and unreasonable. Notices to appear?! How does anyone get their court notices to appear from arrests that happened over sixteen years ago? *No one* can get those. Period. Notices to appear are not even archived. I would have to track down each independent case file and hope to find the clerk of court mailings enclosed.

9/3/13:   I submitted a response to the Board stating, "I contacted the clerk of courts for each of my respective arrests and was informed on each occasion that the clerk of courts does not keep a record of any of the notices to appear."

9/18/13:   The Board responded indicating that they had received my letter and the supporting documents.

9/23/13:   The Board notified me that I was not authorized to take the Oath of Attorney.

What could I do?

How much more clearly could I explain that "the clerk of courts does not keep a record of any of the notices to appear"? Did they think I kept a scrapbook of my legal indiscretions? These were *their* courts. How could they hold my fitness to practice hostage for a ransom they knew I couldn't produce?

9/26/13: I drafted a response stating, "I have complied with all requests for documents that your office has asked me to provide. I have been in constant contact with your office and am a bit perplexed by your most recent letter indicating that my application is about to become 'stale.' I am resubmitting all documents I have previously provided your office in order to ensure that you have a copy of everything your office has requested, and I am willing to answer any and all additional questions, requests, etc. posed by your office. I want nothing more than to be licensed in my home state of Florida and then be able to practice in the Miami-Dade County community, where I grew up, helping others in need."

It was war. I knew it. The members running the Florida Bar had a lot in common with the cops in Miami-Dade County. How would admitting a minority thirteen-time arrestee with a shortsale and a significant amount of student loans help those Board members retain their positions?

And that—not justice, not integrity, not rehabilitation—is what mattered to them.

10/1/13: The Board responded stating, "Amendments must be sworn and notarized and are considered timely when made 30-days of any occurrence that would change any response made to an application question."

10/4/13: I responded stating, "The reason these were not notarized is because they have been previously submitted to the Board. If it will assist the Board in processing my application, I would be more than happy to meet the Board in person."

10/17/13: The Board acknowledged receipt of my letter.

10/21/13: The Board mailed me a Notice of Rights and Responsibilities form which requested that I personally appear before the Board at an Investigative Hearing. Apparently, they wished to inquire into the final dispositions for each of my misdemeanor, felony, and traffic violation arrests, as well as the HSBC shortsale.

Good.

I was done with all this back and forth administrative red tape. I wanted to see the people I was fighting, and I wanted them to look me in the eyes and hear my story with their own ears.

In the Notice of Rights and Responsibilities form, the Board indicated that I have the right to be represented by counsel. It instructed on which attorneys were prevented from representing applicants before the Board, none of which exempted my boss, Arora, from representing me at the hearing.

Arora was not a member of the Florida Bar. However, we made sure that nothing in the notice would prevent Arora from representing me at the hearing. In addition to the counsel representation instructions, a list of hearing dates and locations to choose from was included. Those dates were November 15 – 16, 2013; January 10 – 11, 2014; and March 14 – 15, 2014.

10/28/13: I submitted a formal request to schedule the Investigative Hearing on the earliest date possible, November 15th – 16th, 2013.

11/4/13: I received a response from the Board stating, "I regret to inform you that the Board's schedule for the November 2013 and January 2014 meetings are full at this time; therefore your hearing has been placed on the calendar for the March 14 – 15, 2014, meeting of the Board in Tallahassee, Florida."

Naturally.

People say that the definition of insanity is attempting the same feat over and over and expecting different results. And it's true that most sane people probably would have withdrawn their applications by this point. But I'd sunk too much time and money to back down now.

12/19/13: I received a notice stating, "In an effort to minimize the wait time for your Investigative Hearing, the following hearing date has been added to the Board's schedule: Monday, February 24, 2014 in Tampa, Florida." On the same date, I confirmed the February 24, 2014, Investigative Hearing date via a phone call with Board representative Tammy Fraser.

1/22/14:   I received confirmation from the Board that the Investigative Hearing was scheduled for 10:00 am on Monday, February 24, 2014 at the Tampa Convention Center.

The Board's letter indicated that I should pay special attention to item number three of the Notice of Rights and Responsibilities form I received on October 21, 2013.

Item number three instructed that I was permitted to present witnesses, affidavits, or other evidence in my own behalf relevant to the subject matter of inquiry, and that any briefs must be submitted fifteen days prior to the Investigative Hearing.

1/27/14:   I indicated that I would not be presenting a brief and emphasized that my attorney and I would be present at the scheduled hearing.

2/3/14:   The Board delivered a letter requesting that my attorney submit a Notice of Appearance.

This was odd. On the Notice of Rights and Responsibilities, there were no instructions requiring that attorneys submit a Notice of Appearance. I checked the Florida Bar rules on the website to confirm, and, as I suspected, the rules did not require a Notice of Appearance.

2/6/14:   Arora submitted a Notice of Appearance.

2/11/14:   The Board responded stating, "Because your attorney is not admitted to the Florida Bar, please have Mr. Arora submit a motion requesting to represent you before the Board *pro hac vice*."[23]

This was thirteen days before the Hearing. I had already purchased flights and reserved hotels. The Notice of Rights and Responsibilities did not mention anything about attorneys not barred in the state of Florida being exempt from such hearings. In addition, the Board is not a tribunal and it does not legally require a pro hac vice motion. I researched the Florida Rules of Professional Conduct

---

[23] A *Pro hac vice* motion permits attorneys not barred in a specific state to practice in that state on a temporary basis.

and discovered that Florida Bar rule 4-5.5(c) authorized a lawyer admitted in another United States Jurisdiction to practice law in Florida on a temporary basis.

2/17/14:   Arora submitted a motion requesting to appear *pro hac vice*.

By noon on the Friday before Monday's hearing, we had yet to hear whether Arora was approved to represent me. Finally at 3:30 p.m., almost literally at the last minute, we received approval via phone call from Board representative Fraser.

We were going to Tampa.

21

POETIC JUSTICE

Arora and I landed at the Tampa International airport at 3:00 p.m. on Sunday, February 23, 2014. We picked up our rental car from Hertz, checked in to the Tahitian Inn on South Dale Mabry Highway, and went out for an early dinner at the Columbia Restaurant, where we discussed the next day's hearing and went over my testimony.

The next morning, as we drove to the Tampa Bay Convention Center, I realized that a year had passed since I'd sat for the Florida bar examination in that same building. I never thought I would be back to Tampa, let alone to the Convention Center. Yet, here I was, a year later and still in limbo.

The Convention Center was right on the coast of the Hillsborough Bay off the Gulf of Mexico. The enormous building, covering 600,000 square feet, sat on a triangular piece of property: one side facing S. Franklin Street; another side is on Channelside Drive; and the third side gave access to Riverwalk and a beautiful view of the bay.

After we made it to the top of the massive steps, we were instructed to take the elevator to the third floor and follow the signs from there. Just outside the elevator, I spotted an easel with a sign pointing us to a security room. The room held several other suit-clad individuals and a police officer with a sign-in sheet. I added my name to the list and grabbed a seat next to Arora.

About two hours later, Michele Gavagni, the Executive Director of the Board, walked into the waiting room and called my name. Gavagni was a Caucasian woman with long straight brunette hair, light eyes, thin lips, and an attractive, if emotionless, face. Arora and I followed Gavagni into a windowless room that was about half the size of a basketball court with four large foldable picnic tables pushed together into one large makeshift table. Positioned on each side were three members of the Board. Document folders, computers, and books cluttered the tabletop. Gavagni instructed Arora and me to sit in the two empty seats on one end, and she took a seat alone at a desk in the corner of the room to listen in on the hearing.

Arora took the seat next to me. As he opened his MacBook and collected his notes, I took the opportunity to scan the nameplates in front of each of the members.

Valerie J. Davis sat to our left. A pale, cold-looking Caucasian woman in her fifties, Davis was the most intimidating of all three Board members. She was dressed in a nondescript grey suit. She had long curly brown hair and brown eyes. Her face had no trace of blush or lipstick. Her features, like her suit, were all plain—except for her chilly, false smile.

Seltzer sat to our right side. He was a clean-shaven Caucasian man in his forties. He looked harmless, like a nice, regular guy. Next to Davis, he looked practically jolly. His thin salt and pepper hair was cut short and he wore reading glasses. Seltzer had on a blue button up shirt without a tie covered by a charcoal coat. Throughout my hearing, Seltzer made solid eye contact with Arora and me, nodding politely and jotting a few words on his notepad.

Pittman, a dark skinned African-American woman, sat directly in front of us. Even though she was clearly the youngest—she appeared to be in her late thirties—she seemed to be the one in charge. She had a no-nonsense, sophisticated air, accentuated by her black button up blouse and short, severe crop haircut. She had very dark eyes and bright red lipstick. No smile. No smirk. Nothing gave away her temperament. She was very professional as she read through a file folder, the contents of which were, presumably, about me.

When Arora was ready to begin, Pittman sat the folder down, folded her hands on top of it, and looked directly at me.

"We are on the record with Mr. David Lee Windecher, bar applicant ID number 38300," Pittman said, breaking the silence in the cavernous ballroom.

"Mr. Windecher why are you here?" she asked.

"Madam Pittman, I am here for an investigative hearing to determine the status of my bar application," I responded, keeping our eye contact.

"And what is the Board to do with you?"

"Ma'am, the Board is to determine whether my character is fit to practice law in the state of Florida when handling other's personal affairs and finances," I replied.

"Fit to practice law, Mr. Windecher?" interjected the icy Davis, sarcasm in her voice. "You were arrested thirteen times, sir. Why?"

Davis narrowed her eyes, leaving no sign of the stiff smile she'd worn just minutes ago.

My tone was composed and serious as I responded, "Madam Davis, I repeatedly made poor decisions because I grew up angry and bitter due to the poverty I experienced. I don't have excuses for my actions. But I cannot apologize for them either, because, while unfortunate that the arrests occurred, they were part of the process that got me here today. And I am grateful to be here, to even have the opportunity to accomplish such a feat after overcoming so much."

"David, all of your arrests happened by the age of nineteen. Where were your parents?" Davis pushed on.

"My parents did the best they could under the circumstances they had. As a matter of fact, they are the reason why I am here today. Without their encouragement and support, I could not have endured this journey," I paused. She looked as if she doubted this greatly. So I went on. "Parents cannot stop gang fights in front of schools. Parents cannot stop bullets in the streets. Parents cannot stop police officers from abusing their discretion. Parents can only try to teach their children to think better for themselves. It is up to the person to understand how to make the decisions that are in their best interests. I made all of the decisions I needed to make to survive the neighborhood I grew up in. I chose to survive. I chose to break the law. But I also chose to be here today. The decisions I made as an adolescent landed me in jail. The decisions I made as a man landed me a license to practice law in Georgia and hopefully Florida. My parents supported me through each decision because they always knew that my heart was in the right place. My parents will be the first phone call I make when I walk out of this room today. So to answer your question, my parents were always there. Right by my side."

"Where is this neighborhood you survived?" asked Seltzer.

"Miami, Mr. Seltzer, Miami-Dade County," I quickly responded.

"Dade County, eh?" sighed Seltzer.

"Yes, sir," I affirmed.

He leaned back from the table eyeing me as he rolled his pen between his right thumb and index finger.

"Habla Espanol?" asked Seltzer with an accent that indicated Spanish was a learned language for him.

"Si, senor," I responded.

"Where is your family from?"

"My parents are both from Argentina, sir. From Buenos Aires, Argentina. We moved to Miami in 1989," I informed him.

"Messi," asserted Seltzer, in reference to Lionel Messi, the captain of Argentina's national futbol team.

"Yes! I am very excited about the World Cup, sir," I said.

Davis picked up the volley. "1989. That was one year before your first arrest at age eleven. Eight years later, you'd accumulated thirteen arrests. Then nothing. What happened? Why'd you stop? Did you have a sudden awakening?"

"No ma'am. My brother, two sisters, and my parents were my first catalysts. I was a terrible son. I was being a bad example to my younger siblings. I was not a good big brother. My siblings were following my footsteps. It broke my heart to watch them become who I was. I did not want to destroy my family. I could feel the pain I saw in my parent's faces and the confusion I saw in my sibling's. I knew then that I had to start making better decisions. I had to change for the better. For myself and for my family. So from the moment of my last arrest, little by little, I worked to get to this moment, here today."

"I can see that on top of your thirteen arrests you also accumulated twenty-three traffic infractions before the age of nineteen. Were your driving privileges ever suspended?" asked Davis.

"Yes, ma'am."

"So on top of all of your arrests, you also allowed your driving privileges to be suspended. Why?" inquired Davis.

"I did not feel good about the people I had to talk to in order to get the traffic issues resolved. I was skeptical about the court process. I did not trust police officers, judges, or prosecutors. I simply did not trust the judicial system whatsoever."

"Yet now you want to become an attorney," Davis said sharply.

I nodded. "Yes, ma'am. I've matured and see things much differently as a man today compared to as a juvenile in 1997. I truly understand that driving is a privilege and I treat it as such."

Davis continued her hard line of questioning. "Is that why you allowed your driver license to be suspended again in 2010, thirteen years *after* you matured into a man?"

"No ma'am. That was a clerical error committed by the Florida Department of Motor Vehicles. That is why the reinstatement fee was waived. And as a matter of fact, the instant I learned of the suspension, I stopped driving. I asked a friend to give me a ride to the Georgia Department of Driver Services in order to rectify the matter," I replied easily.

Pittman jumped back into the fray, "The last time your license was suspended was in 2010, but that was in error. When was the last time you used marijuana, Mr. Windecher?

"Madam Pittman, frankly speaking, I cannot remember the exact date I last smoked marijuana. However, I do remember that it happened while I was attending American Intercontinental University during my undergraduate studies," I responded.

"So you were using drugs while you were in college?" continued Pittman.

"Yes ma'am. I did use marijuana while I was in college," I answered.

"Where did you get the marijuana, Mr. Windecher?" asked Seltzer.

"On campus, sir. I bought it from a student who I knew sold marijuana."

"Instead of reporting a known drug dealer on campus, you proceeded to purchase marijuana from them and smoke it," directed Seltzer.

"Correct, sir. I did not report them to the authorities. I was used to seeing those things. It was not out of the ordinary for drugs to be sold on campus."

"Speaking of smoking marijuana, I see that one of your arrests was for driving intoxicated. Are you still condoning such behavior, specifically from yourself?" asked Davis.

I shook my head. "Madam Davis, no. I do not. I seldom drink alcohol because I am addicted to working out and alcohol consumption is counterproductive to results."

"How often do you drink, Mr. Windecher?" she asked.

"On special occasions, such as birthday parties, weddings, social network gatherings. Events of that sort, ma'am," I responded.

"And how do you get home from these events when you have consumed alcohol?" continued Pittman.

"Uber, ma'am," I replied.

"Excuse me?" Pittman asked, eyebrows raised, head cocked to the side.

"Uber. It is a cab service that anyone can employ by downloading an app to his or her smartphone. You select the location and time that you want a cab to pick you up. You submit payment through the app. And you're home safe. It is a neat seamless service. It is also great for preventing DUIs," I informed Pittman.

"Uber, eh?" Seltzer said.

"Yes, sir. It's brilliant," I commented.

"What about your HSBC shortsale?" asked Davis, changing the subject.

"Yes ma'am," I said. "I did not want to let that property go. It meant a lot to me. It was the first property I owned in my life. I bought it when I first moved up to Georgia. I planned on living there through and after law school. It was difficult to make that strategic decision—"

"What do you mean *strategic*?" asked Davis, her tone hard.

"I mean that it was the best strategy I could choose out of the options I had at that moment. I ran out of federal disbursements in January of 2012, and realized I would no longer be able to sustain the mortgage payments because I could not work. I had to study for the bar exam in July," I explained.

"And so you decided to stop making payments on a piece of property you signed a contract for?" continued Davis.

I explained, "No, ma'am. I consulted with a property attorney, John Hollingsworth. I was informed that my property was upside down by more than 50% and even if I continued to pay, I stood to lose significant amounts of money because the property would never yield a return on investment. Hollingsworth believed that a strategic shortsale made most sense. He explained the legalities and consequences of the process and indicated that it would only work if HSBC consented. He said that mortgage companies were allowing mortgagors to request discharge of the negative balances on their property, that is, if those properties were sold for less than the mortgage's balance. Hollingsworth suggested that due to the balance of my mortgage being near $100,000 and the property appraisal reflecting $40,000, it was likely HSBC would consent to a shortsale."

"Do you plan on being as strategic with your student loans?" questioned Davis.

"I am not in default on any of my student loans, nor am I at risk of defaulting. I'm gainfully employed. And I plan on doing everything I can to repay the loans I had to incur to get to where I am today," I responded.

"How much do you owe?" asked Seltzer, removing his glasses.

"About $290,000, sir. Currently, I am paying over $200 per month on my private loans; however, my federal loans are in forbearance, so a payment isn't due yet," I explained.

"And how exactly are you going to pay all of that back?" questioned Davis.

"The only way I know how, ma'am: through hard work. I'm writing a book detailing the story of my life to attempt to inspire kids growing up like I did. Some of the proceeds will be for the kids, some for my loans. But I'm not putting all of my eggs in the book basket, I'm a lawyer in Georgia and I am going to work as much as I possibly can to earn a significant income," I said.

Davis tilted her head and met my eyes. "If that honest living does not pan out, would you revert back to your adolescent ways?"

I returned her bold gaze. "No, ma'am. I could never go back. I was not proud of who I was. I am proud of who I have become. It took years of never quitting and always doing the right thing to get to where I am. I want to continue to lead with that example. I am going to work hard to remain solvent with my student loans because I understand the value. Had it not been for the money I borrowed, I would never have been able to obtain a legal education. Now, that is not to say that if Congress were to enact a forgiveness law for student loans, that I would not take advantage of the opportunity; I absolutely would. Just like the forgiveness in place for people that paid too much for properties, if it turns out that I overpaid for my education, then I want to remit only what is considered fair."

There was silence for a full twenty seconds. The Board members shared un-readable looks and each nodded in the others' direction.

Pittman leaned forward, again resting her folded hands on the table in front of her.

"Mr. Windecher, this is your opportunity to tell us whatever it is you would like for us to hear."

I nodded and then began.

"I want to be licensed to practice law in Florida. My family still lives in Miami. My childhood was spent here. This was home to me. And I left because of all of the bad memories. But that is in the past. I am focused on today and the future. There are so many others like me, and I am inspired by them. I live with a tremendous guilt for having found a way out of that situation and onto a successful career as an attorney. I feel guilty because I cannot answer 'Why me?' Why did God help me find a way out?"

I paused, looking at each Board member in turn.

"There is a reason. A purpose. And I want to fulfill it. But I will never be able to fulfill that purpose unless I can overcome this final obstacle. A long time ago, I realized this journey was not about me anymore. This is about the change I can bring about if I finish what I started. If I can save just one child from making the same mistakes I did in order to preserve his or her bright future, then all of my struggles will have been worth it. Just one kid. *One* will be worth it. I am aiming higher. But I cannot do it without your help.

I need you to empower me to have a voice. A voice that understands and cares and knows how to make a difference. I was fortunate to have a family that stood by me. Without them I would not be here today. Not everyone has that. But that does not mean they cannot be saved too. So, all I am asking for is an opportunity to show that it doesn't matter how or where you start, but what you do along the way and how you finish.

I don't want to be measured by the short time in my life in which I behaved like a criminal. I don't want to be condemned for that. I want to be measured by the totality of my existence. Because when it is all said and done for me, the good I will have caused with my life will far outweigh that short period in which I was very troubled. But I need you to give me one chance. That is all I need. Allow me to swear into the Florida Bar so I can fulfill my purpose and give back to others like me."

No one said anything for a moment. Seltzer was nodding, almost imperceptivity to himself, and rolling his pen. Davis was motionless, her lips drawn in a tight line.

Finally, Pittman spoke. "Thank you, Mr. Windecher. Mr. Arora, is there anything you'd like to add?"

Arora leaned forward.

"Well, I've been doing this close to twenty years now. During that time, I practiced in the Air Force, at the District Attorney's office, in private practice, and now in my own firm. I've met a lot of people along the way. David may be the most interesting of all. This is someone who, as a kid, didn't have much other than a good family. He grew up poor. He overcame that. He grew up in a tough environment. He overcame that. He was arrested thirteen times. He overcame that. He wanted to go to college. He finished at the top of his class. He wanted to go to law school. He got in despite his criminal record. And he got in because of his attitude. He will not quit pushing himself toward his goals. I learned that about him when we first interviewed him. That is why we hired him. This is a man who made mistakes as a child but has corrected himself to lead an admirable adult life. A life any parent would be proud of. Now, if we don't help people like him, then what is the point? What is the point of our profession? This is inspiring. This is really helping people. Our firm stands behind David 100%. If he were to be given an oath of attorney and wanted to move back to his hometown to work in his own community, then we will help him make the move back. He'll make a difference. He deserves to be licensed in Florida."

"Thank you, Mr. Arora. Mr. Windecher, the Board will deliver formal notice of its decision within three weeks. Gentlemen, have a safe trip back to Georgia," said Pittman.

On March 18, 2014, the Board recommended me for admission to the Florida Bar and issued an Oath of Attorney.

There was only one courthouse that I wanted to take that oath in.

It was time to close the circle.

On March 25, 2014, the morning of the hearing, my entire family arrived early at the Richard E. Gerstein Justice Building (the Miami-Dade County

Criminal Courthouse). We went through the security gates and took the escalator up to the judge's chamber. My family waited out in the corridor while I checked in with the Judge's assistant, Monica Galo.

Judge Nushin G. Sayfie walked out of her office while I was speaking with Galo.

"Morning," the Judge welcomed me. "Are you here to get sworn-in?"

"Good morning, your Honor," I said, extending my hand to the Judge. "Yes, my name is David Lee Windecher. It's nice to meet you."

"Very well," Judge Sayfie replied, giving my hand a firm shake. "Please give Ms. Galo your oath and she will get it to me before I take the bench. See you in court shortly."

"Thank you, Judge," I said, unable to conceal my smile.

I entered the courtroom and was immediately reminded of walking through those same hallways in an orange jumpsuit. My journey began a long time ago when I was born into circumstances I didn't choose. It was about to end on my terms.

I had been working toward this moment for half of my life. I was utterly exhausted. There had been so many obstacles, so many opportunities to quit or to take an easier path. But none of that mattered now. No one could ever take this achievement away from my family or me. It was my proudest moment.

My family sat in the gallery inside the courtroom. Karina waved me over, and I took a seat between my parents and my brother and sisters. We watched the judge hear a few jail calendar cases before she finally called mine.

"Mr. David Lee Windecher," called the judge.

I stood up, squeezed my mom's hand and let it go as I made my way up to the podium. The plaque above the judge's tribunal caught my eye. *We Who Labor Here Seek Only The Truth.*

"I have an Oath of Attorney here with your name on it," declared the Judge.

"Yes, your Honor. Thank you. It has been a long time coming."

"Mr. Windecher, will you approach so that I may swear you in?" she requested.

I walked up to the tribunal and stood face to face with Judge Sayfie.

"Raise your right hand and repeat after me," instructed the Judge.

"I do solemnly swear: I will support the Constitution of the United States and the Constitution of the State of Florida; I will maintain the respect due to

Courts of Justice and Judicial Officers; I will not counsel or maintain any suit or proceedings which shall appear to me to be unjust…"

I could feel my mouth moving, repeating the solemn words Judge Sayfie spoke, but I couldn't hear the sound.

I felt powerful and deeply humbled. I thought about the past: my parent's struggles, the bitterness of growing up impoverished, getting jumped-in to a gang, selling dope to make money to eat, thirteen arrests, sitting in jail for months, Torres. But mostly I thought about the future. I'd thought this moment would feel like closure, but I was wrong. This wasn't the end of a journey.

Yes, I'd fought hard. Yes, I was tired. But my life wasn't really about me and my journey anymore.

It was about the people who needed my story.

For them, I would keep to the path. For them, I would share what I'd learned. For them, I would fight for the America I believed in: the America that defends what is right and honorable and just; the America that once gave a poor, angry kid a chance at redemption.

I would fight for the American dream, and I would fight for those whose every hope depends on it.

I looked out at my family and smiled.

"So help me, God."

ACKNOWLEDGEMENTS

The AmerIcan Dream would have been impossible without the love and support from the people and organizations that energized and motivated me to push forward.

To my Heavenly Father, Jesus Christ, for blessing me with the chance to make a difference in the lives of others;

My father, Raul Windecher, for teaching me what it means to be a man and to protect my family; my mother, Laura Windecher, for her unrelenting efforts to ensure that I was raised right; my brother, Christian Windecher, and my sisters, Giselle and Karina Windecher, for being the best friends I could ask for in this life;

Joey Torres for taking this ride with me, though our paths have diverged; Nichole Logiudice for the compassion you showed while I was still a troubled individual; James McGuire, Jon Neuman, Danny Castanon, Zach French, Kevin Haviv, Boris Milter, Brad Griffin and Holly Waltman for being the closest thing I have to family; Professor Sharon Reid for teaching me that if I always do what I've always done, I'll always get what I've always got; Joan Melville for teaching me how to trust in my faith;

John Marshall Law School for giving me an opportunity when others wouldn't; Manny Arora and Michael LaScala for taking me under your wings and being the best mentors an attorney could ask for; Knippenberg Literary for your amazing editing skills; Omar Chadli for designing the perfect book cover;

NoBox Creatives and Jamie Wiggins for creating an online presence for *The AmerIcan Dream* and helping me share my journey with the rest of the world, thank you.

ABOUT THE AUTHOR

David Lee Windecher was born on October 16, 1978, in East Los Angeles, California, the son of Argentinean immigrants. Windecher graduated summa cum laude from the American Intercontinental University in Fort Lauderdale, Florida, with a Bachelor's Degree in Business Administration in June of 2005 and in May of 2012 received a Juris Doctorate degree from John Marshall Law School in Atlanta, Georgia.

Windecher is a defense attorney admitted to the Georgia Bar in 2012 and the Florida Bar in 2014. He is a member of the Georgia and Florida Court of Appeals, the Georgia and Florida Supreme Court, the Northern District of Georgia United States District Court and the American Bar Association. Windecher represents clients facing major felony and misdemeanor charges. He is an expert in criminal defense, juvenile law and expungement procedure.

Windecher is a recipient of Martindale-Hubbell's Client Distinction Award in 2013, 2014 and 2015. He was named "40 Under 40" by Georgia Trend Magazine and the Atlanta Business Chronicle. Windecher is a frequent guest on local and national news outlets as a legal expert.

Windecher founded RED in March of 2015. RED (Rehabilitation Enables Dreams, Inc.) is a domestic non-profit 501(c)(3) organization. RED engineers and administers restorative justice programs for pre and post adjudication first time non-violent offenders.

Connect with David Lee Windecher and RED ...

www.windecherfirm.com

www.hisstoryinthemaking.com

www.stoprecidivism.org

www.davidwindecher.com

Made in the USA
Monee, IL
13 April 2021